The Rock Observed

The Rock Observed

Studies in the Literature of Newfoundland

PATRICK O'FLAHERTY

UNIVERSITY OF TORONTO PRESS

Toronto Buffalo London

© University of Toronto Press 1979
Toronto Buffalo London
Printed in Canada

Canadian Cataloguing in Publication Data

O'Flaherty, P.A., 1939–
The rock observed

Includes index.
ISBN 0-8020-2351-7

1. Canadian literature (English) – Newfoundland –
History and criticism.* 2. Newfoundland in
literature. 3. Newfoundland – History – Sources.
I. Title.

PS8131.N4045   c810'.9'9718   C79-094319-0
PR9198.2.N4045

For Frankie

and our sons, Keir, Peter, and Padraic

Contents

Preface

My purpose in this book is to provide a survey of literary responses to Newfoundland and Newfoundlanders over the centuries. The study will, I hope, prove of interest to students of Newfoundland (and hence Canadian) literature and culture, but I trust it will have an appeal to a wider audience. The general Canadian view of Newfoundland and, more significantly, Newfoundlanders' conceptions of their own history and character have been shaped to some extent by the written word, and if this book helps in some way to indicate the nature of this influence, then my purpose will have been achieved.

I have tried to relate the literature of Newfoundland to the context of Newfoundland history, since without such a context discussion of books has limited value. In these brief excursions into Newfoundland history, I have leaned heavily on the work of recent scholars, whose books and articles have been acknowledged. Needless to say, such errors as remain in this study, whether of fact or interpretation, are my own.

I would like to acknowledge the assistance of the Canada Council, which provided me with a Leave Fellowship to enable me to write this book. The Vice-President (Academic) of Memorial University of Newfoundland, Dr Leslie Harris, kindly recommended me for two grants from his research fund, to help defray the costs of travelling and typing. I am grateful for the continuous help I received from librarians and researchers at the Centre for Newfoundland Studies in Memorial University's Henrietta Harvey Library, the A.C. Hunter Library in The Arts and Culture Centre, St John's, and the Public Archives of Newfoundland and Labrador. Mr Ben Hansen allowed me to take advantage of his expertise in photography. D.G. Pitt, head of the Department of English Language and Literature at Memorial University, willingly offered departmental co-operation. G.M. Story, professor of English at Memorial University, read my manuscript in a late draft and made a number of valuable suggestions.

I wish to acknowledge the advice and encouragement of Frankie O'Flaherty, who has put up with my talking about Newfoundland for many years. Peter Neary, too, has influenced my thinking on many matters, and first got me interested in writing about Newfoundland. Mrs Paulette Evans typed my manuscript with speed and accuracy. Mrs Mary Doyle prepared the index. Publication of this book has been made possible by a grant from the Canada Council.

P.O'F.
11 December 1978

Illustrations

1 Migratory fishermen, c. 1700

2 George Cartwright

3 William Cormack

4 William Carson

5 Patrick Morris

6 Charles Pedley

7 D.W. Prowse

8 Moses Harvey

9 R.T.S. Lowell

10 Norman Duncan

11 A house in northern Newfoundland, c. 1900

12 A scene in Labrador, c. 1900

13 A family in Labrador, c. 1900

14 Flatrock, c. 1930

15 A Bell Island miner

16 Gunner A.N. Ryan
    of Bonavista Bay,
    in Italy, 1944

17 Pouch Cove, c. 1930

18 E.J. Pratt

19 Margaret Duley

20 Arthur Scammell

21 Ron Pollett

22 Harold Horwood

23 Ted Russell

24 Percy Janes

25 An original Grenfell cartoon

Maps

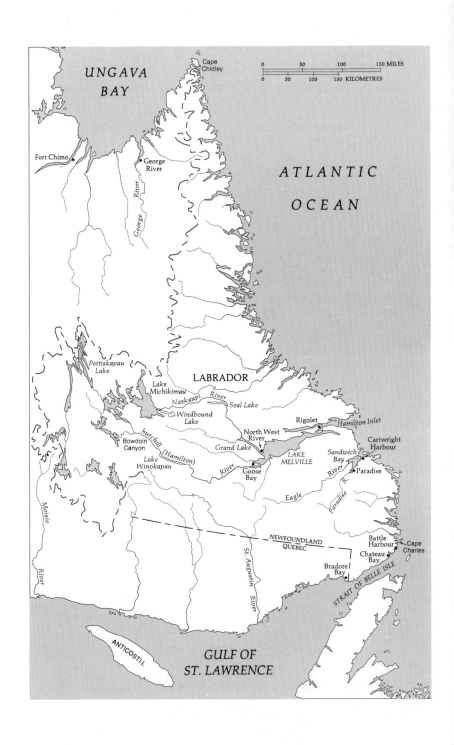

UNGAVA
BAY

Cape
Chidley

0   50   100   150 MILES
0   50   100   150 KILOMETRES

ATLANTIC

OCEAN

Fort Chimo

George
River

George River

Pettiskapau
Lake

Lake
Michikimau

LABRADOR

Naskaupi River   Seal Lake

Windbound
Lake

Bowdoin
Canyon

Churchill (Hamilton)

Lake
Winokapau

Grand Lake

River

North West
River

Rigolet   Hamilton Inlet

Goose
Bay

LAKE
MELVILLE

Sandwich
Bay

Cartwright
Harbour

Paradise

River

Eagle

Paradise R.

Moisie

NEWFOUNDLAND
QUEBEC

Battle
Harbour   Cape
Charles

Chateau
Bay

St. Augustin River

Bradore
Bay

STRAIT OF BELLE ISLE

ANTICOSTI I.

GULF OF
ST. LAWRENCE

River

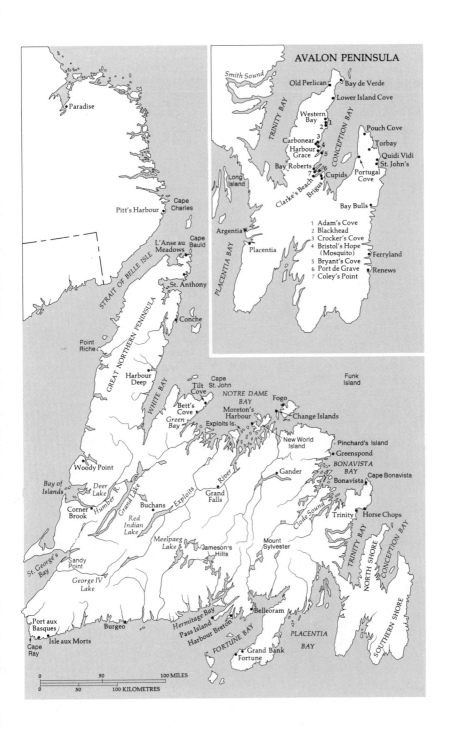

AVALON PENINSULA

Smith Sound

Old Perlican
Bay de Verde
Lower Island Cove

TRINITY BAY

Western
Bay
2 1
Pouch Cove

Carbonear
3
Torbay
Harbour
4
Quidi Vidi
Grace
5
St. John's

CONCEPTION BAY

Bay Roberts
6
Portugal
Long
7
Clarke's Beach
Cupids
Cove
Island
Brigus

Bay Bulls

Pitt's Harbour
Cape
Charles

Paradise

Argentia

1 Adam's Cove
2 Blackhead
3 Crocker's Cove
4 Bristol's Hope
   (Mosquito)
5 Bryant's Cove
6 Port de Grave
7 Coley's Point

Placentia
Ferryland

Renews

PLACENTIA BAY

L'Anse au
Meadows
Cape
Bauld

STRAIT OF BELLE ISLE

St. Anthony

Point
Riche

Conche

GREAT NORTHERN PENINSULA

Harbour
Deep

Funk
Island

Cape
St. John

Tilt
Cove

NOTRE DAME
BAY

Fogo

WHITE BAY

Bett's
Cove

Moreton's
Harbour

Change Islands

Green
Bay

Exploits Is.

New World
Island

Pinchard's Island

Greenspond

Woody Point

River

Gander

BONAVISTA
BAY

Cape Bonavista

Bay of
Islands

Deer
Lake

Grand Lake

Bonavista

Corner
Brook

Humber R.

Buchans

Exploits

Grand
Falls

Clode Sound

Trinity
Horse Chops

Red
Indian
Lake

Meelpaeg
Lake

Jameson's
Hills

Mount
Sylvester

TRINITY BAY

NORTH SHORE

CONCEPTION BAY

St. George's
Bay

Sandy
Point

George IV
Lake

Belleoram

SOUTHERN SHORE

Port aux
Basques

Burgeo

Hermitage Bay

Pass Island

Harbour Breton

FORTUNE BAY

PLACENTIA
BAY

Isle aux Morts

Cape
Ray

Grand Bank

Fortune

0   50   100 MILES

0   50   100 KILOMETRES

The Rock Observed

1 🏴 'It passeth England'

LITERATURE OF DISCOVERY
AND EARLY SETTLEMENT / 1497–1670

On 24 June 1497, John Cabot, after a thirty-five-day voyage westward from Bristol, saw what most authorities think was the Newfoundland mainland. Disembarking with a crucifix, he 'raised banners with the arms of the Holy Father and those of the King of England.' At the very spot where he and a few of his men landed, near 'tall trees' and 'rich' grasslands, there were signs of human habitation: a trail leading inland; manure, possibly (as they thought) of farm animals; and a carved and painted stick, pierced at both ends. Sensing danger, Cabot went inland no further than 'the shooting distance of a cross-bow.' He and his men then retreated to their ship and spent one month exploring the coastline of the new land. Codfish, they noted, were plentiful. As they sailed along the shore they saw fields 'where they thought might also be villages' and 'a forest whose foliage looked beautiful.' Once they spotted 'two forms running on land one after the other' but could not determine if they were humans or animals. Without venturing to step on shore again, Cabot then returned to England to report his discovery to Henry VII.[1]

Thus about five centuries after the Norsemen abandoned their settlement near L'Anse au Meadows on the Great Northern Peninsula, white men rediscovered Newfoundland and planted on its shores the insignia of their civilization. Cabot's news spread quickly from Henry's court to the capitals of continental Europe, and we can see in the first excited accounts of his discovery by European ambassadors in London the mixture of greed, fantasy, and idealism that constituted the usual Renaissance response to the New World. In sighting or nearing what was variously thought to be 'the country of the Grand

Khan,' 'the Seven Cities,' the islands of 'Brazil,' and 'Cipango,' Cabot awakened visions of precious stones, spices, silks, island kingdoms, and bishoprics in the entourage at the English court, and before he set out on his second and fatal voyage across the Atlantic even his barber had hopes of owning an island.[2] Slightly more realistic dreams of plunder and power were stirred up by the reports of Gaspar Corte Real's expedition of 1501, which brought back to Portugal 'about fifty' kidnapped native people from Newfoundland or Labrador, the promise of 'plenty of men-slaves fit for every kind of labour,' and accounts of 'abundance of most luscious and varied fruits, and trees and pines of such measureless height and girth, that they would be too big as a mast for the largest ship that sails the sea.'[3] As knowledge of western geography expanded during the subsequent decades, such airy fancies and high hopes faded, and in time European enterprise concentrated on Newfoundland's most readily available commodity, codfish. However, in sixteenth-century descriptions of Newfoundland we can expect to find what is, indeed, common in much Elizabethan and Tudor travel literature, an element of distortion and fantasy that amounts at times to downright lying. This was a time when travellers were expected to return from such mythical kingdoms as Norumbega and Saguenay with stories of unipeds, 'shepe, which beareth redde woole,' and 'men whose heads / Do grow beneath their shoulders,' and even Jacques Cartier and Sir Richard Whitbourne could not resist satisfying the European appetite for hearing 'strange newes.'[4]

While the earliest reference to the 'new fund Yle' in British imaginative literature dates from the early 1500s,[5] it was not until the latter decades of the century that English commercial interests began to exploit the island's rich fishery. English voyages of discovery to North America prior to Sir Martin Frobisher's (1576–8) and Sir Humphrey Gilbert's (1583) were infrequent, and the images they provide of Newfoundland are a medley of fact and fable. Sebastian Cabot's voyage of 1508–9 was apparently undertaken to locate a northwest passage to the Orient. According to a report printed by an Italian historian, Cabot paused in Newfoundland to enjoy this spectacle:

near the shores are many tall trees, the leaves of which fall into the sea, and the cod come to feed on them in shoals. The bears, which eat nothing but these fish, stand in ambush on the shore, and when they see the approach of the shoals of these fish, which are very large and shaped like tunny, they rush into the sea, linked with another of their kind, and striking their claws under the scales, do not let them go and try to pull them on shore; but the cod, which are very strong, turn round and plunge into the sea, so that, these two creatures being grappled together, it is a great sport to see now the one under the water and now the other on top, splashing the foam into the air; and in the end the bear pulls the cod ashore and eats him.[6]

John Rut's voyage of 1527 provides us with the earliest firsthand English description of Newfoundland. Like Sebastian Cabot, Rut was searching for a northwest passage, but was driven south by fear of 'great Ilands of Ice.' At 'Cap de Bas' (possibly Cape Charles or Cape Bauld) Rut saw a 'mayne Land' which he gloomily described as 'all wildernesse and mountaines and woods, and no naturall ground but all mosse, and no inhabitation nor no people.' Proceeding to St John's, he counted fourteen ships from Normandy, Brittany, and Portugal, 'all a fishing.' For some reason he continued on to the West Indies, where he told a Spanish officer that in northern waters he had run into 'a sea as hot as water in a boiler' and had altered course for fear that the water 'should melt the pitch of their vessel.'[7] A similarly incredible tale was told of the voyage of the *Minion* in 1536, under the command of Richard Hore. Hore had persuaded a number of lawyers and other 'gentlemen' to accompany him to North America 'to see the straunge things of the world.' In Newfoundland they saw, among other wonders, bears, great auks, and Beothuck Indians, but growing 'into great want of victuals' they were obliged to go ashore to steal the fish which an osprey brought to her young. Eventually they were driven to harsher measures, and one day a member of the crew was discovered in the forest broiling a piece of a comrade's buttock. For this crime he was sternly reprimanded by the captain, who had noticed that his company had been steadily diminishing in number. Before necessity made cannibals of still others, 'the mercie of God' sent a well-victualled French ship to the coast, which Hore's gentlemen raided before returning to England.[8]

The only further glimpse of Newfoundland that we catch in the 1530s is Cartier's grim remark about the coastlines of southern Labrador and part of the Great Northern Peninsula: 'the land should not be called the New Land, being composed of stones and horrible rugged rocks. [Labrador] is the land God gave to Cain.'[9] The first English geographer to describe Newfoundland, Roger Barlow, echoed Cartier when he wrote in 1541 that the region had no 'riches of gold, spyces nor preciose stones.'[10] Still, as the previous accounts indicate, Newfoundland had already become a fertile source of lies; and by 1570 a tradition of telling 'merrie tales'[11] about the island seems to have been established. Anthony Parkhurst, a merchant who first went to Newfoundland to fish in 1574, deals wittily with this habit in his 'Report of the True State and Commodities of Newfoundland,' contained in a letter to Richard Hakluyt in 1578. Parkhurst's letter is an attempt to give a factual report on the island's climate, vegetation, and animal life, but he humorously and pointedly inserts details about such phenomena as 'fish like a Smelt' (caplin) which at his command 'cometh on shore' in such numbers that it is possible to catch 'sufficient in three or four houres for a whole Citie' and another variety (flounder) that can be caught with a simple tool 'as fast as one would gather up stones.' These appear to be 'notorious lies,' he told Hakluyt, but 'each tale is true.' Parkhurst's essay, the first detailed report on Newfoundland by an Englishman, was a clever rejoinder to fantastic accounts circulated by earlier visitors, but his wit was such that he seems occasionally to be as concerned with creating wonder as exposing lies. One of his stories, about a dog that catches fish, borders perilously on fiction.[12]

ACCOUNTS OF THE GILBERT VOYAGE OF 1583

Newfoundland comes more sharply into focus in the 1580s as a result of the expedition of Sir Humphrey Gilbert. A Devonshire man and a half-brother of Sir Walter Raleigh, Gilbert by 1583 had already followed a complicated and uneven career as a soldier, member of Parliament, and incorrigible schemer. As colonel of the English army in Munster in 1569, he had distinguished himself by an unmitigated savagery towards the Irish, of whom he once remarked that 'he thought his Dogges eares to good to heare the speeche of the greatest noble manne emongest them.'[13] From 1576 Gilbert's heart was set on western adventure and colonization, and in 1578–9 he assembled a squadron at Plymouth, intending, probably, to harass and rob Spanish ships in the Caribbean. The enterprise was a total failure, and it was with great difficulty that Gilbert won support for another expedition, for Queen Elizabeth now rightly regarded him as 'a man noted of no good hap at sea.'[14] But Gilbert persisted, and in June 1583 he sailed from Plymouth with five ships and two hundred and sixty men, bound initially for Newfoundland and ultimately for the American coast north of Florida, where he planned to establish 'a colonial Utopia' in which he would be 'the governor and universal landlord.'[15] The largest ship in the little fleet mysteriously turned back after only two days at sea, but the four others reached Newfoundland late in July and assembled off St John's harbour on 3 August. On its way through the St John's Narrows Gilbert's ship, the *Delight*, grounded on Chain Rock and had to be towed off by men from some of the thirty-six European fishing ships in the harbour.

Among the various surviving accounts of Gilbert's experiences in and near Newfoundland the most elaborate is that of Edward Hayes, the captain and owner of the *Golden Hind*, who incorporated in his narrative 'A brief relation of the New found land, and the commodities thereof.' Hayes judges Newfoundland from the point of view of the potential settler. He admits the truth of the 'common opinion,' that the island is colder in winter than European countries at equivalent latitudes, and reasons that the sun, after passing over the Atlantic, has become too 'infeebled' by 'moyst vapours' to produce heat. But for this 'only defect' of 'sharpe cold,' nature has given ample recompense in the form of 'incredible quantitie, and no lesse varietie of kindes of fish in the sea and fresh waters.' Among these he lists 'Oysters having pearle'; but, he adds carefully, 'not orient in colour.' Turning with less enthusiasm to the land, he notes that with 'time and industrie' products such as 'hempe, corne, cables, cordage, linnen cloth, mettals and many more' could be produced in Newfoundland as readily as they can in the 'East and Northerly countries of Europe.' The trees, he found, yielded 'Gumme and Turpentine' but little fruit. He saw cherries 'no bigger than a small pease' and the pear trees he thought he saw were, alas, 'fruitlesse.' The soil along the coast, though 'not deepe of earth' – a choice phrase – produced peas, berries that were 'good and holesome to eat,' and wild roses, and the grass 'doth fat sheepe in a very short space.' As for the animal life of the country, Hayes knew that in his brief visit he probably saw only a 'hundreth part' of the 'creatures in those unhabited lands,' but he received sufficient information about the presence of 'Beares, ounces or leopards, ... wolves, foxes, ... Otters, bevers, marternes,' and even sables, to induce him 'to glorifie the magnificent God, who hath superabundantly replenished the earth with creatures serving for the use of man.' Hayes learned too that the mountains of Newfoundland 'generally make shew of minerall substance: Iron very common, lead, and somewhere copper,' adding cautiously 'I will not averre of richer mettals,' but 'more then hope may be conceived thereof.' This prudent, cautious note is sounded throughout his appraisal of Newfoundland, setting him apart from many later propagandists for colonization. Hayes nevertheless remained an advocate for settlement, dismissing fears about the harsh climate with the briskness of a man of the world, and telling Englishmen that it is preferable 'to adventure as becommeth men' in Newfoundland than 'very miserably to live & die' in a country 'pestered with inhabitants.'[16] Perhaps we can see in his account the natural optimism of a businessman who had invested heavily and unwisely in Gilbert's tomfool enterprise and was reluctant to see his investment utterly without effect.

Stephen Parmenius, the young Hungarian poet and scholar who accompanied Gilbert, left an account of Newfoundland which contrasts strikingly with that of Hayes. Parmenius had come to England in 1581 and had learned of Gilbert's projected commonwealth in America from Hakluyt. He was filled with enthusiasm for the project, wrote a long Latin poem celebrating it, and made the unfortunate blunder of going himself to observe its establishment. He sailed, moreover, on the *Swallow*, whose crew boarded and raided a fishing ship prior to entering St John's and tortured the helpless fishermen – hardly an inspiring scene for one who had praised England's young men for turning from war to 'Study the arts of peace and brotherhood,' and who hoped to help construct a new society across the Atlantic where

> ... people, innocent
> Of crime and falsity, will rather wear
> The crown of lasting purity than sink
> Their minds and bodies into sinful lust
> And base indulgence ...[17]

Parmenius's response to Newfoundland is contained in a letter to Hakluyt from St John's, dated 6 August 1583. In it we possibly see idealism foundering on harsh reality. He can find very little to say of the island's people, customs, and territories: 'what shall I say, my good Hakluyt, when I see nothing but a very wildernesse?' A particular irritant to the poet was the thick coniferous forest in the vicinity of St John's, which was made impassable by fallen trees and which obstructed his view of the surrounding countryside. He made representations to Gilbert 'to set the woods a fire, that so we might have space, and entrance to take view of the Countrey.' Gilbert favoured the proposal but desisted when he was advised that the flow of turpentine from the burning woods might injure the fishery. In the suggestion by Parmenius, who was a man of sensitivity accustomed to sing in praise of 'shapely cedars' and 'lofty firs'[18] in more congenial settings, we see how small a part sentiment played in early attitudes to Newfoundland. In St John's Parmenius did indeed come upon grass that 'little differeth' from English grass, 'bushe berries ... of great sweetnesse,' and certain indications that the soil 'is fitt for corne.' But Newfoundland seemed too hot in summer, and he heard reports of peril and cold during the winter. Even 'the ayre upon land is indifferent clear,' while at sea 'there is nothing els but perpetual mistes' and 'no day without rayne.' With God's help, he told Hakluyt, he would 'passe towards the south,' where he hoped to find 'much greater ... thinges.'[19]

In Hayes and Parmenius similar experiences evoke contradictory responses, reminding us that even in the earliest literature about Newfoundland we are receiving impressions of the island filtered through the author's personality and influenced by his hopes and fears. The same point can be made of Gilbert's own opinion of Newfoundland, which was conveyed to Sir George Peckham in a short letter on 8 August: 'Be of good cheare, for if there were no better expectation, it were a very rich demaynes, the country being very good and full of all sorts of victuall, as fish both of the fresh water and Sea-fish, Deere, Pheasants, Partridges, Swannes, and divers Fowles else. ... I have comforted my selfe, answerable to all my hopes.'[20] This represented a considerable change of heart in Gilbert, who 'had never before good conceit of these North parts of the world.' The reason for the change was simple: he had become convinced that his 'minerall man and refiner,' a man named Daniel, had discovered silver near St John's. 'I have seen ynough,' Gilbert told Hayes, 'and were it but to satisfie my private humor, I would proceede no further.' However, he had made a promise to subscribers to sail south. Gilbert sent the *Swallow* back to England with sick and disaffected men, and on 20 August, having supplied their wants 'commodiously' from the provisions of the ships in St John's and taken specimens of the 'silver ore,' the remaining three ships of the expedition left the harbour. But Gilbert's mind 'was wholly fixed upon the New found land,' and he lingered in Placentia Bay, sending men ashore 'to take view of the soyle' along the coast. A week later, following a course that Gilbert insisted should be taken, the *Delight* was wrecked on a shoal near Sable Island, and a hundred men, the 'silver ore,' and Stephen Parmenius were lost with her. The *Golden Hind* and the *Squirrel*, having barely avoided shipwreck, changed their course for England, with Gilbert sailing on the much smaller ship, the *Squirrel*, to refute 'hard reports given of him, that he was afraid of the sea.' On two occasions in mid-Atlantic Gilbert came aboard the *Golden Hind*, the second time 'to make merrie together with the Captaine, Master, and company.' Remembering his lost silver and 'not able to containe himself, he beat his boy in great rage' for forgetting an order to bring the ore to him from the *Delight*. He was now determined to return to North America in the spring of 1584, and would reserve 'unto himselfe the North, affirming that this voyage had wonne his heart from the South, and that he was now become a Northerne man altogether.' A few days later the *Squirrel* was 'devoured and swallowed up' in 'outragious Seas.' Gilbert was last seen sitting aft in the ship, with a book in his hand. He shouted, again and again, 'We are as neere to heaven by sea as by land.'[21] Even his death features the note of fanaticism and drama that was the authentic mark of his character.

PROPAGANDISTS AND SETTLERS

Following the failure of Gilbert's expedition of 1583, English interest in colonizing North America was interrupted by events in Europe until the first decade of the seventeenth century. When war between England and Spain ended in 1604, interest in formal colonial enterprise revived, and between 1610 and 1661 no less than seven attempts were made to found colonies in Newfoundland.[22] The motive behind the establishment of these plantations was almost exclusively economic. English companies obtained land grants from the Crown or from other companies, and planted colonies in the hope of profits from the sale of such commodities as the island afforded. No thought was given to developing the country for its own sake. Accompanying these attempts at colonization was what the historian J.D. Rogers called 'a plethora of poetry,' and indeed, if we can judge not only from literature dealing directly with Newfoundland but also from imagery and subject matter in the work of John Donne, Shakespeare, Michael Drayton, Francis Bacon, and others, it was in this period that the idea of western discovery appealed most strongly to the English imagination.[23]

The writing from the period that focuses on Newfoundland consists mostly of tracts written by propagandists to promote settlement and encourage investment. Though usually based on actual experience of life on the island, these are filled with exaggerations, deliberate oversights, and judicious side-stepping of the country's shortcomings, and we may expect to find in them, not the true picture of Newfoundland they pretend to give, but rather the flourish of many fine phrases. Typically, they rehearse the economic and political advantages to England of settlement on the island, and offer to colonists and investors the prospect of boundless opportunity; as in this excerpt from John Mason's *Briefe Discourse of the New-found-land* (1620), which climaxes a long recital of the island's manifold resources: 'But of all, the most admirable is the Sea, so diversified with severall sorts of Fishes abounding therein, the consideration whereof is readie to swallow up and drowne my senses not being able to comprehend or expresse the riches thereof. For could one acre thereof be inclosed with the Creatures therein in the moneths of June, Julie and August, it would exceed one thousand acres of the best Pasture with the stocke thereon which we have in England. ... Cods [are] so thicke by the shoare that we heardlie have been able to row a Boate through them ...'[24]

Another observer in 1623 noted that 'The Vines which were sent thither, doe prosper very well, whereby it is to be assured that anie thing that growes in *England*, will thrive and flourish there exceedingly.'[25] Sir William Vaughan's foppishly mannered book *The Golden Fleece* (1626) provides an illustration of the figurative and patriotic excesses which characterized this promotional literature: 'God [has] reserved the *Newfoundland* for us *Britaines*. ... This is our *Colchos*, where the *Golden Fleece* flourisheth on the backes of *Neptunes sheepe*, continually to be shorne. This is *Great Britaines Indies*, never to be exhausted dry.'[26] This fine frenzy is but a step away from poetry, if not a little beyond it; and the actual book of poems inspired by Newfoundland at this time, Robert Hayman's *Quodlibets, lately come over from New Britaniola, Old Newfoundland* (1628), may seem by comparison somewhat prosaic. Hayman's verses were written during his tenure as governor of the English colony at Bristol's Hope, Conception Bay. His good opinions of Newfoundland and exhortations to reluctant countrymen to settle there are delivered in what he truthfully calls 'bad unripe Rimes,' but it may well be that his artlessness was partly cultivated and that a touch of irony lingers below his accent of praise. It is hard to believe that he did not write with tongue in cheek in his blatant lie about the Newfoundland winter ('They love it best, that have once winter'd there') or in his poem 'To all those worthy Women, who have any desire to live in Newfound-Land':

Sweet Creatures, did you truely understand
The pleasant life you'd live in Newfound-land,
You would with teares desire to be brought thither:
I wish you, when you goe, faire wind, faire weather:
For if you with the passage can dispence,
When you are there, I know you'll n'er come thence.[27]

Hayman himself may have spent only one winter in Newfoundland. He died of a fever in 1628 while on a journey up the Amazon River.

Sir Richard Whitbourne's *Discourse and Discovery of New-found-land* (1620) belongs in this general category of promotional literature, but it is set apart from similar pieces of rhetoric by the wider knowledge of the island revealed in it and by the genuine note of warmth and sincerity in Whitbourne's character. Whitbourne had been voyaging to Newfoundland since 1579 and knew the coastline of the country well. According to his own report, he had made little money from his Newfoundland adventures, but he did not attribute his failures to lack of opportunity around the island. Beneath his 'rough style' and occasionally surly manner there is, in fact, a new feeling in literature about Newfoundland: regard for the country, not for what it could return in the way of profit, but for itself. There is a real anger in Whitbourne when he lists the abuses committed in Newfoundland by visiting European fishermen: practices such as burning down the forests around the bays and mindlessly dropping ballast into harbours that are 'so beautifull, and so excellent, ordayned by God, for ships to ride safe in at anchor.' To him the island's woods and valleys were 'delightful,' her hills 'enticing,' and her coasts 'wholesome.' In his view, only those who 'have bin accustomed to sit by a Taverne fire, or touched with the French disease' will complain of the cold. Whitbourne dismisses the argument that the country is 'so rockie, and mountainous, and so overgrowne with trees and bushes' that 'it will be an endlesse trouble to bring it to good perfection,' and delivers his own view of Newfoundland's resources in a style of passionate oratory: 'What receive wee from the hands of our owne Countrey, which in most bounteous manner wee have not had, or may have at hers? Nay, what can the world yeeld to the sustentation of man, which is not in her to be gotten? Desire you wholesome ayre? (the very food of life) It is there. Shall any Land powre in abundant heapes of nourishments and necessaries before you? There you have them. What Seas so abounding with fish? What shores so replenished with fresh and sweet waters? Sure, no other part of the world hath better.'[28]

The claims of such enthusiasts as Whitbourne were put to the test by the ordinary men and women who, from 1610 onwards, went to live in various harbours on the Avalon Peninsula. Some of the written responses of the new settlers to their environment survive, and a few have found their way into print. Even those that favour Newfoundland make a poignant contrast to the windy rhetoric of writers like Vaughan and Mason. A tradesman in Lord Baltimore's colony at

Ferryland in 1622 reported that 'concerning our health, there is not any man amongst our company that hath been sick scarcely one day since he came but hath been able to follow his work. The climate differs but little from England, and I myself felt less cold here this winter than I did in England the winter before, by much. The air is sweeter; for I never smelt any evil savour in the country, nor saw any venomous creature. God's blessings upon this land are manifold. As for wood and water, it passeth England: the one most sweet in growing and burning, the other most pleasant to taste and good to drink.'[29] In this letter and in similar ones by John Guy (1611), Daniel Powell (1622), and Edward Wynne (1622), we see men responding simply but eloquently to the physical sensations of new surroundings, charged with the hope of success, and relieved, perhaps, to have escaped from the 'ancient bone-heap of Europe.'[30] Another such document from 1612 depicts the only known friendly encounter between groups of white settlers and Beothucks, a meeting impressive in both the sincerity shown by the Europeans and the simplicity and gaiety of the Indians.[31] From the very beginning of organized settlement there were, however, dissenting voices, complaints about 'labour verie much and harde,' doubts about 'the goodnes of our land,' and anxious petitions to be allowed to return home. 'I have spent my time I cannot tell how availinge me nothinge at all,' a disgruntled yeoman wrote from Cupids, Conception Bay, in 1612.[32] Lord Baltimore took his wife and children to Ferryland in 1628 but sent them back to England the following summer, with this explanation: 'I have sent them home after much sufferance in this wofull country, where with one intolerable wynter were we almost undone. It is not to be expressed with my pen what wee have endured.'[33] All the organized English colonies were failing, and the hope of turning a profit through such ventures had proved to be baseless. There was as yet no economic alternative to the century-old migratory fishery, carried out in the spring and summer by west country fishermen who had no interest in settling permanently. However, the colonies around Conception Bay and on the Southern Shore left behind a trickle of permanent settlers, and by 1660 a resident white population, however small, had become established on the island.

JAMES YONGE

By comparison with the reports of jaundiced settlers and eager promoters on conditions in seventeenth-century Newfoundland, that of

James Yonge seems remarkably free of bias. Yonge was born in Plymouth in 1647 and at the age of ten was apprenticed to a naval surgeon. His first voyage to Newfoundland as a ship's surgeon took place in 1663, when he accompanied a crew of migratory fishermen to Renews. Over the next seven years he returned to Newfoundland on three more occasions, twice to St John's and once to Bay Bulls, but in the spring of 1670 he became so terrified of ice conditions on the voyage westward that he resolved thereafter to 'try Land luck.' Yonge's *Journal* was published in 1963, and his factual, workmanlike account of his experiences in Newfoundland is now recognized as an invaluable literary document.

Yonge's curiosity was keen, and his account of the economics and procedures of the migratory fishery is minutely detailed. How many men fished at Renews in 1663, what preparations were necessary before fishing could begin, how fish were split, salted, washed, and dried, how much the surgeon and fishermen were paid, what diseases he had to treat and how he treated them – all this he faithfully records, with much more. Throughout his account we catch vignettes of a harsh, laborious, and risky life. On his initial voyage he noted the risks taken by the 'mad Newfoundland men' who were 'so greedy of a good place' along the coast that they 'ventured in strangely' to land with their ships in foggy weather. The work of fishing sometimes became so onerous that the 'shore men' who processed the catch could rest 'not above two hours in a night'; and boys employed as helpers would become 'so tired with labour' that they would steal off and sleep in the woods, unaware of the bites of mosquitoes, which would leave them temporarily blind with their faces 'prodigiously swoln.' One little boy – perhaps one of the 'inhabitants' Yonge refers to – lost 'the top of its nose, several fingers, part of the glans and prepuce, both heels to the bones, and several toes' to frostbite, a complaint Yonge thought was caused by the 'very ill vapors' which emerged from the uncultivated ground inland. Infected sores, scurvy, colds, coughs, 'vexatious hemorrhages of the nose,' and other complaints gave Yonge 'much to do in my profession,' although he also found 'leisure to study, to walk, to fish, and take pleasure.' He seems to have been the only one of the crew to escape the pressures of a hard environment.[34]

The Newfoundland historian D.W. Prowse, after quoting a description of the cod fishery from Marc Lescarbot's *Nova Francia* (1609), commented in 1895 that in Lescarbot's account 'we have an ancient picture of the mode of fishing, the stage, the water-horse, the splitting table, the pews, the flakes, the hand-barrows; all are exactly like those to be found to this day around our shores.'[35] A similar remark can be made of Yonge's *Journal*, for in many of the details he supplies and in the general atmosphere his words evoke there is a resemblance to day-to-day activity of outport life in Prowse's time and, indeed, in the outport of living memory. What Yonge brings home to us is the essential continuity of life in Newfoundland over the centuries. From the primitive beginnings of organized society which he observed around the coast, the 'planters,' 'inhabitants,' and 'interlopers' who would stay on in Newfoundland after the migratory fishermen had gone home, would grow a people shaped by the same fickle, relentless pressures of geography that dominated life in Renews in 1663. A process of 'merciless winnowing' had begun, and from it would come 'a race apart.'[36]

2 Fishers of men

THREE MISSIONARIES IN
EIGHTEENTH-CENTURY
NEWFOUNDLAND / 1764–98

A CENTURY OF ANARCHY

When the attempts at establishing private colonies in Newfoundland failed, the island's history entered a long period of obscurity and neglect. The historian Keith Matthews has shown that between 1660 and 1700 the official policy of the British government towards New-foundland fluctuated among three alternatives: encouraging settle-ment, discouraging settlement, and having no policy at all.[1] During this period Newfoundland was a pawn among warring British mer-cantile interests, some of which argued that settlement would inter-fere with the rich migratory fishery, while others held that settlement was necessary to ensure English control over the island. In 1699 a policy that amounted to a compromise between these two viewpoints was established, and an act known as 'King William's Act' was passed which in effect allowed limited settlement 'but decided against any form of residential law or government.' This act was designed deliber-ately to retard the development of the colony and to permit unim-peded exploitation of the fish resource by English merchants. It 'formed the basis of British policy for the next hundred years.'[2]

Eighteenth-century Newfoundland thus presents the unusual spectacle of a society developing, or at any rate existing, without the benefit of government. It is hard to think of a situation in colonial history that more closely approximates the anarchist model. There was, indeed, from the beginning of the century a rudimentary form of government. King William's Act made the commander of the naval convoy which annually accompanied the fishing ships 'a sort of appeal judge,'[3] and in 1729, after a period of disorder and crime in the colony, the commander was made a governor and was permitted to appoint magistrates. In addition, as the century progressed, a primitive legal system evolved in response to the growing needs of the population. However, until 1817 the governor resided in Newfoundland only for the duration of the fishing season, roughly from June to September or October, and for the remaining months there was no effective authority in the colony. The resulting precariousness of life during the long Newfoundland winters combined with the natural rigour of the climate, the harshness of the terrain, and the vicissitudes of the fishery to keep the number of settlers to a minimum and guarantee the success of British policy. Nor were these the only factors that retarded the growth of a resident population. Though far removed from the purview of European statesmen, Newfoundland throughout the eighteenth century felt the reverberations of foreign wars, and settlements along the coast were subjected to occasional devastating raids by the French and harassment by privateers. In looking through documents related to the period, it does not take long to find examples of common people, similar to those in Hardy's *Dynasts*, 'writhing' and 'crawling,' 'distressed by events which they did not cause.'[4]

Why anybody would have chosen to settle on Newfoundland's bleak coastline seemed to one early eighteenth-century observer, a chaplain on a British ship who had a knack for rhyming, to be a source of amazement:

> Who then can represent this dismal Place?
> (Thrown by itself to be the World's disgrace)
> For whate'er offers to my present view,
> Looks truly frightful with a ghastly hue,
> Numbers of craggy Rocks hang o'er the Sea,
> Yielding an horrid prospect from each Bay:
> The Mountains lofty Tops do mount so high,
> As if they proudly meant to reach the Sky:
> The Land within is all a Wood entire,
> That any home-bred Mortal must admire,
> What frenzy could unhappy Men besot,
> To settle where scarce Food is to be got.
> If Eatables within the Country grows,
> Its hitherto what no Enquirer knows:
> No painful Peasant breaks up this hard Ground,
> Nor scarce a Blade of Grain can here be found;
> No studious Need doth useful Arts explore
> From well-till'd Fields to reap the fruitful Store.

Tough Spruce does choak the Land instead of Corn,
And an unthrifty Crop of Weeds is borne:
Nay truly this bad Soil all Good denies,
And nothing can be sown, and nothing rise.
Thus the whole Island, or by Nature curst,
Or Fate's decree, is certainly the worst
Of any Spot, which on the Globe doth lie,
Beneath the Covering of the starry Sky.[5]

But in spite of adverse conditions, a year-round population clung to the shoreline of the Avalon Peninsula, slowly spread further around eastern Newfoundland, and gradually increased in number. By the terms of the Treaty of Utrecht in 1713, the French were driven from their settlement in Placentia and, as a kind of compensation for the loss, were permitted to land and dry fish on the northern coastline between Cape Bonavista and Point Riche. One effect of the treaty was to open up Placentia Bay and the south coast of the island to British settlers. At the end of the seventeenth century, there were only about twelve hundred permanent residents in Newfoundland. This number, while subject to yearly fluctuations, had increased to around three thousand five hundred by 1732; by 1770 it had reached nearly twelve thousand and in 1790 about thirty thousand.[6] As the population grew, the number of Irish settlers came to equal those of west country stock, and the ratio between numbers of permanent settlers and visiting fishermen also changed. In 1750 that ratio was approximately 5:8; at the end of the century 90 per cent of the summer population consisted of year-round residents. By 1800 the migratory fishery from England had virtually ended, and a large settled population had emerged which knew 'no home but Newfoundland.'[7] The appearance of the coastal landscape had also changed. On a large portion of the eastern shoreline the thick coniferous forest had been replaced by what geographers call 'a discontinuous strip of cultural fabric.' Or, as a sympathetic poet might have put it, the land was becoming 'scored with the print of perished hands.'[8]

There is no shortage of statistical information about eighteenth-century Newfoundland, for both visitors and 'Newfoundlanders' (the term seems to have been first used in print to describe permanent residents of the island, as distinct from the English and Irish, in 1765[9]) were counted annually by the agents of the naval governors, who were obliged to report to authorities in London on the population and economic activity around the island. These surviving dispatches together with other information constitute a rich 'data source'[10] from which geographers can deduce much about the shape and progress of settlement. But lists of numbers, and neat diagrams and graphs based upon them, do not get us very close to the lives of ordinary settlers, to an understanding of 'the inner springs of the life of human society; the constructive work of the unknown masses, which so seldom finds any mention in books, and the importance of that constructive work in the growth of forms of society [and] in the accomplishment of all important historical events.'[11] In order to understand something of this invisible process we need, not long rows of figures and collections of laws, but a native literature or a literature based on prolonged, firsthand observation of common life. The closest equivalent to this in the period we are considering was the writing of missionaries.

JAMES BALFOUR

The Society for the Propagation of the Gospel in Foreign Parts, the most important Anglican missionary society, was established by Royal Charter in 1701, and in 1703 began its formal connection with Newfoundland by appointing its first missionary in St John's, John Jackson.[12] Continuous SPG involvement with Newfoundland did not, however, begin until 1725, with the appointment of Henry Jones to Bonavista. In 1731 Robert Kilpatrick was sent to Trinity Bay, and, as we shall see, Conception Bay was sent its first SPG missionary in 1767. None of these four missions was continuously occupied in the eighteenth century, but in the lengthy annual reports sent back to the society by its ministers we see, or seem to see, how ordinary people lived in the outharbours of Newfoundland.

Missionaries sent by the SPG to Newfoundland in the eighteenth century were men who, by birth and education, seem on the whole to have been ill-prepared to cope with the harsh conditions of life in the colony or to understand the ways of the people they were meant to serve. Their letters and reports were filled with complaints: about the weather, isolation, threats from Irish malcontents, inadequate housing, scarcity of food, the immorality and wilfulness of the people, and above all, their parishioners' reluctance to pay for their support. It is wise to bear in mind as one reads such letters that it was sometimes in the interest of the missionary to exaggerate the backwardness of his parishioners and the precariousness of his own circumstances, since such indications of labour and duress could, and sometimes did, prompt the SPG to supplement his salary. On the other hand, when a missionary calls attention to his unexpected success, he may also have his eye on the effect his letter will create in London. This is not to say that the SPG missionaries had no hardships to endure; there can be no doubt that on occasion, and especially during wartime, they suffered grievously. They also responded with pity and concern to the greater sufferings of their unsalaried parishioners. But it is hard to read their accounts of Newfoundland without detecting their conspicuous concern for their own status and welfare, and, all too often, a barely suppressed aversion for the manners and circumstances of ordinary people.

James Balfour was a young graduate of Oxford University who was sent to the SPG mission at Trinity in 1764. On his arrival in St John's he was briefed by the resident missionary there, Edward Langman, another Oxford man, about the people who were to be his parishioners. 'They may be led, but not drove,' Langman told him.[13] A month later Balfour reported from Trinity to the SPG in the following terms: 'To be sure nothing can be more laudable, than to instruct the ignorant, more especially the poor creatures here: who are in a manner in an original state of nature, or if you please, little better than savages.'[14]

In October 1765, having endured a winter 'so inclement and ghastly' that it was 'beyond any description that I can give of it,' he noted that one of the most 'shocking' features of 'this uncomfortable part of the world' was 'to see vices of every kind so very familiar as to loose their deformity, & become agreeable.' Balfour was evidently referring to the common law marriages he saw in several families. In the course of giving these grim accounts of Trinity, and noting the people's 'licentious way of living,' he also acknowledged that his parishioners 'have built me a good convenient new house, valued at one hundred & thirty pounds English money, ... more than ever I expected here.' In 1766 he wrote of 'the most agreeable harmony & contentment, subsisting between my people & me,'[15] but a year later he sent the following tale of woe:

Trade declines very much here; and the spirits of the people are quite sunk. – The bad voyage of fishing this year has almost entirely ruin'd the richest of them. – And the miseries of the poor are inexpressible. There were I think seventy subscribers for a missionary. – A great many of them are either bankrupt – dead – or gone from the country, and those that remain give themselves no concern, how a missionary is to be supported, notwithstanding everything here costs three times the value of what it does in England. – They plead that paying yearly for a seat is unconstitutional, and tho' their predecessors did always so, that is no reason they should be fools too. They value themselves upon never having properly agreed to give any church dues but according to their own pleasure. – The church is so ruinous that it is almost ready to drope down, & altho' their forefathers, were so pious as to build it, their children are so impious, they will not repair it. I live among a people that love heartily to vex & plague one another, no description can equal their malice & envy that way, and every family seems at open war with its neighbour. I make no doubt but they have intercepted my letters that are miscarried. I know very well, when here, I must put up with innumerable ill wages of this kind from them. … I have unluckily again engag'd to give bill (before your letter came to hand) until [26 March 1768] in order to keep the raging famine that now prevails in this part of the world, from coming within my walls this winter. If the next year be no better than this: this whole harbour will certainly be depopulated. I am settled at present in the most uncomfortable mission, that can be. Necessity obliges the Irish here to mob frequently, & the wickedness & obstinacy of the people prevent any civil magistrate or justices of the peace being made among them by the Governor, for no man dare or will take upon him that charge. – For fear of house-breaking; I have been on my guard night & day this twelve months past: & every person of property the same. … I chuse Sir, thus to write you in this free manner, fairly to lay open the genius of my people.'[16]

The next year brought no improvement in Balfour's spirits or the alleged behaviour of his parishioners. His letter of 20 June 1768 expressed his continuing dislike of 'this terrible clime' and noted that his people, 'one & all of them, take a mighty pleasure, in cheating, defrauding & disappointing one another.' Balfour by now had found a wife in Newfoundland and had a family of 'two promising youths.' By 1769 he had found something else to complain of, in addition to the 'terrible severe winter here of six month's intense frost.' The 'Deistical opinions of traders from England,' he claimed, were now having 'a bad effect upon the minds of the generality of these people.' He promised, however, to use his 'assiduous exhortations' to gain more communicants for the church.[17]

So much for Balfour's impressions of the island and people during the first five years of his long service as an SPG missionary. He will cross our path again later in this chapter. In his letters between 1764 and 1769 it is hard to separate facts from, not lies, but the subtle distortions caused by self-righteousness, a lack of sympathy for common life, and a wish to create a good impression in London. There is still another feeling one gets from reading his letters, and this is felt as well in reading such nineteenth-century missionary accounts as Edward Wix's *Six Months of a Newfoundland Missionary's Journal* (1836) and F.E.J. Lloyd's *Two Years in the Region of Icebergs* (1886). It is this: that the missionary and the people inhabit different universes. The priest enforces, by precept and exhortation, a scrupulous code of morality upon the people and expects from them appropriate generosity; they are accustomed to a milieu in which a nice conscience has no place, which requires of men brute strength, vigilance, and guile to ensure survival. It was a gap of sensibility and outlook that many SPG missionaries could not bridge. Balfour was among them. To believe his accounts, eighteenth-century Newfoundlanders were pathetic savages, reluctantly clinging to a barren rock, quarrelsome, promiscuous, and capricious. As we shall see in subsequent pages, there is plenty of evidence to suggest a contrary view.

LAURENCE COUGHLAN

In November 1764 Edward Langman told the SPG that he had heard reports from Harbour Grace in Conception Bay that the people had 'fixed up the frame & gone a great way towards finishing' a new church, and, further, that they had already begun to raise 'a subscription' in support of a minister.[18] A year later, a number of prominent inhabitants of Harbour Grace, Mosquito, and Carbonear authorized George Davis, a London merchant who was probably about to leave Newfoundland for the winter, 'to procure and agree with a Protestant Minister of the Gospel' to come and reside among them.[19] The following April Davis informed the Earl of Dartmouth, president of the Board of Trade, that Laurence Coughlan seemed 'a proper Person' to fill this role as minister 'if he could obtain Holy Orders,' and urged Dartmouth to 'use your endeavours to get him ordained.' Coughlan was made deacon on April 25, licensed by the Bishop of London 'to perform the ministerial office in the province of Newfoundland' the following day, and ordained priest by Edmund Keene, Bishop of Chester, on the 27th. Since Dartmouth on 18 April indicated that a ship was waiting for Coughlan at Poole '& will sail as soon as he gets thither,'[20] the date of Coughlan's arrival in Newfoundland was therefore 1766, probably in June. After his initial visit to Newfoundland, Coughlan returned to England in the fall of 1766 with a petition to the SPG from the people, asking that he be appointed as their minister. The request was granted, and Coughlan arrived back in Harbour Grace with his wife and daughter in September 1767 to begin his six-year ministry.[21] It is apparent that neither the SPG nor the 'principal inhabitants' who had asked for his appointment knew Coughlan's real purpose in coming to North America.

Coughlan was a Methodist. An Irishman, he had converted from Roman Catholicism at Drumsna, County Leitrim, in 1753, and after 1755 had become an itinerant preacher in Ireland and England.[22] In 1760 he was preaching in Waterford, a port through which a great number of Irish servants travelled annually to Newfoundland and where Coughlan would probably have learned of the opportunities for missionary work in the colony.[23] By 1763 John Wesley regarded Coughlan as one of his most valued helpers but when Coughlan arranged to have himself ordained by Erasmus, a Greek Orthodox bishop, now thought an impostor, who had turned up in London in 1763, Wesley was angered and embarrassed.[24] In Wesley's view, Coughlan was 'a person who had no learning at all' and accordingly did not qualify for ordination. A letter by Wesley in 1768 states that Coughlan had brought another 'blot' upon him when he 'married and ruined' an unnamed woman. The ruin alluded to was evidently financial. In addition, there were theological differences between the two men.[25] In any event, by 1765 Coughlan's formal connection with Wesley was at an end, and he was available for another mission.[26]

The record of Coughlan's ministry in Harbour Grace from 1767 to 1773 shows that he led a kind of double life. As an Anglican priest, according to his annual reports to the SPG, he administered the sacraments to a growing number of communicants, held regular services in Harbour Grace and, after 1768, in nearby Carbonear, and on occasion preached in the Irish language to Irish fishermen to make them see 'the errors of Popery.'[27] In addition, on his arrival in Harbour Grace in 1767 he opened a school and hired a schoolmaster, and maintained the school, despite financial difficulties, during his ministry. By 1772 Coughlan could justly claim that he had served the SPG with distinction.[28] However, this appearance of success as an Anglican cloaked his real Methodist ambition, which was to be an instrument of evangelical conversion among the people. In this effort he met with no success for almost three years, though he 'laboured Night and Day,' preaching 'from House to House' in the manner favoured by Wesley. Coughlan at length grew discouraged, and determined he would not stay 'in such a poor desolate Land, and spend my Strength for naught'; but his dogged efforts eventually bore fruit, and a Methodist revival began and spread '*like Fire.*' According to Coughlan, the 'awakening' occurred in a 'very remarkable Manner,' manifesting itself in public testimonies, 'loud Songs of Praises,' extraordinary deathbed protestations of faith, and a widespread reformation of morals. Prior to the revival, he said, the 'Natives' had spent 'much of their Time in Rioting and Drunkenness.'[29]

As this revival spread, and reports circulated around Conception Bay that 'the People at *Harbour-Grace* and *Carbonear* were going mad,'[30] Coughlan started to meet opposition from his more orthodox parishioners. His Methodist enthusiasm and theology now began to appear in sermons to his regular congregations, and he openly encouraged Anglicans to attend the private meetings which he was organizing in houses throughout his parish.[31] The merchants who had initially promised to support the missionary now informed him that his 'Way of preaching was Madness.'[32] A series of ugly incidents followed in 1771 and 1772, provoked, in part, by Coughlan's own zealousness. In 1771 he publicly denounced a merchant named Hugh Roberts for living in adultery and advised his congregation to avoid dealing with the merchant in future. He also tried physically to prevent some of Roberts's labourers from working on Sunday. These incidents led the merchants to petition the governor to have Coughlan 'silenc'd or remov'd,'[33] and when yet another ferocious, open quarrel broke out in 1772, this one partly caused by Coughlan's refusal to allow an 'immoral' merchant to sponsor a child in baptism, the governor asked the SPG to recall their missionary.[34] Late in 1773 Coughlan returned to England and resigned his mission.[35] He died in London, probably in 1784.

In the surviving documents dealing with Coughlan's relationship with the merchants, there is the violent language of controversy and personal antagonism. This contrasts strikingly with the note of affection and loyalty sounded in letters to him from the ordinary people who joined his movement.[36] That movement caught hold and flourished as the opposition of the merchants increased, spreading from Harbour Grace and Carbonear to coves in the immediate vicinity, and northward as far as Blackhead on the North Shore of Conception Bay. The establishment of societies beyond Carbonear indicates Coughlan's desire to 'travel up and down in this land' to spread the message of Methodism. If he could have continued in this itinerant way, he told Wesley in 1772, he would have stayed in Newfoundland, 'but as I cannot, except by water, in small boats, I am not able to stand it.'[37] Coughlan's 'dreadful Apprehensions' of the sea made his life in the colony 'one continued Martyrdom,' and the willingness of the people to come to Harbour Grace from neighbouring communities 'over the mighty waters at the hazard of their lives, with their little babes in their arms' filled him with admiration.[38]

Coughlan's *Account of the Work of God in Newfoundland* (1776) consists mainly of pious letters sent to Coughlan by his followers after his departure from Newfoundland and accounts of 'Experiences' or individual conversions. Such 'artless Language' is provided as a means of 'stirring up the dear Children of God.' There is not, in fact, much direct description of the people's way of life in Coughlan's little book. What distinguishes it from similar accounts by many other spg missionaries is the attitude displayed in it towards ordinary Newfoundlanders. Coughlan is able to describe their rather primitive houses without calling the people savages, and there may even be a hint of humour in his recollection of waking up in some of them on a winter's day:

The Winters in *Newfoundland* are very severe, there being great Falls of Snow, and hard Frost; the Houses there are mostly very disagreeable to those who are not used to them; in general, they are all Wood; the Walls, so called, are Studs put into the Ground close together, and between each, they stop Moss, as they call it, to keep out the Snow; this they cover with Bark of Trees, and put great Clods over that; some are covered with Boards: In such Houses I have been, and in the Morning my Bedside has had a beautiful white Covering of Snow; my Shoes have been so hard frozen, that I could not well put them on, till brought to the Fire ...

His description of the building of a new church at Blackhead in the winter of 1768 contains his most revealing statement about his parishioners:

They proposed to me, to point out a Place where I would choose to build a Church, which was agreed upon; accordingly all Hands went into the Wood, and cut down as much of it as they wanted, which they hauled out upon what they call Slides. When they had the Timber upon the Place, they sent for me, and I went, thinking there was not one Stick hewn; however they had made great Progress in the Work; the People there in general are good Hatchet Men (there are very few Carpenters in *Europe*, who are able to hew a Piece of Timber with those in *Newfoundland*, this they take up naturally;) they are People of a very bright Genius: I have known a Man, who could not read a Letter in a Book, go into the Wood, and cut down Timber, bring the same out with the Help of a Servant, and build a Boat, rig it, and afterwards go to Sea with the same Boat. – But to return; the said Church was framed, and covered in, in less than fourteen Days, which contained about four hundred People. – God raised up here a precious People ...

Perhaps the most significant feature of this passage is the recognition it contains of the distinctiveness of the people, a distinctiveness evident to Coughlan in the impressive way they had learned the special skills demanded by the Newfoundland milieu. The same point is made elsewhere in his book when he distinguishes between the ordinary people he served and '*Europeans*, who came annually to fish.'[39] Coughlan's perception, based on years of working among the people, that Newfoundlanders were in some ways superior to Europeans, may be contrasted with the hasty judgments formed by other observers, some of which were so patronizing and abusive that they convinced a modern historian that eighteenth-century settlers on the island represented 'the gradual degeneration of a splendid stock.'[40] Such a notion finds little support in the writings of the early Methodists, those who knew Newfoundlanders best. Nor can the differences in attitude between Coughlan and, say, Balfour, be accounted for by pointing to disparate economic and living conditions in different bays. When Balfour came to Conception Bay from Trinity, there was no perceptible change in his view of the common people.

WILLIAM THORESBY

When Coughlan vacated his mission, James Balfour saw an opportunity to leave Trinity Bay and obtain a parish where 'the emoluments, as well as trust, will be both greater.' He accordingly asked the SPG to authorize a transfer, and arrived in Harbour Grace with his family in October 1775. Balfour soon learned how profoundly Coughlan had influenced the people of Conception Bay. In Harbour Grace he was for some years forbidden the use of the manse unless he agreed to pay rent. When, in 1775, he tried to enter the little chapel in Carbonear, the doors were shut against him, and in another incident in 1778 he came close to being physically assaulted in the pulpit. The people in Carbonear insisted that they wanted 'a Methodist, or Presbyterian' as their minister, and that 'the Meeting house was their own, and ... they would do with it what they pleased.'[41] Late in 1775 Balfour sent the SPG a description of his new and (to him) combustible parishioners:

I think proper to drop this short line, as a sketch of what I have observed of the genius of this people. They are fond of holding private conventicles two or three times a week, in sentiments unfriendly to our civil government, and give the Magistrates sometimes a good deal of trouble. Were they numerous, and enterprising men to head them, they would exactly resemble the Americans on the continent. But happy for us, our people of property here are strictly loyal. It is only our lower classes that affect these things. – I act with the greatest moderation, because to oppose religion, as they term their enthusiasm, would kindle a fire. They are scheming to have a Methodist preacher recommended to them by their former missionary, or a Presbyterian which would render their neighbours of a different way of thinking very uneasy, and create a great deal of trouble: and which I hardly think government will allow ...[42]

Soon Balfour was relating the familiar tale of the people's 'low cunning' and meanness. Late in 1778 he at last managed to gain 'quiet possession' of the missionary's house in Harbour Grace, and in 1779, a year of 'raging famine, nakedness & sickness' throughout Conception Bay when a great number of people were forced to emigrate to America, an order from the governor forced the people to allow him to conduct divine services in the Carbonear chapel.[43] But while he had won a legal victory at a time of crisis, he could not stem the tide of Methodism and 'Popery,' and in 1785 he reported to the SPG that he had again been insulted at Carbonear and continued to be 'involved in a great deal of trouble by means of hot headed Enthusiastic people.'[44] In 1788 he asked to be recalled to England and in 1790 he once again noted that the 'generality' of his parishioners 'are a barbarous, perfidious, cruel people.'[45] He returned to England in 1792 and died in 1809.

From 1773 to 1784 Methodism was kept alive in the Conception Bay area by lay preachers. In October 1785 John McGeary became the first missionary sent by the British Methodist Conference to Newfoundland, but his years in Conception Bay (1785–8, 1790–2) were not marked by notable success, and when William Black, a Nova Scotia Methodist, visited McGeary at Wesley's request in 1791, he thought he saw signs that the movement was flagging.[46] Black's visit may have revitalized the movement, and although there seems to have been no formally appointed missionary on the island between 1792 and 1794, the arrival of George Smith (1766–1832) in 1794 ensured the continuing strength of Methodism in Conception Bay. Smith established new societies in Trinity Bay, Bonavista, and as far north as Greenspond. In 1796 he was sent back to Newfoundland accompanied by a second missionary, William Thoresby, who was about thirty-six years of age and already a veteran preacher on the English circuit.[47] Smith was to continue his work, already tentatively begun, in the Bonavista area, while Thoresby was to preach in the older societies in Conception Bay. Thoresby's journal of his life in Newfoundland from 1796 to 1798 was published as *A Narrative of God's Love to William Thoresby* (1799). It is a valuable book which offers intimate glimpses into the domestic and religious life of ordinary Newfoundlanders.

From October 1796 to July 1798 Thoresby was what Coughlan had wished to be in Newfoundland: an itinerant Methodist preacher among the common people. He preached in houses and churches along the coast between Old Perlican in Trinity Bay, where Methodism had been established by John Hoskins in 1784, and Brigus in Conception Bay, a shoreline that presented the greatest difficulties to the traveller. There was no road, and Thoresby was forced to use small boats, or labour through the woods, over the barrens, or along treacherous cliffs, in order to pass from community to community:

On Wednesday [Jan. 18th. 1797] in the afernoon, I went to a place at a little distance to preach; I had to go down a high mountain, and then on a path-way which led close by the side of a hill; I was obliged to walk on creepers, (two pieces of iron made to fit the feet, having prods to pierce the ice to prevent the foot from slipping) the sea roared in a tremendious manner under us, which made it very frightful, and more so in the situation we were in, for had our feet slipt we must have unavoidably tumbled headlong into the sea; but God preserved us in safety, glory be to him for ever.

[Jan. 26th. 1797] I parted with my friends in this harbour [Bay Roberts] in peace, and seven men rowed me ten miles in a skiff to Harbourgrace; they had to beat through much ice, and the frost was very severe. I lay with seven great coats around me at the bottom of the boat; and it was with difficulty that I escaped being burnt with the frost; but I bless God that I was not.

Feb. 13th. [1797] This day I left [Lower] Island Cove, conducted by a young man through woods and waste places to Old Perlican, much fatigued; the snow frequently broke in (being a thaw) and let me up to the middle; many rocks and stumps of old trees we have to pass over and by; well, he in whom we live and move, brought me safe to Mr. Mark's, where I was kindly received by the heads of the family.[48]

These episodes occurred during Thoresby's first winter in Conception Bay. The simple, direct account of that hard season is the most memor-

able part of his book. The bitter cold once froze the ink in his pen as he
was writing. Conception Bay itself froze over, and the effect of the cold
upon farm animals was pitiful:

[Apr. 4th 1797] My mind is greatly affected sometimes when I look at the dumb
creatures in this island, especially those who had their limbs froze; some with
one leg, and here and there with none. Numbers of the fowls had their toes
froze off this winter, and likewise the combs of the cocks.

'How long and severe the winter continues on this island!' he
exclaimed in Carbonear on 16 March, the thought of the winter even
driving from his mind the rumour that a Roman Catholic priest and
his people were going to attack him next day. From October to April
there was no news of what was happening in the world beyond
Conception Bay. Finally, after a number of false reports that ships had
arrived from England, the *Stag* sailed into Carbonear on 13 April,
relieving the people's sense of isolation but bringing 'the awful tid-
ings of a Spanish war.'[49]
    The winter made the missionary's work 'great and very laborious'
and sometimes caused awkward moments while he was conducting
services. At one house he was 'much disturbed, as I sung, by the
grunting of a pig that lay under the long-settle,' where the animal had
apparently taken refuge from the cold. The presence of farm animals in
people's homes was not uncommon:

The men that live in Newfoundland are in general of a hardy race, for many of
their houses or tilts are not proof against wind or weather, numbers of them
are open on every side. Several times this winter I have been snowed upon
both as I sat in the house and lay in bed; and in some of their houses you might
see the men and women, boys and girls, sheep and hogs, hens and ducks,
dogs and cats scrambling in every direction to catch a bit of any thing eatable;
though it is so in many houses, it is not the case with every one: my heart has
been pained many times on their account. With respect to myself, I have
reason to be thankful, for wherever I go I meet with kind friends; they
endeavour to make me as comfortable as the nature of things will allow ... [50]

The primitive scene would produce sneers about 'savages' from un-
sympathetic observers, but Thoresby's observations are marked by
gentleness and fairness. He never grumbles. While there are references to 'bigotted' Anglicans and 'wicked' Roman Catholics, there is
not a hint of complaint in his book about the people he served.

Thoresby's book shows the people leading a disasterprone, tremulous existence, subject to the buffetings of unpredictable weather, disease, and the high risks of a seafaring way of life. Infectious diseases or 'fevers' were a source of particular terror. Between October and January in his first year in Newfoundland, Thoresby had to bury 'more than forty' people who died of 'fever' at Carbonear and three adjacent coves, and fear of catching the disease was so acute that at the burial of a beloved inhabitant of Adam's Cove 'the people were afraid of coming near the corps.' The following June the fever appeared again. Every month brought news of wrecks, drownings, or miraculous rescues, with the seal fishery, 'dangerous beyond description,' taking a high toll of lives. During Thoresby's stay in Conception Bay the seal fishery was conducted by men and boys who simply walked out on the treacherous Arctic ice as soon as it came near shore, and a change in the direction of the wind could prove disastrous. On the road to Crocker's Cove in April 1797, Thoresby met a man 'in tears, who told me that his two sons went in the morning on the ice, and had not returned.' The following day Thoresby got 'melancholy news' at Harbour Grace that ten men had been lost at the ice-fields.[51]

The ice, snow, wind, frost, and ocean seemed to dominate life, presenting daily obstacles to Thoresby as he made his rounds, demanding constant watchfulness and persistence, punishing and frightening. Yet neither the missionary nor his people became brutalized, dumbly submissive, when confronted by the harsh elements. Thoresby himself was occasionally struck by the wonder and beauty of what he saw. Once, going by boat past a very high rock, he was 'delighted with the sight of an eagle that flew therefrom; it was a beautiful large bird.' The quick freezing of the whole of Conception Bay made him exclaim: 'how astonishing!' In June 1797, on 'the first summer's evening' after the long winter, he was 'greatly delighted with the prospect I was favoured with of several islands of ice,' one of which 'was as large as St. Paul's in London.'[52] His parishioners too, in their vigorous, emotional participation in Methodist services, and in their kindly treatment of the minister, show unexpected reserves of warmth and generosity. Any theoretical notion that a life lived close to the elements must of necessity coarsen or deaden a people's sensibility must be qualified after reading Thoresby's *Narrative*.

The population of Newfoundland in the eighteenth century has been described by one historian as 'small, scattered, and shifting.'[53] As a general observation on the whole island, this can perhaps be defended, but it does not seem true of Conception Bay in the years

1796–8, as described by Thoresby, nor indeed does it seem to square with Coughlan's earlier observations. Though subject to a variety of disruptive influences, and deprived of political institutions, Thoresby's parishioners appear to have been a settled people, who had learned how to vary their occupations to seasonal requirements and whose lives were perhaps no harsher than those of rural people in, say, the remote corners of England. Data sheets and dull statistical reports of governors' agents hide their human reality from our eyes, and one wishes, even while reading the letters and books of missionaries, to see them better. But we do see them faintly, ordinary men and women in Newfoundland crawling in labour and obscurity to their graves, caught in 'the monotonous moils of strained, hard-run Humanity.'[54]

3 ~~Walking new ground

BOOKS BY TWO NEWFOUNDLAND
PIONEERS / 1770–1822

With the signing of the Treaty of Paris in 1763, the history of Newfoundland entered a new phase of expansion and exploration. Although the French 'liberty' to catch and process fish on the Treaty
Shore between Cape Bonavista and Point Riche was reaffirmed in the
agreement, the British government 'emphasized that this was not an
exclusive right,' and the interests of the merchants and settlers who
had moved into Notre Dame Bay, and even west of Cape St John,
during the Seven Years War were thus in a sense formally recognized.[1]
In effect, a new coastline lay open for English fishermen and furriers to
exploit. By signing the Treaty of Paris, the French also handed over all
of New France, including Labrador, to England, whereupon the Labrador coast was placed under the control of the governor of Newfoundland. An energetic governor, Hugh Palliser, was appointed in
1764 and immediately took steps to consolidate the English hold on the
Newfoundland and Labrador fisheries. His zeal reflected a growing
awareness in the British government of the importance of the Newfoundland fishery, which was becoming recognized, in the words of
Edmund Burke, as 'the most valuable branch of trade we have in the
world.'[2]

During Palliser's tenure as governor (1764–8) James Cook completed his surveys of the north, south, and west coasts of Newfoundland, and of Chateau Bay on the coast of Labrador.[3] Thus by 1767 the
cartography of coastal Newfoundland was established on a firm scientific basis, and after 1768 Cook's successor as Surveyor of Newfoundland, Michael Lane, continued the task of mapping the coast of
Labrador. A further indication of British scientific interest in New-

foundland during this period was the extended visit of the naturalist Joseph Banks in 1766, which produced the first study of the colony's flora and fauna. Cook's and Lane's charts, however, had an interest beyond the merely scientific. They facilitated the British policy of strictly enforcing the geographical terms of the Treaty of Paris and of extending their fishery further around the coast. The new governor, for his part, was determined to pursue this policy aggressively. In traditional Newfoundland historiography, Palliser is usually pictured as a reactionary or villain for his attempt to discourage permanent settlement on the island, and it is true that he regarded 'inhabitant fishers' as 'abandoned savage wretches';[4] but his efforts to revive the migratory fishery at the expense of settlers ultimately had little effect and he deserves a better name in textbooks. He certainly did not lack decisiveness or courage. In June 1765 he arrested French crews discovered fishing near the south coast of Newfoundland and seized their ships; three months later he banished two Quebec merchants from Cape Charles in Labrador, where they had been carrying on 'a most pernicious illicit trade' with the French.[5] Palliser's plan for the Labrador coast was to preserve it for English migratory fishermen, and to prevent not only other nations but also other British colonists and even inhabitants of Newfoundland from gaining access to it.

The earliest French adventurers in Labrador seem to have succeeded in establishing friendly contact with native peoples, but by 1765 the relationship between the Eskimos and the English was marked by fear and suspicion.[6] Palliser realized that the only way to make the riches of Labrador available to English merchants was to placate the Eskimos, whom he regarded as 'the most Savage of all Savages.'[7] Accordingly he supported the attempts of the Moravians to establish missions along the Labrador coast. Jens Haven, a Danish carpenter and Moravian missionary, made the first successful contact with the Eskimos in a dramatic encounter in 1764, approaching the people in their own language, which he had learned in Greenland.[8] A year later he returned with three companions, and Palliser himself turned up at Pitt's Harbour in Chateau Bay in August 1765, and with the help of the Moravians spoke to an assembly of about three hundred Eskimos, promising peace and friendship. One of the chiefs struck Palliser on the chest, kissed him, and said: 'We will remain good friends.'[9] By 1766 English merchants were beginning to exploit the cod fishery in southern Labrador. Palliser had a stockade built in Chateau Bay, which was garrisoned year-round between 1766 and 1775 to protect English enterprise on the coast. Despite these careful tactics, in 1767 the merchant Nicholas Darby was driven from his fishing establishment near Cape Charles by the Eskimos, who killed three of his men. The attackers had been angered by American whalers, who evidently made a practice of hunting and plundering the people at will. This setback notwithstanding, the next couple of decades would see the English moving cautiously northward in search of fish, seals, and furs. Three years after the deadly skirmish with the Eskimos, at a time when 'no British Subject in Labrador would venture to reside further northward than Chatteau Bay,'[10] George Cartwright arrived to take Darby's place in Charles Harbour. Cartwright's eventual description of his experiences, the voluminous *Journal of Transactions and Events, during a Residence of nearly Sixteen Years on the Coast of Labrador* (Newark 1792) was the earliest published record of a white man's prolonged encounter with the Labrador wilderness. It is one of the two most impressive early literary responses to the 'undiscovered country' at the colony's frontiers.

CARTWRIGHT'S 'LOV'D LABRADOR,' 1770–86

Cartwright was born in Marnham, Nottinghamshire, in 1739, the second son of a respectable family of ten children which included Edmund, the poet and inventor of the power-loom, and John, an influential pamphleteer. George Cartwright's youth was spent in military service in India, Ireland, and Germany, and by 1757 he had risen to the brevet rank of captain. His superiors not seeming inclined to give him a higher rank, Cartwright began to look elsewhere for employment and pleasure, and indulged his 'insatiable propensity for shooting'[11] by making excursions to Scotland and, in 1766 and 1768, to Newfoundland, where he joined his brother John, then a lieutenant in the navy, in an expedition up the Exploits River in search of the Beothuck Indians. The expedition, which will be discussed later in this chapter, was commanded by John Cartwright, but in his *Journal* his older brother seems to take much of the credit for it – a piece of fraternal buccaneering, almost humorous in its openness, that illustrates the latter's considerable self-esteem. In 1770 Cartwright disentangled himself from the army altogether and was permitted to retire at half pay in order to begin 'carrying on various branches of business upon the coast of Labrador' in partnership with a naval colleague and two Bristol merchants.[12] On 30 July 1770, he took possession of Nicholas Darby's abandoned premises in Charles Harbour which he initially decided would be his own residence during his sojourn in

Labrador. By arrangement with his partners, he would stay in Labrador throughout the year to collect fish and furs and supervise the shore establishment, while they would supply such materials and provisions as could not be obtained locally and ensure delivery of his accumulated products to market. Every third winter he would spend in England. Cartwright had what he liked to call his 'family' with him. It comprised initially a housekeeper and mistress, Mrs Selby, two servants, two carpenters, a mason, a blacksmith named O'Brien, and O'Brien's wife, but in later years the number of employees and servants would increase in summertime to about seventy and include such companions as an Eskimo slave girl, whom Cartwright purchased from her father, and four English convicts. In addition to this odd entourage, Cartwright brought with him seven dogs of various species, two tame rabbits, two goats, and some chickens. On his first night in Charles Harbour he sent two men ashore to take care of the animals, but since none of his crew 'had ever been in this part of the world before, they were greatly terrified with the continual crying of the loons.' On the following day Cartwright himself landed with his servant Ned 'and took a walk upon the barrens.' He saw no caribou, but 'I got shots at an otter, a black-duck, and a spruce-game, with my Hanoverian rifle, and killed them all.'[13]

Thus began a yearly round of hunting, trapping, and fishing which Cartwright recorded with astonishing persistence until his departure from the coast in 1786. His strategy to ensure survival and make a profit was simply to kill whatever animal came his way, for though a creature might not yield furs or be otherwise marketable, it could almost certainly be eaten. The list of animal species killed and eaten by Cartwright and his crews is extraordinarily long, spanning the entire range of subarctic creatures from polar bears to whiskey jacks. At one point we find the hunter deliberating over whether he prefers 'loin of wolf' to 'loin of white-bear,' and at another contemplating having to resort to 'bow-wow-pie.' The killing was both highly organized and, given Cartwright's apparently phenomenal appetite and the number of servants in his retinue, highly necessary. Every season brought certain varieties of game and fish within range of the hunters, and if the caribou were not killed when the opportunity arose, or if the fishermen were not prepared to kill salmon or seals during the brief appearance of those species, then the little community could run dangerously short of food or ultimately would not prosper. Even with Cartwright's determined pursuit of game, hunger threatened him more than once during his stay in Labrador, and three of his men who were sent to winter in Sandwich Bay in 1774 starved to death after eating their dogs and part of their furs.[14] When these circumstances are considered, it is perhaps ungracious to laugh, as the young poet Robert Southey laughed, at Cartwright's attentiveness to detail in his *Journal*, at 'the importance he attached to his traps.'[15] What seemed a trifling matter to an habitué of London literary society, the daily yield of trap or rifle, may have had an unimaginable urgency on the Labrador coast in the dead of winter. Still, there is something amusing in the plodding literalness and repetitiousness of the *Journal*. Cartwright never tired of sitting down at nightfall and recording, with a solemnity that would not have been out of place in the diurnal jottings of Napoleon or Caesar, how many curlews and gulls he shot during the day. His self-importance disarms criticism, and his indefatigable counting of birds, eggs, martens, and squirrels gives a childlike aura of 'strange simplicity' (to use Coleridge's phrase)[16] to what is in truth a narrative of relentless slaughter.

Only once in the huge *Journal* do we sense that Cartwright indulged in unnecessary killing. This episode occurred in 1778, after he had moved his headquarters from Charles Harbour to a more favourable site further north in Sandwich Bay. On 22 July Cartwright went exploring on foot along the Eagle River. Half a mile inland he spotted several 'white bears' fishing in the stream, and soon a cub sat still on a rock, offering a fair shot. Cartwright shot it, at a distance of a hundred and twenty yards, and soon afterwards heard it 'crying mournfully' in the woods. The noise brought other bears down to the river from the neighbouring forest, and he fired at a she-bear, struck her in the head, and killed her. Her cub then charged the hunter 'with great ferocity' and, having no time to reload, he was forced to use his shotgun: 'I saluted him with a load of large shot in his right eye, which not only knocked that out, but also made him close the other.' Pawing his face and roaring 'most hideously,' the cub charged towards Cartwright again, 'mad with rage and pain,' and 'I gave him a second salute with the other barrel, and blinded him almost completely.' The cub's entire head was now covered with blood, and Cartwright caught a last sight of him 'blundering into the wood, knocking his head against every rock and tree that he met with.'

He now saw yet another she-bear and cub. He realized that shooting the mother would be dangerous in the circumstances, but 'I could not resist the temptation' and 'fortunately sent my ball through her heart.' Proceeding still further inland, he soon came upon a scene so beautiful that it stirred the pioneer's artistic impulses:

I came opposite to a beautiful cataract, and to the end of a small woody island which lies near the south shore. There I sat down upon some bare rocks, to contemplate the scene before me, and to observe the manoeuvres of the bears; numbers of which were then in sight.

The cataract is formed by the river being confined between two elevated points, with a flat rock extending across the bed of it; the perpendicular fall of which is eight feet; from whence there was a gradual descent for about forty yards, with several rude cubical rocks standing upon it. These made a most complete and magnificent cascade; far superior to the best artificial one I ever saw. Immediately beneath was a deep pool; and the river widened in a circular form, into a spacious basin of three hundred yards diameter, which taking a short turn below, resembled a circular pond. ... The whole was surrounded by small, detached hills, covered with spruces and firs, interspersed with larches, birch, and aspin, forming a most pleasing landscape; a drawing of which I greatly regretted that I was not able to take. In the lower part of the pool were several island-rocks, from one to two yards over; with salmon innumerable, continually leaping into the air, which had attracted a great concourse of bears. Some of them were diving after the fish: and I often observed them to get upon a rock, from whence they would take a high leap, fall head foremost into the water, dive to the bottom, and come up again at seventy or eighty yards distance. Others again were walking along shore; some were going into the woods, and others coming out. I had not sat there long, ere my attention was diverted, from the variety of objects, which at first presented themselves, to an enormous, old, dog bear, which came out of some alder-bushes on my right and was walking slowly towards me, with his eyes fixed on the ground, and his nose not far from it; at the same time he presented a fair forehead to me: I turned myself round to front him, drew up my feet to elevate my knees, on which I rested my elbows, and in that position suffered him to come within five yards of me before I drew the trigger; when I placed my ball in the centre of his scull, and killed him dead: but as the shore was a flat, reclining rock, he rolled round until he fell into the river; from the edge of which, he dropped at least four yards.

On casting my eyes around, I perceived another beast of equal size, raised half out of the water. He no sooner discovered me, than he made towards me as fast as he could swim. As I was not then prepared to receive him, I ran into the woods to make ready my unerring rifle. Whilst I was employed in that operation, he dived and brought up a salmon; which he repeatedly tossed up a yard or two in the air, and, letting it fall into the water, would dive and bring it up again. In this manner he diverted himself for some time, falling slowly down with the stream until he was shut out from my sight, by some bushes, which grew a little lower down. Being now ready, I advanced to the attack, and presently perceived him, standing in the water with his fore paws upon a rock, devouring the salmon. I crept through the bushes until I came opposite to him, and finding myself then within fifty yards, I interrupted his repast, by sending a ball through his head; it entered a little above his left eye, went out at the root of his right ear, and knocked him over; he then appeared to be in the agonies of death for some time; but at last recovered sufficiently to land on my side of the river, and to stagger into the woods; where I found he bled so copious a stream, that it was impossible he could go far.

Cartwright perceived that he had come upon 'the finest sport that man ever had.' Unfortunately, he had failed to take with him his usual large supply of balls, and his total kill for the day amounted to only six bears. He would certainly have killed 'four or five brace more' if he had been properly supplied. Moreover, Cartwright had shot the bears in a place so difficult of access that the eventual yield was only one skin and 'not one morsel of flesh.' And so 'the noblest day's sport I ever saw' ended in 'disappointment.'[17]

'O, let the hours be short,' Hotspur exclaimed before the Battle of Shrewsbury, 'Till fields, and blows, and groans applaud our sport!'[18] The word 'sport' seems almost equally inappropriate in Cartwright's account of the bloody scene on the Eagle River. It could be taken as a paradigm of vicious European intrusion into a North American idyll. Yet Cartwright must not be judged harshly. By 1778 he had become accustomed to scarcity, to making a living by slow accumulation and dogged effort. The winter especially was a long succession of lean days and weeks, marked in the *Journal* by anecdotes of empty traps, elusive game, and missed chances. When a hunter used to these grim circumstances unexpectedly came upon plenty, his natural response would be to take whatever he could get. The Labrador peninsula in the 1770's was no place to nurture a tender conscience. Cartwright had to be ruthless to survive. We see this roughness of character not just in his imperturbable slaughtering of animals but in his behaviour in his own household. 'I broke the stock of my Hanoverian rifle by striking a dog with it,' he noted coolly in December 1771. He administered frequent 'trimmings' to his employees, once giving a man named John MacCarthy twenty-seven lashes with a dog whip on the bare back for insubordination; on another occasion two obstreperous servants were given three beatings each to teach them good manners. One of the unfortunate convicts who came to Labrador with Cartwright on his sixth voyage was forced to eat the smelly guts of a caribou, as a lesson in how to dress an animal properly. Such cruelties as these were

commonplace. And yet, for all his severity, there was a compassionate
and even a courtly side to Cartwright which one is surprised to see
surviving in a man following his pursuits. This emerges particularly
in his relationship with the Eskimos, whom he treated on the whole
with courtesy and decency. It is true that on his first voyage we see him
taking advantage of the Eskimos in trade, for example exchanging a
2½d. comb for a silver fox worth four guineas,[19] but such mercantile
greed was accepted practice in his day. There is good reason to accept
his later claim that he was partly responsible for overcoming Eskimo
hostility towards the English, and it is worth noting that in a conversation with John Bland unrecorded in the *Journal* Cartwright declared
that 'he had always found [the Eskimos] more deserving of confidence
that his own countrymen.'[20]

The description of the Eagle River also displays Cartwright's liking
for the picturesque in nature, which some might misinterpret as a
mere literary flourish. He was in fact keenly interested in the natural
history of Labrador, writing elaborate accounts of the habits of the
beaver, caribou, and other animals which are minor classics of exact
observation. The flora of the region also interested him, and his habit
of searching in April and May for the first flowers of the Labrador
spring is one of the most poignant features of his *Journal*. Cartwright
was the first English writer to describe in some detail the rocky and
treacherous coastline between Cape Charles and Sandwich Bay,
which he saw for the first time in June 1775, during a period of poor
weather and rough ice conditions. His initial impressions were similar to those of the English poet William Falconer, who in *The Shipwreck*
(1762) claimed to have sailed

> From regions where Peruvian billows roar,
> To the bleak coasts of savage Labrador.[21]

The 'dreary' shore filled Cartwright with 'horror.' The 'astonished
mariner,' he wrote, 'is insensibly drawn into a conclusion, that this
country was the last which God made, and that he had no other view
than to throw together there, the refuse of his materials, as of no use to
mankind.' However, on leaving the coast and entering a deep bay,
'the face of nature' changed. Cartwright was so struck by the beauty
and fertility of Cartwright Harbour that he felt 'as if we had shot
within the tropics.' There he saw hills covered with a variety of trees,
'the different hues of which caused a pleasing variety,' 'verdant grass'
around the shore, water 'mottled over with duck and drakes, cooing

amorously,' and other attractions of a warm day in summer. In 1775 he gave one of his shore establishments in Sandwich Bay the name of Paradise.[22]

When we consider the risks and labour involved in his enterprise in Labrador, Cartwright's principal achievement will appear to be simply that he survived. Reading the *Journal*, we sense the nearness of disaster and marvel at the aplomb with which he confronted peril and responded to brushes with death. The constant danger in winter was of course the cold. Two men lost their way and froze to death during his years in Labrador, and once a dog that was accompanying him on a hunt succumbed to the weather and perished. Cartwright's own 'Herculean frame'[23] and careful habits protected him, but even he was once on the point of giving in: 'Finding [my] people could not keep pace with me, I pushed forward by myself, and felt very stout until I passed Black Head; but then, the snow growing lighter and deeper, (by being sheltered from drift) I sunk up to my knees even in Indian rackets [snowshoes], and soon was tired so completely, that it was with the utmost difficulty I got home; and even when within gun-shot of my own house, I was almost ready to lie down and give it up.' Other risks were presented by unpredictable ice conditions along the coast, fire, wild animals, and the toilsome nature of the men's occupations. At the height of the salmon and cod fisheries Cartwright's employees would become so sodden with fatigue that they were accident prone. One man fell asleep while attempting to wash himself and toppled into the ocean. Another staggered while carrying a heavy beam, which fell upon his head with such force that 'the blood gushed out of his eyes, nose, ears, and mouth [and] his face instantly turned black.' Cartwright became skilled at treating frostbite and snow blindness, suturing wounds, pulling teeth, bleeding, delivering babies, with which his 'family' was occasionally blessed, performing minor surgery, and a variety of other medical skills. He never seemed to be discomposed by pain. Once his little finger was 'burnt from end to end' when he unwisely touched a trap on a bitterly cold morning. Cartwright spent the rest of the day chuckling over the wisdom contained in this couplet from Samuel Butler's *Hudibras*:

And many dangers shall environ
The man who meddles with cold iron.[24]

The greatest threat to Cartwright's business came from forces beyond his control in the outside world. He was obliged to depend on a succession of partners for supplies of fishing equipment, salt, and crucial winter provisions, and these were not always forthcoming. Politics also interfered with his work, and he had to make direct representations to British authorities to convince them that Palliser's efforts to restrict the Labrador trade to migratory fishermen were unworkable.[25] Increasing English enterprise along the coast, which continued despite the temporary return of Labrador to Quebec in 1774, brought competition and uncertainty and cut into his once profitable trade with the Eskimos. But none of these equalled the menace posed by the war with America. In August 1778, a Boston privateer named the *Minerva* arrived at Cartwright's fishing station at Great Island in Blackguard Bay. She was manned by a crew of one hundred and sixty men, who, in four days of plundering, reduced the helpless Cartwright to a near pauper. The Americans took back to Boston thirty-six of his seventy-three employees, two of his ships, and goods and provisions valued at fourteen thousand pounds. They even rifled his private baggage. When Cartwright begged 'a few nails' prior to the *Minerva*'s departure, he received this reply from the first lieutenant: 'G-d d--n you, sir, if I commanded this ship, I would not leave you a rag to your a--e by God.' After the ship left he took stock of his position with his accustomed sang-froid. Two would-be deserters who had been sent back to shore by the Americans were given 'a most severe beating with a stout stick.' Then, back to work:

The rest of this day was spent in landing the provisions which [Captain] Grimes had returned, and in picking up the few things which were left scattered up and down; and I had the pleasure to find, that they had forgot a puncheon of olive oil, and my three live swine. As soon as they were gone, I took up my gun, walked out upon the island, and shot a curlew.
    A very fine day.[26]

    It would take more than American malice or the stern face of nature to drive a man of this temperament off the Labrador coast. However, although he lived until 1819 his sixth voyage would be his last, for persistent 'sciatica' interrupted his hunting and kept him indoors for a great part of the winter of 1785–6. Even in this last winter of confinement and pain, Cartwright never grumbled. As in the past, he had to cope with a number of perplexing situations. He now had no mistress, and, being 'in great want of one,' he asked an Eskimo named Eketch-eak if he would spare one of his two wives, 'a young girl about sixteen years of age' who struck his fancy. Eketcheak was willing to oblige

him, but the young lady, to Cartwright's amusement, replied to his
addresses with: 'You are an old fellow, and I will have nothing to say to
you.'[27] And so the affair ended. In addition to this, he had to adjust to
his physical inability to pursue game, and the *Journal* records a
number of occasions when the weakened hunter had to rest on some
rock or promontory and watch his quarry escape. Thus he was a failure
at both types of venery. Knowing Cartwright, it should not be difficult
to guess which of the two he regarded with greater consternation. But
no matter what afflicted him, he remained throughout his stay in
Labrador essentially a happy man.

The most impressive feature of Cartwright was, oddly, his ordi-
nariness. We find no trace in him of the rhetoric associated with later
romantic adventurers and tourists, nothing about breaking through
'the portals of the unknown' or fighting for existence 'on the edge of
the Labrador wilderness.' His temper was even and sober, his eye
fixed on the particular, his will dedicated to the common instincts: to
endure and, if possible, to succeed. Succeed he may have done, in the
end, for documents show him scrambling for territorial grants along
the coast after his own departure, and in 1793 we find him declaring
'that his trade has been very flourishing, having cleared above one
hundred per cent for the last three years.'[28] His own years on the
Labrador, though marked by no such success, were nevertheless
triumphs of persistence and nerve, a demonstration of an ordinary
man's ability to adapt to harsh and unfamiliar conditions. It is worth
noting, as a contrast to some later explorers and visitors, that Cartwright's affection for Labrador did not diminish, but grew, the longer
he stayed there, and in 1785, on the eve of his last voyage, he was
capable of writing a long poem in praise of what he now called, in a
rare show of feeling, 'my lov'd Labrador.'[29] This was his poetic finale.
His prose, lean and earthy as ever, ends more typically with the
practical suggestion that what he had learned about the use of ma-
nures in Labrador could be applied, with great benefit, in England as
well.

WILLIAM CORMACK, 1822

Until the Treaty of Paris Newfoundland could truly be described as 'a
golden casket full of mocking emptiness,'[30] but the growth of enterprise and settlement around the coast after 1763 coincided with a new
interest in exploring the interior of the colony. Following complaints
by Griffith Williams, a soldier, in 1765, and by Joseph Banks in 1766,

about the English ignorance of the 'Interior Parts of the Island,' James Cook in 1767 went up the Humber River into Deer Lake, and reported favourably on the potential for timber and salmon.[31] But it was to be the Exploits River that would first conduct Europeans into the heart of the island. In August 1768, John Cartwright, authorized by Governor Palliser, led an expedition of fourteen men up the Exploits for this threefold purpose: 'to explore the unknown interior parts of New-foundland; to examine into the practicability of travelling from shore to shore, across the body of that island; and to acquire a more certain knowledge of the settlements of the natives or Red Indians, as well as to surprise, if possible, one or more of these savages, for the purpose of effecting in time, a friendly intercourse with them.'[32] The journey was one expression of the growing humanitarian and scientific interest in the Beothucks, who were now confined by expanding English settlement to the coastline at the mouth of the Exploits and were recognized as being in danger of extinction.[33] Though Cartwright's party set out in 'high spirits,' and before long came upon a 'beautiful cascade' which seemed 'highly romantic,' they were quickly discouraged by the thick bush and rough ground in the vicinity of the river, and unnerved by fear of the Indians. Eight members of the expedition turned back before reaching Lieutenant's Lake (now Red Indian Lake). Cartwright saw numerous Beothuck habitations and artifacts, but no people, and after viewing the 'one unvarying scene of thick woods' on the shores of the newly discovered lake, he returned to the coast 'with as much speed as broken shoes and very rainy weather would admit of.'[34]

In the fifty years following Cartwright's adventure on the Exploits other efforts were made by successive governors to establish contact with the surviving Beothucks. None succeeded. Formal proclamations and threats of legal reprisal against settlers who murdered or robbed the Indians had little effect. The Beothucks were relentlessly driven back to an ever diminishing territory between the Europeans in Notre Dame Bay and their other enemies, the Micmacs, south and west of Red Indian Lake, and their nomadic way of life, which depended in part on gaining access to the seacoast during the summer, was doomed. The return of a captured Indian woman to her people, unharmed, in 1804 brought no result. In January 1811, another expedition to Red Indian Lake led by Lieutenant David Buchan succeeded in locating and, by the expedient of surrounding their tents early in the morning, confronting about seventy-five Beothucks, but a misunderstanding led to the murder of two of Buchan's soldiers, and Buchan had to return empty-handed. He went back to the lake in 1820 with the body of Waunathoake, another captured Indian who had died of tuberculosis on the ship escorting her to her people. At this time, as Shanadithit, the last Beothuck seen by white men, later reported, only twenty-seven Indians remained alive.[35]

The plight of the Beothucks was one factor that attracted the young scientist William Cormack to Newfoundland in 1821 or 1822.[36] Cormack was born in St John's in 1796, but his Scottish father, a merchant, died while William was still a boy of about seven, and his family moved to Scotland. There he became a student at the universities of Glasgow and Edinburgh, at a time when scientific interest in the subject of geology was keen throughout Europe, and especially so, it seems, in Scotland. Cormack studied under the Regius Professor of Natural History at Edinburgh University, Robert Jameson, acquiring an interest in mineralogy and various branches of natural history which persisted during his lifetime, and enjoying 'boyish rambles' in the 'pleasing and classic scenery' of the Scottish lowlands.[37] Humane and romantic by nature, he was deeply stirred by reports about Newfoundland's aboriginal tribe, and a determination to learn more about them, together with scientific curiosity about the interior, led him to make a daring walk across the island from east to west in 1822. He set out with a Micmac guide named Joseph Sylvester from Smith Sound in Trinity Bay on 5 September; on 2 November he reached St George's Bay. The record of his trip was the publication *Narrative of a Journey across the Island of Newfoundland in 1822*, which first appeared in abbreviated form in the *Edinburgh Philosophical Journal* of 1824 and was later expanded into a book.[38]

Cormack's *Journey* was a work of science, presenting the first geological map and topographical description of the part of the interior over which he trekked and masses of detail about the flora and fauna of the region.[39] He described such phenomena as beaver houses and dams, the Newfoundland bogs and barrens (which he grandly called 'savannas'), the geology of Mount Sylvester, and the varieties of berries and birds he encountered on his way. However, he was no plodding cataloguer of rocks and animals. Even the scientific portions of the *Journey* are enlivened by the imprint of his distinct personality, by his sense of participating in a great adventure, and youthful enthusiasm and curiosity. One notices the studied formality with which he assigned appropriate terminology to the various lakes and hills. His mentor Jameson was twice honoured. A series of ridges east of Meelpaeg Lake was called Jameson's Mountains (now, more accurately, Jameson's Hills) and, this single designation not being sufficient for the eminent mineralogist, Meelpaeg Lake itself was renamed Jameson's Lake. The lake has since reverted to its original name, but other names such as Mount Sylvester and George IV Lake survive to show Cormack's influence on the island's toponymy.

There is a boyish naïveté in these experiments in nomenclature, as there is, indeed, in many of Cormack's excited observations early on his journey overland. After a few days of hard walking from Smith Sound, he became aware of entering 'retreats ... never before invaded by man' and of forcing 'his way fearlessly onward' in an 'untrodden boundless wilderness.'[40] The schoolboy vocabulary proved surprisingly durable. On 10 September, after nearly a week laboriously plunging westward through a dark, thick coniferous forest, tortured by mosquitoes and 'suffocating heat,' Sylvester and Cormack broke out of the woods onto high, rocky ground, where the young adventurer experienced sensations of triumph and elation, and delivered the earliest sustained imaginative response to the Newfoundland landscape. Looking eastward over the forest 'through which we had pilgrimaged,' he saw 'a novel picture' of woods 'spotted with bright yellow marshes and a few glossy lakes on its bosom.' But in the west,

... to our inexpressible delight, the interior broke in sublimity before us. What a contrast did this present to the conjectures entertained of Newfoundland! The hitherto mysterious interior lay unfolded below us, a boundless scene, an emerald surface, a vast basin. The eye strides again and again over a succession of northerly and southerly ranges of green plains, marbled with woods and lakes of every form and extent, a picture of all the luxurious scenes of national cultivation, receding into invisibleness. The imagination hovers in the distance, and clings involuntarily to the undulating horizon of vapour, far into the west, until it is lost. A new world seemed to invite us onwards, or rather we claimed the dominion, and were impatient to proceed to take possession. Fancy carried us quickly across the Island. Obstacles of every kind were dispelled and despised. Primitiveness, omnipotence, and tranquillity were stamped upon everything so forcibly that the mind is hurled back thousands of years and the man left denuded of the mental fabric which a knowledge of ages of human experience and of time may have reared within him. Could a dwelling be secured amid the heavenly emotions excited by the presence of such objects!

It was manifest on every hand that this was the season of the year when the earth here offers her stores of productions; land berries were ripening, game birds were fledging, and beasts were emerging to prey upon each other.

Everything animate or inanimate seemed to be our own. We consumed un-sparingly our remaining provisions, confident that henceforward, with our personal powers, which felt increased by the nature of the objects that pre-sented themselves (aided by what now seemed by contrast the admirable power of our firearms), the destruction of one creature would afford us nourishment and vigour for the destruction of others. There was no will but ours. Thoughts of the aborigines did not alter our determination to meet them, as well as everything living, that might present itself in a country yet untrod-den and before unseen by civilised man.[41]

Consuming provisions quickly in the belief that nature would supply plenty was an impossibly romantic gesture to make on a rock in the middle of Newfoundland. Perhaps Cormack had read widely in con-temporary English poetry and was schooled to see, in every vista, mere pastoral. Indeed, at one point in the *Journey* he quotes a famous stanza from William Cowper's poem about Crusoe:

> I am monarch of all I survey,
>   My right there is none to dispute;
> From the centre all round to the sea,
>   I am lord of the fowl and the brute.[42]

The very imagery Cormack used in his early responses to the New-foundland landscape, phrases such as 'paps of granite' and 'bosom of the interior,' betrayed his unrealistic expectations of the island's sternly masculine terrain. So too his delusion of imminent mastery over his surroundings showed inexperience. Cormack would soon learn that taking 'possession' of Newfoundland was no easy matter. In fact, the land he walked over remains today in essentially the same primitive condition he found it in a century and a half ago, and none of the developments he expected to take place, the use of the 'savannas,' for example, as pasture, has come into effect. One sees why the histo-rian J.D. Rogers said of Cormack's walk that it 'seemed to prove noth-ing and to lead to nothing.'[43] This may be harsh; but history shows that Cormack's dream of dominion was, to speak mildly, premature, and that nature has, to date, dominated and shaped man on this island to a far greater extent than he has succeeded in influencing it.

Our game pedestrian would see something of this as he continued his journey westward into the bosom of the interior. However quickly his fancy might carry him across the island, his feet were obliged to proceed with mortifying slowness. Ahead lay fifty days of peril, cold, and exhausting work. The sight of huge, stark, granite boulders near Mount Sylvester impressed upon him 'his own feebleness' and 'the power of time.' He and Sylvester killed game, but never seemed to get enough food. They struggled through marshland and scrub spruce, waded through swift brooks, toiled around long lakes which crossed their path at awkward angles. Once the two became separated, and Cormack experienced such intense loneliness that he risked firing his rifle to attract an unidentified Indian on a nearby lake. (The Indian turned out to be a Montagni from Labrador; Cormack saw not a trace of the Beothucks on his journey.) Complicating matters further, Sylvester became grumpy quite early on the trip and remained somewhat refractory throughout, despite a formal agreement drawn up on 14 September in which Cormack made various promises to keep the Micmac from abandoning the trek. On 16 October the two 'weakened and miserable' men awakened to find three feet of snow on the ground.[44] Two days later, now dangerously short of provisions, they were lucky enough to obtain food at a Micmac encampment, but Cormack was so 'enfeebled by want of sustenance' that he 'could only eat a few mouthfuls.' He calculated on 28 October that his body 'would not obey the will, and drag along the frame, beyond two weeks more.' By late October the kind of vocabulary he was using to describe nature had changed radically. The 'aspect of the country' now appeared to be 'dreary,' with mountains of 'coarse' granite, 'bald' near the top and 'shrouded' with firs, while the snow lent an air of 'monotonous sublimity' to the scenery. On 1 November he saw the ocean in the west. Had he viewed it a month earlier, he admitted, 'it would have created in my mind a thousand pleasures, the impression of which I was now too callous to receive.' Callous: a far different state of mind from that of the young pathfinder of early September. It would be an appropriate word to use of George Cartwright's disposition. But Cormack's long excursion, described at the end as a mixture of 'toil, pleasure, pain, and anxiety,' was over, and he now hastened to return to England and 'the delight of being again restored to society.'[45]

The process we witness as we follow Cormack on his tramp is the bludgeoning of sensibility. Not that he was permanently soured or coarsened by his experiences. The high-minded, even quixotic, streak in his nature stayed with him to the end of his life and was illustrated in two of his later impractical enterprises: founding an elaborate 'Beothuck Institution' in 1827, two years before the last Beothuck on earth died of tuberculosis, and planning another walk, this time across Australia. These were very much in keeping with his first great adventure of blazing a trail across Newfoundland that nobody else would follow. But the significance of the *Journey* is more than geographical. It dramatizes another human encounter with Newfoundland's inhospitable hinterland, indicating, in ways similar to Cartwright's *Journal*, that romantic sentiment, together with the stock phraseology about 'vistas,' 'sylvan scenery,' and 'heavenly objects' that accompanies it, seems singularly out of place in this still primitive 'frayed edge'[46] of North America, where nature is more often a force to be confronted than a scene to be enjoyed. Such beauty as Newfoundland possesses and occasionally manifests is a kind to which Cormack was oblivious: 'The huge island ... stands, with its sheer, beetling cliffs, out of the ocean, a monstrous mass of rock and gravel, almost without soil, like a strange thing from the bottom of the great deep, lifted up, suddenly, into sunshine and storm, but belonging to the watery darkness out of which it has been reared. The eye, accustomed to richer and softer scenes, finds something of a strange and almost startling beauty in its bold, hard outlines, cut out on every side, against the sky.'[47] Thus R.T.S. Lowell, writing in 1858, nine years before William Cormack died in the new frontier territory of British Columbia.

4 🏠 *The triumph of sentiment*

COLONIAL SELF-ASSERTION

Throughout the second half of the eighteenth century, Newfoundland continued on her course as 'something more than a fishing station, something less than a colony.'[1] Lacking the year-round political institutions that had been granted to other British territories overseas, it was to be expected that progress in developing many of the usual amenities of civilized life – agriculture, roads, communications, religious and educational facilities – was necessarily slow or nonexistent. Some improvements had, however, been made, and it is a mistake to think of eighteenth-century Newfoundland as stagnant and repressed. The complicated legal system that had emerged in the island prior to 1775, in which the governor, his surrogates, the magistrates, and the fishing admirals played a variety of sometimes overlapping roles, had given way by the end of the century to an arrangement of new and properly constituted courts. An historian has argued recently that even the older legal system was 'in many ways' superior to that of England itself,[2] thus implicitly challenging the traditional image of the fishing admirals as unconscionable and ignorant tyrants, distributing justice 'according to their caprice, over a bottle of rum.'[3] The first school on the island was established by the SPG missionary Henry Jones, who began his ministry in Bonavista in 1725, and other schools appeared under the auspices of the SPG as the society's presence became more widespread in the colony.[4] Religious toleration in Newfoundland dates from 1784, when a Roman Catholic priest, J.L. O'Donel, was given permission to work in St John's. Difficulties in obtaining supplies during the American Revolution forced Newfoundlanders to turn increasingly to agriculture, and by 1785 military personnel and 'others not concerned in the Fishery' had 'enclosed and improved extensive Tracts of Land' in the vicinity of St John's.[5] The American war had other important effects: it undermined the English migratory fishery, brought an increase in the resident population, and enhanced the stature of St John's among Newfoundland's ports. Throughout the war, St John's had apparently prospered because it had remained relatively safe from American privateers. When, in October 1786, George Cartwright visited the city after an absence of sixteen years, he was 'astonished to observe the difference between the manners of the inhabitants, and also the face of the country now, and what they were when I was here formerly. Many elegant houses are built; the merchants live comfortably, and even luxuriously; the numbers of settlers are greatly increased; abundance of horses are kept; the country is cleared, and under cultivation for a great distance from the town; great plenty of potatoes, barley, oats, &c. are grown; and the crops appear to be as fine as the same sort of soil would produce in England.'[6] Also in 1786 Newfoundland was honoured by the visit of HRH Prince William Henry, Duke of Clarence and St Andrew's and Earl of Munster (later William IV), another sign, perhaps, that the colony was on the highroad to civilization. The prince became a naval surrogate to the current governor and reportedly distinguished himself by sentencing an innocent man to receive one hundred lashes.[7]

By the end of the century, no indication had been given by Britain that she was willing to grant representative institutions to Newfoundland. Nor, indeed, did there seem to be any desire whatever among the people for such institutions. The first suggestion that the colony might benefit from a local legislature came, remarkably, from Governor James Gambier in 1803. His request was ignored by British authorities and, as the historian D.W. Prowse dolefully remarked in 1895, 'poor Newfoundland had still to struggle thirty years more for this great boon.'[8] However, with the rapid growth of a sedentary fishery and resident population in Newfoundland during the Napoleonic Wars, and the rise of a permanently settled merchant class in St John's, Harbour Grace, and elsewhere, it was inevitable that requests for the 'boon' of local government would soon be heard. Significantly, when the first such demand was made in 1812, it came not from a native Newfoundlander but from a Scottish doctor, William Carson (1770–1843), who had set up practice in St John's in 1808. Carson was soon joined by another agitator, Patrick Morris (1789–1849), a merchant who had come to Newfoundland from Ireland in 1800. Thus the nationalist movement in the colony originated with two middle-class outsiders, who were probably not so much responding to local pressures and grievances as articulating the commonplace sentiments of 'the élite in all the white colonies' – sentiments that would have been the same no matter what country they chose to settle in.[9] But where no real social grievances among the mass of the people were apparent, some had to be contrived to provide the foundation of nationalist rhetoric. Carson, and especially Morris, found such largely imagined grievances in the past history of the colony. They began, and later nineteenth-century historians and commentators endlessly echoed and extended, a view of Newfoundland's past that is still a part of the mythology of the island. The work that innocently provided nationalists with the hints they needed to sentimentalize Newfoundland's past was, as Keith Matthews has pointed out,[10] John Reeves's *History of the Government of the Island of Newfoundland* (1793).

REEVES AND NATIONALISM

Reeves, a barrister who had been educated at Eton and Oxford, came to Newfoundland in 1791 as chief judge in a newly instituted Court of Judicature. His 'short History of the Government and Constitution of the island of Newfoundland' was based on a study of records pertaining to the colony in the files of the Board of Trade and Plantations in London. Reeves saw the dominant theme of Newfoundland history as a struggle between 'two contending interests': 'The *planters* and *inhabitants* on the one hand, who, being settled there, needed the protection of a government and police, with the administration of justice: and the *adventurers* and *merchants* on the other; who, originally carrying on the fishery from this country, and visiting that island only for the season, needed no such protection for themselves, and had various reasons for preventing its being afforded to the others.'[11] He included in his *History* the so-called 'Star Chamber Rules' for the Newfoundland fishery (the 'Western Charter'[12]) and the now notorious additional regulations of 1671, which specified 'That no planter should cut down any wood, or should plant within six miles of the sea shore – That no inhabitant or planter should take up the best stages before the arrival of the fishermen. – That no master or owner of any ship should transport seamen, or fishermen to Newfoundland, unless they belonged to his ship's company,' and 'That no seaman or fisherman should remain behind, after the fishing was ended.' He further recorded the decision taken by the Committee for Trade and Plantation in 1675, in which it was proposed that *'all plantations in Newfoundland should be discouraged*; and, in order thereunto, that the commander of the convoy should have commission to declare to all the planters, to come voluntarily away; or else that the western charter should, from time to time, be put into execution; by which charter all planters were forbid to inhabit within six miles of the shore.' The committee, Reeves noted, ordered that these regulations be put 'into effectual execution.'[13]

Reeves went on to develop his thesis of confrontation between merchant and settler in his account of eighteenth-century Newfoundland. The documents he selected and summarized effectively revealed the English policy of withholding government in order to limit settlement. Reeves, however, was more of an advocate than a historian and was not content to let the documents speak for themselves. Throughout his book his sympathies clearly lay with the settlers and against the west country merchants and fishing admirals. The admirals, he noted, 'were the servants of the merchants, inasmuch as they were the masters of some of their ships,' and 'in many cases, therefore, justice was not to be expected from them.' In general, 'a poor planter, or inhabitant, (who was considered as little better than a law-breaker in being such) had but small chance of justice, in opposition to any great west-country merchant.' Reeves ridiculed the admirals for their 'inactivity, neglect, and contempt,' and seemed angered that legal authority had been 'lodged in such feeble hands.' As for the merchants, Reeves was confident that he could guess the motives behind their effort to keep Newfoundland in 'weakness and anarchy.' This course, he argued, 'was favourable to their old impressions, that Newfoundland was *theirs*, and that all the planters and inhabitants were to be spoiled and devoured at *their* pleasure.' This sentence represents the strongest piece of rhetoric in his usually calm appraisal of the documents. He concluded his book with a long and still useful appendix in which he printed 'The [British] Statutes relating to Newfoundland.'[14]

The book had two chief weaknesses. First, it seemed to equate legislative intention with actual implementation. With a couple of exceptions, there seemed to be little questioning of the assumption that what was enacted in London was carried out in Newfoundland. In fact, apart from the general success of the policy of denying the colony a year-round government, there was little, if any, formal attempt to enforce such unworkable statutes as the six-mile rule – a rule ludicrously inappropriate to the colony, given the nature of its resources and terrain – and Keith Matthews has concluded that 'almost none' of the seventeenth-century laws pertaining to Newfoundland was 'ever successfully enforced.' Again, there was no sustained, effective attempt to drive out settlers. Convoy commanders in 1675 and 1676 did not obey an order-in-council requiring the removal of settlers, and although the fishing admirals themselves 'took the law into their own hands and in St. John's at least attempted to remove the settlers from their coastal possessions'[15] during the fishing season of 1676, this effort was effectively countered by a representative of the residents who travelled to England to defend settlement in the colony.[16] Thereafter such harassment ceased, although there undoubtedly were occasional quarrels over fishing rooms and the sporadic brutality one would expect to find on a frontier without government. No evidence has been produced showing that any person or family was ever evicted from Newfoundland by British authorities acting under the regulations and orders of 1671 and 1675. When we look away from the statutes to inquire about what actually happened in seventeenth- and eighteenth-century Newfoundland, the picture conveyed by Reeves in parts of his book of 'poor labouring fishermen' 'spoiled and devoured' by merchants and 'left wholly at *their* mercy' was a distortion of the truth. There was no suggestion of such a pattern in, for example, Yonge's *Journal*, where its existence would almost certainly have been noted. Eighteenth-century Newfoundland history cannot be reduced to the simple formula provided by Reeves, and it may be a moot question whether living conditions for the mass of the people improved significantly in the century following. The second defect in Reeves's *History* was his failure to understand the significance of King William's Act of 1699, which he dismissed in one short paragraph as 'little more than an enactment of the rules, regulations, and constitution that had mostly prevailed there for some time.'[17] On the contrary, the act was a careful attempt to outline the respective rights of migratory fishermen and settlers, favouring the former but granting important concessions to the inhabitants. Section VII of the act, as Grant Head has recently reminded us, specifically permitted settlement: 'Provided always, That all such Persons, as since the twenty-fifth Day of March one thousand six hundred eighty-five, have built, cut out or made, *or at any Time hereafter* shall build, cut out or make, any Houses, Stages, Cook-rooms, Train-fats, or other Conveniences, for fishing there, that did not belong to fishing Ships since the said Year one thousand six hundred eighty-five, shall and may peaceably and quietly enjoy the same to his or their own Use, without any Disturbance of or from any Person or Persons whatsoever.'[18] Even William Carson realized that this proviso gave statutory protection to the rights of all settlers in Newfoundland.[19]

Despite these limitations, Reeves's *History* was a carefully researched and impressive work. It is possible that it was the most influential book ever written about Newfoundland, for so stunningly simple and plausible was his reading of the colony's past that most subsequent historians merely repeated or amplified his ideas, which then passed into school textbooks and the popular imagination. Reeves, however, was not responsible for some of the emotional excesses of nineteenth-century nationalist historians, whose embellishments of the documentary evidence supplied by his book led to such myths as the illegality of settlement and agriculture in the island. Reeves nowhere stated that settlement or agriculture had been prohibited. These notions were the figments of more fertile imaginations.

For Carson and Morris, Reeves supplied a convenient explanation for the lack of progress in the colony and for its failure to attract a large population. They could now blame this retarded condition, not on the climate and geography of the island, which would have been unflattering to budding nationalists, but upon the west country adventurers, the Star Chamber, and the fishing admirals. The first angry sally against these straw men took place in 1812 in Carson's pamphlet, *A Letter to the Members of Parliament of the United Kingdom*. Carson's purpose in the tract was 'to expose the evil genius that has hitherto blasted the fortunes of this Country.' This was none other than the west country merchant, who had, according to Carson,

... assailed the planters with all the opprobrious epithets of their language, and circulated, with assiduity and effect, false representations of the country, its climate and soil. With such rivals the honest but illiterate fisherman at a far distance from the seat of Government was but ill calculated to contend. The laborious fisherman and hardy woodman, although they felt their rights as men, knew not how or where to claim them: they were oppressed with Star chamber regulations, and orders of council; they were forbid to approach nearer the Sea Coast than six miles; they were banished into the Woods to perish of hunger, or become a prey to wolves.

Thus Newfoundland history was set on a plunge into sentiment from which it is only now emerging. Carson went on to attack the 'quarter deck' justice administered by naval surrogates, to call for the concentration of all British subjects scattered throughout North America ('one million of people') in Newfoundland, and to note the absence of local government on the island. His view of Newfoundland's natural resources bears a striking resemblance to accounts written by seventeenth-century propagandists – accounts which, indeed, nineteenth-century publicists and historians were fond of citing. Here again it is proper to quote Carson's own words:

The Island is watered by many fine Rivers, some of which are navigable for more than 20 leagues. The lakes and ponds are numerous, many of them beautifully romantic. Of the soil little is known, every possible discourage-ment having been placed in the way of agriculture. There are only a very few spots reclaimed by an imperfect husbandry. Even these are productive of potatoes, turnips, grass and corn. The winters are not so severe as in the same latitude in the continent of America, and do not set in so early. The last week of last December, the thermometer was but seldom under 40, and only one night as low as freezing; at present, the 5 January, there is neither frost or snow on the ground. Iron, copper, and even more precious metals are reported to have been found in the Island. Coal is known to abound in one district.[20]

In Carson's second and final tract, *Reasons for Colonizing the Island of Newfoundland, in a Letter Addressed to the Inhabitants* (1813) – a title which oddly seemed to discount the colonizing that had gone on previously – the agricultural potential of the island was further exag-gerated, with the author declaring himself convinced of 'the capability of Newfoundland to become a pastoral and agricultural country.' If the money spent in buying produce abroad were to be invested in local agriculture, he wrote, the effort, in 'a few years, would convert the wilds and morasses into corn fields, and cause towns and cities to arise, where the untameable savage now rears his wigwam.'[21] Carson, like some other literary commentators on Newfoundland in the nineteenth century, came from a background in which fishing was not a conspicuous activity and was consequently inclined to overestimate the colony's agricultural potential. One of the chief themes of their books was an emphasis upon the land rather than the sea as the key to the island's future prosperity, and typically they were at pains to indicate how the addition of farming to a fishing way of life could make the inhabitants more comfortable and secure. Small-scale ag-riculture had, in fact, been carried on by fishermen as far back as the seventeenth century, and had been permitted as long as the activity did not encroach on fishing rooms.[22]

As for the 'one hundred thousand' people living in Newfoundland, Carson pictured them as 'calling loudly for their civil rights.' In his pamphlets we can, perhaps, see the beginning of that perennial, sturdy myth, the 'hardy Newfoundlander': 'The inhabitants of Newfoundland may be characterized as a hardy race, fearless of danger, and capable of undergoing the greatest corporeal exertion. They have no strong antipathies, violent prejudices, or unjust prepossessions; they have that fondness for liberty which all men possess, that are not subdued by fear, or unseduced by the illusions of vice. Their love of liberty is chastened by a sentiment of just subordination, and a respectful demeanor towards those in superior situations.' Carson wavered between this view of Newfoundlanders and another, at times equally useful attitude – seeing them as deprived and oppressed by outsiders, to the extent that their 'span of human existence is considerably shortened, and it but seldom happens, that a native obtains a large size, or arrives at an advanced age.' He did not attempt to explain this apparent contradiction. He again may be accused of failing to explain how a people having a 'fondness for liberty' could suffer willingly 'an insulting and contumelious disregard of their rights' and still feel 'a pride in being subjects to the King of England.'[23] Similar paradoxes recur in most of the fanciful history created by nineteenth-century nationalists.

Carson's rhetoric seems mild by comparison with the shrill demagoguery of his successor in political and historical propaganda, Patrick Morris, three of whose pamphlets of the 1820s showed a rising crescendo of anger against Newfoundland's imagined enemies. After studying Reeves's book, Morris concluded in his first set of *Observations* (1824) that Newfoundland history was a chronicle of 'ruthless tyranny' by a set of 'unprincipled adventurers' who held the 'unhappy people' of Newfoundland 'smarting under the most intolerable yoke' and maintained their system 'with more than eastern despotism.' He was the first 'historian' to suggest that there had been a massive expulsion of settlers in the 1670s, when 'the most wanton acts of violence were committed, the houses of the inhabitants were burnt and destroyed, and every other violent means resorted to, to force them from the country.' (It will be noted that he did not actually state that they were driven off the island.) King William's Act, he wrote, was founded on the 'barbarous policy' of past decades and merely gave that policy 'legalized form.' Moreover, 'not one in ten' of the naval commanders given authority in the act could write his own name.[24] In *Remarks on the State of Society, Religion, Morals, and Education at Newfoundland* (1827) Morris's criticism of the fishing admirals became harsher. He now claimed that on arriving in the colony each spring, the admirals behaved 'like Persian satraps or Turkish bashaws' and 'plundered, oppressed, and flogged the people at their pleasure.' He also expanded on suggestions made in the first tract about the enormous profits made by Englishmen from the fishery in Newfoundland. 'Cities, towns, and whole districts in England,' he wrote, 'have been raised to wealth and importance by the capital there accumulated; vast fortunes were made by persons who came to the country without a shilling, and were soon enabled to retire and live in splendour in other countries.' The settlers were pictured by Morris as enduring this exploitation 'without scarcely a murmur of complaint,' even though they were abused and calumniated by their oppressors. He came vigorously to their defence, answering, for example, the charge which he had somewhere heard that there was religious bigotry in Newfoundland. 'The people of the various religious congregations,' he wrote, in a sentence which does not square well with the subsequent history of the colony, 'have complied with the recommendation of our divine master, – *they love one another*.[25] In a third tract published in 1828 the ranting against the merchants reached a frenzied peak. He now called them 'Hannibals' and 'monopolists' – the latter a favourite term in later histories – who had sworn 'eternal enmity to that country which raised their fathers and themselves to wealth and importance' and had held Newfoundlanders 'in bondage and barbarism' or 'in chains of worse than feudal despotism.'[26] Morris's turbulent imagination and zeal were such that it is hard to find his equal among Newfoundland's orators.

The solutions to all of Newfoundland's problems, to Morris, were the acquisition of local autonomy and the development of agriculture. The fisheries alone, he believed, were not capable of providing Newfoundlanders with a secure livelihood. He fiercely attacked 'the unnatural restrictions on the cultivation of the soil,' which had been caused, in his view, by the false reports about the island spread by the monopolists. His opinion was that there were 'millions of uncultivated acres capable of producing food' in the colony, and that if these were developed 'the country would afford a comfortable settlement' to a much greater population.[27] Morris, like Carson, was a progressivist, holding out to the people the prospect of triumph over imagined oppressors and repressive laws, and of a new day dawning in which the 'inexhaustible'[28] wealth of the country would become their own.

As with Carson, Morris's rhetoric embroiled him in awkward paradoxes which he side-stepped only with some difficulty. While persistently attacking 'mercantile monopoly,' for example, he admitted that he was not 'prejudiced' against trade itself since 'I am a merchant, carrying on business at Newfoundland.' He revealed the 'frightful, inquisitorial system' maintained by naval governors, adding, however, that the governors themselves were not responsible for this but rather 'certain individuals' who attached themselves to them on their arrival in St John's.[29] Thus he managed to be anti-British and pro-British at once – a balancing act which later commentators also accomplished. Morris also moaned about Newfoundland's 'present unimproved and impoverished state,' calling the colony deficient in 'any of those institutions which are necessary for the well-being of every civilized country,' but he took strong exception to an English bishop's slurs against Newfoundland and at times seemed highly pleased with the progress that had occurred.[30] In the following passage, for instance, he imagined what the old fishing admirals, ancestors of the present monopolists, would think of the present generation of Newfoundlanders, if they were called from their graves to view them:

But, let them not be wafted on the wings of the eastern gale across the Atlantic, for what would be their horror to behold the apostacy of the present degenerate race; to see them sinking from their former state of happy ignorance and barbarism, into one of intellectual improvement; to see some of them skilled in the cabalistic art of writing, impiously daring to read over their merchant's accounts, and profanely questioning their correctness. Instead of the hoops, nailed to the table, out of which they sparingly eat their cod's heads and sound bones with more than Spartan temperance, to see them regaling themselves on fish and bang, off the plate of Staffordshire; and, in place of the ancient boat's kettle, whose well besooted sides bore ample testimony to its long and useful services, to see in the centre of the table a dish of the same precious material as the plates; to see them despising those useful organs with which kind Nature has supplied them for conveying their food to their mouths, and which alone they ever used for the purpose, and substituting in lieu knives, forks, – and even spoons! All this would be *horrible, very horrible*!![31]

By 1832, the year Newfoundland was given Representative Government by Britain, the view of Newfoundland history promoted by Carson and Morris had become current. John M'Gregor's important account of *British America*, published in that year, shows the extent to which the distorted picture had been accepted even by eminent foreign authorities. M'Gregor's description of Newfoundland was derived from Reeves and Morris. The latter he swallowed whole. He repeated Morris's reading of the 1670s and interpretation of King William's Act and, in one startling sentence, credited the act with authorizing exactly the opposite of what the British legislators intended. The resident fishermen, said M'Gregor, 'were driven from time to time out of Newfoundland, by the statute of William and Mary.'[32] For perhaps the first time, in M'Gregor's book, it was stated as fact that settlers had been driven off the island, and driven off more than once, by the dastardly British. His contribution to Newfoundland historiography was thus to out-Morris Morris. From M'Gregor's book the sentimental picture of the island's history passed into other similar influential compilations, such as Hugh Murray's huge work, *An Historical and Descriptive Account of British America* (1839).[33]

OTHER BRITISH OBSERVERS, 1818–42

While the nationalist rhetoric of Carson and Morris would succeed in dominating Newfoundland historiography, a number of other books by British writers in the early decades of the century provided alternative views of the colony's development to the world outside. These works, although different in many ways, had the common element of a British imperialist perspective, and the kind of distortions we find in them are those we would expect, given the usual imperiousness of English visitors travelling overseas in the early heyday of the Empire. In some cases, however, the imperial swagger of these observers gave them an advantage in so far as it enabled them to see beyond local partisan feeling to the true nature of events, and their books cannot be dismissed as merely snobbish. The first work belonging in this general category is Edward Chappell's *Voyage of his Majesty's Ship Rosamond to Newfoundland and the Southern Coast of Labrador* (1818), a strange mixture of military haughtiness, romanticism, and outright lies that does not require extended commentary. Writing to divert a London reading public, Chappell, a naval lieutenant who served in Newfoundland in the summer of 1813, pictured the island as a remote, peculiar, barbarous, and little-known backwater of civilization, a likely setting for improbable and shocking occurrences. He is simply not to be trusted as an authority on any subject. His accounts of the Newfoundland dog (which 'will leap from the summit of the highest cliff into the water in obedience to the commands of their master'), the curlew ('it is not unusual to kill ten or twelve at a shot'), the fox ('it has frequently been seen to discharge the *spring* by dropping a large stone into the trap'), the cod (so plentiful that 'we killed several of them with the oars of the boat'), the cold weather ('it is not an unusual circumstance, in *St. John's*, to find, at the breakfast-table, the tea-cup frozen to the saucer, although filled with boiling water at the moment'), and numerous other phenomena, are just ludicrous exaggerations.[34] Chappell had the lowest opinion of Newfoundlanders, calling the St John's merchants 'vulgar ... upstarts' and mocking the 'burlesque finery' of fishermen's daughters who turned out to dance with the crew of his ship at Sandy Point. He was an insufferable snob. His book nevertheless may have had an influence in spreading romantic nonsense about Newfoundland. He was one of the first writers to caterwaul in public over the fate of the Beothucks, claiming that these 'timorous *Natives*' had been slaughtered by 'inhuman mariners'; and he preceded Morris in denouncing 'the principal mercantile men of this country' for 'monopolizing almost the whole of the external and internal trade' and amassing 'splendid fortunes with an inconceivable rapidity,' to the detriment of the fishermen who 'toil from year to year, with patient and unremitting industry.'[35] *Voyage of his Majesty's Ship Rosamond* was a precursor of a type of work that would become common in late nineteenth- and twentieth-century literature, the type in which the country was seen essentially as entertainment for an outside audience. It is possible to see this motive behind some of the most recent academic studies of the island's political and social history.

A year after the appearance of Chappell's book, Lewis Amadeus Anspach published *A History of the Island of Newfoundland*, the first comprehensive account of the colony's history, resources, and people. Anspach was an Anglican priest who came to Newfoundland in 1799 to be headmaster of a grammar school in St John's. In 1802 he was appointed SPG missionary in Harbour Grace and Carbonear, with the additional office of magistrate and, later, judge of the civil court of judicature. He returned to England in 1812. His book had certain peculiarities which tended to undermine its reputation with later historians. For example, he inserted a fifteen-page narrative of his own activities in Newfoundland, apparently thinking that he was just as important in the annals of the island's history as Sir Humphrey Gilbert, who received equivalent treatment, or for that matter that he was worth as much space as the whole history of the colony between 1776 and 1793.[36] There was also a marked pro-British tendency in the book, together with an occasional shaft of irony directed at the pretensions of St John's politicians. None of these features was calculated to make Anspach a favourite in certain drawing rooms of the capital city. Yet his *History* was an important addition to the colony's literature. Anspach ignored the overriding thesis proposed by Reeves to explain Newfoundland's development (although he did remark of the fishing admirals that they were 'not always the best informed, the most impartial, and incorruptible judges'[37]) and saw the history of the island principally as an extension of the larger Anglo-French rivalry in Europe and North America. Having had no access to unprinted documents, he naturally gave fuller treatment to the early history of Newfoundland, where he could base his observations on printed sources. One notices an inclination to make heroes out of such dubious characters as Gibert – a feature that would become commonplace in subsequent histories. In general, he praised the 'wise and liberal policy' of Britain towards her colonies and tended to be shocked by signs of colonial resentment of the mother country. His narrative of the actual events in the island's history up to 1818 occupied only half of his book. While limited by the kind of sources available to him and distinguished by no bold new thrusts in historical interpretation, this unremarkable chronicle is at least not vitiated by some indefensible thesis.

In the second half of his book Anspach turned from narrating historical events to comment on the island's topography and people. This remains a highly valuable and readable portion of the *History*, and it is no exaggeration to say that Anspach's interest in the actual, quotidian activities of people around the coast made him a pioneer in the social history of the country. His view of Newfoundland's resources and future possibilities for development was shrewdly realistic. After describing the climate, he concluded that 'this island is not calculated to produce any thing sufficient for the support of its inhabitants,' and he placed little faith in 'hopes of success in agricultural improvements.' A list of the common vegetables grown in Newfoundland was followed by the wry comment that 'Even the common dandelion is most eagerly sought after in the spring, as a substitute for the greater delicacies of the fine season.' Anspach discounted the suggestion that Newfoundland could produce good ship's timber and was sceptical about 'the traditionary reports' of mineral wealth. On the whole, he inclined to the view that Newfoundland could 'never be truly valuable but as a fishery.' All of this was a healthy antidote to the dreams of Carson, Morris, and later enthusiasts. Anspach's observations had a homely honesty and stubborn adherence to fact. He was disinclined to believe the sentimental notions, now becoming current, about the Newfoundland dog, since his own member of the breed, a creature named 'Jowler,' did not behave in accordance with them. As far as Anspach could see, Jowler never manifested any sign of a timorous disposition, and, in addition to possessing a fighting temperament, he was likewise 'fond of poultry of the larger kind.' When Jowler wanted a beverage, Anspach noted grimly, 'nothing is equal in his estimation to the blood of a sheep.' Again, while 'we are assured,' he wrote, that Newfoundland lacks 'venomous animals,' this advantage is compensated for by the mosquitoes, which 'fly about in large bands,' generally giving newcomers 'the preference.' As for the Beothucks, Anspach wrote of them with great good sense. The reports of atrocities committed by white men were, he claimed, 'greatly exaggerated, [and] originated in occurrences which were frequently the unavoidable consequence of accidental meetings in the northern parts of the island.'[38] His restrained comments on the indigenous Indians of Newfoundland may be contrasted with other contemporary descriptions. Cormack in 1827 was picturing the Beothucks as 'silvan people' or 'unsullied people of the chase' to whom Britons had been 'a blight and a scourge.'[39]

Anspach's integrity as an observer makes his admiration of the Newfoundland fishermen and sealers the more impressive. His account of 'the precarious and uncertain nature of the cod-fishery' was one of his most perceptive pieces, one that may yet be read with profit by those who choose to write about oldtime Newfoundland. Anspach had observed the activities of the fishermen closely and wrote of them with understanding and respect. He was especially stirred by the exploits of the sealers, of whom he wrote that 'It is impossible to conceive a greater degree of perseverance and intrepidity than the people of Conception-Bay in particular, display' at the ice-fields. His analysis of the general character of Newfoundland outporters cannot be dismissed, as perhaps Morris's and Carson's can, as empty panegyric. When he notes the people's 'kindness of disposition,' their 'confidence in the midst of danger,'[40] and still other admirable qualities, we are not hearing the partisan ranting of a would-be politician, but the judgment of a man not easy to impress or accustomed to bestow praise without good reason.

Anspach's immediate successor as a commentator on Newfoundland was another clergyman, Edward Wix (1802–66), who was the second archdeacon of the Anglican Church in Newfoundland and the first to reside in St John's. Between February and August 1835, Wix conducted a coastal tour of isolated communities on the south and west coasts of the island in order to provide the people with the services of a missionary. The result was a book, *Six Months of a Newfoundland Missionary's Journal* (1836), which was the first extended literary response to southern and western Newfoundland. Wix was an ecclesiastical snoop and prig. He sniffed intoxication and licentiousness in almost every community he visited, and frequently drew attention to his own zeal in spreading the Word in a region 'far removed from the seat of advanced civilization and refinement.' His visitation resembled somewhat 'the excursion of Mr. Cormack,' he noted grandly.[41] In fact, his recounting of various instances of depravity in specific outports – often peccadillos when judged by ordinary standards of morality – resembled nothing so much as loose gossip. Nevertheless, his book is valuable, for even when due regard is taken of his crass British snobbery and pharisaical self-righteousness, there still remains a core of observation which cannot be dismissed and which illuminates much about life in remote outports in the 1830s. Wix presided as judge and jury over the Newfoundlanders he met, and his prying nature was such that he saw mostly the dark side of things: the wreckers, poverty stricken families, drunks, idlers, and Sabbath breakers. But that dark side was there to be seen. The monotony and harshness of a fishing way of life on the bleak south coast created victims as well as heroes, and the ideal portraits of 'hardy Newfoundlanders' in other writers will not stand up to examination.

A thorough and humane overview of Newfoundland at the end of the 1830s was provided by the young English geologist and Cambridge graduate, J.B. Jukes (1811–69), who came to the island in 1839 to carry out a geological survey for the local government and eventually published *Excursions in and about Newfoundland during the Years 1839 and 1840* (1842). The practical results of his long sojourn were few. He found two small coal beds in western Newfoundland which did not 'seem to be of any great thickness.' He added: 'It is perfectly possible, however, that more important beds may be found, should the districts ever be thought worth working.' From this careful sentence and a few other remarks later publicists would concoct a fantasy about a 'great coal basin' in western and central Newfoundland. Indeed, Jukes received an early indication of how his findings would be misinterpreted when, after only a few weeks in the colony during which he had discovered nothing of value, he read a report 'in which I was said to have discovered copper, gypsum, coal, limestone, and, if I recollect rightly, silver.' What he actually found was some gypsum, lime, plenty of stone for building materials, and little else of commercial significance. Thus his view of the colony's mineral resource was not hopeful, and he was even less sanguine about its agricultural potential. The country, he wrote, could never 'under any circumstances, become an extensively agricultural one.' However, he allowed that sufficient beef, mutton, and vegetables 'might be produced to supply the wants of the population.'[42] While Jukes's surveys in Newfoundland were much less extensive than those started in 1864 by the Geological Survey of Canada under the direction of Alexander Murray, it may well be that the earlier geologist had a more accurate idea of the colony's prospects.

Jukes's determined explorations took him into numerous harbours around the coastline and as well far into the interior. He went up the Humber River further than any previous explorer, and he may have been the first white man on record to explore and describe Grand Lake, the largest lake on the island. He also attempted, without success, to reach Red Indian Lake. In his work, as in Wix's, we see the progress of settlement on the west coast and an emphasis upon the attractions offered to aspiring farmers and colonists by St George's Bay ('the most inviting part of Newfoundland') and Bay of Islands. 'Were the western side of the island settled,' Jukes wrote, 'the banks of the Humber and north end of the Grand [Lake] would be by far the most favourable spots for an inland population. The soil is richer, and the inland communication might be greatly extended by means of a few roads between the ponds and rivers.'[43] Jukes's account of the people he met in south coast communities provides a balance to the harsh picture in Wix, and his descriptions of individual outports around the colony refute any notion that such villages were merely collections of huts and tilts.[44] Throughout the *Excursions* we sense the bustle of new life and the expansion of enterprise along the coastline. But we also become aware of Newfoundland's past history, already written on the landscape in the shape of abandoned settlements. On 2 August 1840, Jukes went ashore at Bread Cove in Clode Sound in search of game, and recorded this scene: 'At the mouth of a little brook in this cove there were signs of former habitations, a cleared space or two, namely, in which raspberry-bushes were growing, and in one spot we found a grave neatly railed in and covered with wild roses. A piece of plank had been raised for a grave-stone, on which were two initials carved, and the date of 1755.'[45] *New*foundland it still was in many ways, but by 1840 the island had become, strangely, 'new and old too.'[46]

Of all the literary visitors that Newfoundland attracted during the nineteenth century, it is possible that Jukes threw himself most completely into the life of the colony. His youth, energy, natural curiosity, and adventurous temperament often took him away from the study of rocks into the activities of men. His most remarkable adventure was his trip to the seal fishery, on board a vessel called the *Topaz*, in the spring of 1840. The pursuit of seals in ocean-going ships had begun in 1794, and by 1840 the hunt had already become a part of the mystique of Newfoundland. No writer ever captured the spirit of the hunt as well as Jukes, whose spirit of comradeship with the sealers appeared two days out of port, when the men were ordered overboard to cut a path for the ship through the ice:

> If a large and strong pan was met with, the ice-saw was got out. Sometimes, a crowd of men clinging round the ship's bows, and holding on to the bights of ropes suspended there for the purpose, would jump and dance on the ice, bending and breaking it with their weight, shoving it below the vessel, and dragging her on over it with all their force. Up to their knees in water, as one piece after another sank below the cutwater, they still held on, hurraing at every fresh start she made, dancing, jumping, pushing, shoving, hauling, hewing, sawing, till every soul on board was roused into excited exertion. After looking on some time, I could stand it no longer: so, seizing a gaff, I jumped overboard ...[47]

Before the trip ended, Jukes saw the glamour and horror of the seal fishery: the occasional thrilling beauty and peace of the ice-floes, the grim, tough work of killing, skinning, and towing the whitecoats, and the visceral appeal and 'excitement' of the hunt itself, which on one occasion, despite his revulsion at seeing a 'mass of dying carcasses piled in the boat around me,' kept him out searching for seals through the ice-pans 'till a late hour in the afternoon.' The sealing expedition was but one of a variety of adventures which took him close to real peril around the Newfoundland coast, and Jukes seemed to relish each new experience that came his way. Once he had to travel 'in a filthy little boat in filthy weather' from Fogo to Trinity: 'We did but just manage to scrape round the Horse Chops, and sailed slowly along this lofty shore, with its perpendicular cliffs, at whose foot the waves were boiling and leaping, dead to leeward, and not a quarter of a mile distant. [John] Peyton seemed rather astonished when I called him on deck to look at them; for the parting of a single rope would have sent us where we should not have had a single chance for our lives. It was, however, a grand sight.' At the end of his stay he took stock of his abilities as a traveller and recognized that his experiences while wandering around the remote corners of the island had changed and toughened him. He realized too that growing accustomed to 'rough living, rough fare, and rough travelling' had not been an unpleasant experience.[48]

Jukes was not above making occasional haughty remarks about the politics and people of Newfoundland that betrayed his more enlightened upbringing in the mother country. He noticed a 'want of manly independence and self-reliance' among 'the lower classes,' for example, and proposed a solution to the political squabbling in the colony that had in it more snobbery than cleverness. Noting that there seemed to be no real division between the two contending interests in the colony in political principles, he claimed that 'if the two parties could agree among themselves as to the distribution of the public offices, their quarrels would die away simply for want of anything further to dispute about.'[49] This was a remark at roughly the same level of sensitivity as that of the British wit who suggested that the votes in the new Newfoundland legislature of 1833 be taken in this manner, 'As many as are of that opinion say – bow; of the contrary – wow; the bows have it,' or that of the Oxford scholar, J.D. Rogers, who suggested that the political history of the colony between 1818 and 1910 be entitled 'Much Ado About Little.'[50] Jukes also had a habit of praising any pleasant-looking, prosperous outport as 'quite an English sort of place.' However, such remarks were rare in his book, and his observations on ordinary Newfoundlanders, quoted above, were qualified by his final assessment of them. Any visitor to Newfoundland, he wrote, will have to 'get rid of all delicate and fastidious notions of comfort, convenience, and accommodation he may have acquired by journeying in England.' But 'so far as the inhabitants are concerned, under a rough exterior, he will meet with sterling kindness and hospitality.'[51]

To pass from Jukes's *Excursions* to Sir Richard Bonnycastle's imposing study *Newfoundland in 1842* (1842) is to leave common sense for imperialist bluster and military pomposity. Bonnycastle (1791–1847) was a colonel in the Royal Engineers who served overseas in the War of 1812 and the Canadian rebellions of 1837. Having become convinced during a stay of two years in Newfoundland that the island was 'the most neglected of our colonies,' he set about writing a book to point this 'sea-girt fortress,' this 'island gem,' in the direction of progress and to help 'develop its resources'[52] – an ominously early appearance of this tag, which has fuelled the careers of many Newfoundland politicians. Bonnycastle was a Victorian optimist through and through. Newfoundland's climate was, to him, one 'of extraordinary salubrity'; her people were 'very orderly and respectful to their superiors'; her interior, despite what such 'young authors' as Jukes may have written, 'will not only be fitted for agricultural purposes, but develop likewise mineral treasures and resources'; her fish resources were 'vastly superior, in consequence of their effects upon man, to the pearls, diamonds, and precious stones of the Eastern and warm countries of the globe.' And on he ran, calling on Britain throughout to cherish and protect Newfoundland as 'the key and fortress' of all her North American colonies and as 'the main stay of British Transatlantic power,' advocating a plan of 'promoting agriculture, education, and internal resources, roads, and steam vessels,' and professing dismay at what the mother country had done to 'the most ancient colony of Great Britain.'[53] This last sobriquet, soon to be firmly established in Newfoundland historiography, belongs really to Ireland.[54] To explain why Newfoundland had not progressed far prior to 1841, Bonnycastle fell back on the theories of Reeves and Morris, conjuring up images of tyrannical fishing admirals and the poor settler who had 'his miserable hut burned about his ears, and his family turned out to wander for protection to the ship which was appointed to carry them off.' But it seemed to him that 'a new era' had 'dawned upon Newfoundland' in the summer of 1841, when Sir John Harvey, a military man, had been appointed governor, to be hailed on his arrival by 'the Newfoundland subjects of her majesty' as the forerunner of an age of prosperity. Everywhere Bonnycastle looked, he saw the evidence of this new era:

A new race of inhabitants is springing up, who, born on the soil, cherish and fondly adhere to it; the population is no longer a fluctuating one; the island has obtained a representative government; it has been discovered that it is by no means so barren and infertile as was uniformly stated by interested persons, and that it is not that foggy country where lantern light is requisite at noon-day, but is possessed of a climate of extraordinary salubrity. Its population is steadily advancing; roads are opening; agriculture rears its head; and in short, from having been a mere mercantile depôt, it now bids fair to take its rank amongst the more flourishing colonies of the neighbouring continent.[55]

Thus in Bonnycastle's unrelenting rhetoric, Newfoundland history was lumbered with imperial and progressivist baggage, another addition to the welter of delusions already clouding the colony's past and future.

THE PEOPLE AND PROGRESS

Reading textbooks on Newfoundland's history and politics, and especially those in which the nineteenth century is quickly passed over as a prelude to developments in the twentieth, one gets an impression of the colony's history in the 1800s as a series of advances towards political and social maturity. There were the successive stages in political growth: resident governor without a council (1818–25); governor with a token council (1825–32); Representative Government (1832–43, 1847–55); an amalgamated legislature (1843–7); and, finally, Responsible Government (1855 onwards). Accompanying this evidence of progress, there may be data showing improvements in agricultural methods, road building around St John's and in Conception Bay, the increasing emphasis on education, the replacement of dogs by horses, the coming of the telegraph, the opening up of the west coast to settlers, and then finally the development of the railway and commencement of large-scale mining in Notre Dame Bay and on Bell Island. For the most part, however, these compendia concentrate on the island's constitutional development and its political and diplomatic history. They tell the reader 'Who loses and who wins, who's in, who's out'[56] on the local scene, and, in the international arena, show Newfoundland toying with the idea of joining the Canadian confederation and promoting her position vis-à-vis the French Shore question. (This complex question, which was not resolved until the Entente Cordiale of 1904, centred on the continuing French rights on the Newfoundland coast, after 1783 between Cape St John and Cape Ray.[57]) But when we turn away from such elevated discussions as Newfoundland's role in the Quebec conference on confederation to examine the lives of ordinary people in outports, a different image of the island emerges. From that perspective, politics seems a game of limited significance played by the St John's élite,[58] and diplomatic negotiations seem of little consequence. It is true that the French Shore dispute may have had an effect in deterring settlement on the west coast, but even that commonplace assertion by historians may be an exaggeration, and to blame Newfoundland's general failure to thrive on the French presence, as Patrick Morris was somewhat inclined to do in 1847, may well be another fallacy of our history.[59]

Newfoundland history in the nineteenth century – the real history, that of the common people – seems to exhibit continuity rather than progress. Whatever took place in high-level discussions in London or St John's, for the mass of the people the essential conditions of life remained unaltered. Every year brought its laborious contest with an unpredictable ocean, and life was a succession of ifs and chances. If the fish failed, hardship and possibly famine followed the next winter: it was that simple. A decade of 'progress' could be wiped away by a single bad summer. Life in nineteenth-century Newfoundland was less a succession of wonderful advances than a series of disasters, caused primarily by the failure of the fishery but also by potato blight and other factors. The period 1815–18, for example, was noteworthy for two calamitous fires in St John's, savage frosts, and widespread famine around the island.[60] Following the failure of the fishery, the winters of 1831–3 brought 'great distress in different parts of Conception Bay,' in New Harbour, Trinity Bay, and in Bonavista, and the government was obliged to distribute relief in the form of bread and molasses.[61] In 1846 a number of disasters struck the colony. On 9 June St John's burned to the ground. On 19 September a fierce storm caused enormous destruction of property on land and sea around the island. In addition, the potato crop was hit by blight and the fishery was a partial failure. Fearing food riots, local authorities unsuccessfully petitioned the British government to send a man-of-war to the island. Once again, famine was widespread, and the people remained in a perilous condition for some years, with the government once again doling out cornmeal (the hated 'Indian meal') as relief.[62] The urgent need for the cornmeal was indicated in a letter from the Bay de Verde merchant Thomas Hutchings to the magistrate in Harbour Grace on 12 April 1848: 'Half the Inhabitants are now in want,' he reported, 'this owing partly to the failure of the potatoe crop.' He went on to say that without the cornmeal, 'hundreds would have died of starvation ere this.'[63] Those requiring government assistance were now referred to in documents as 'paupers' and were sometimes obliged to work on the public roads to pay for what they had received. A few years after the disasters of 1846–8, in 1853, the fish again failed in Conception Bay, and the winter of 1853–4 is revealed in the documents dealing with the distribution of relief as one of the grimmest in the history of the colony. Widespread hunger became evident in early February 1854, far in advance of the beginning of the seal fishery, which outporters traditionally looked forward to as the beginning of economic revival after the long winter. Families were literally on the brink of starvation: 'The bearer hereof is John Fling who has a family of *nine* & have not at this moment a *morsel to eat* – this is the truth & nothing but the truth – the children go from door to door *daily* – unless the Government affords them relief I know not what they and the others are to do.' This note, dated 9 February 1854, is one of scores of surviving letters from Conception Bay in that harsh winter. As the merchant Hutchings wrote later in February, 'it can no longer be doubted that in this District many are in a state of calamitous destitution with no other prospect before them, humanly speaking, than still greater distress for three months to come.' A year later, the potato crop and the fishery having once more failed on the North Shore of Conception Bay, the people were again 'in great distress.'[64] In 1857 complaints were made about the number of beggars from neighbouring communities seen in Harbour Grace and Carbonear.

These periodic reversals in the people's struggle for a livelihood – reversals which by no means ended in 1854 – give the lie to the progressivist view of the colony's history in the nineteenth century. Whatever Patrick Morris may have fancied about the advantages of local government, government in fact affected most people's lives hardly a jot, except as the reluctant dispenser of eleemosynary aid in times of emergency. A missionary living in Portugal Cove in 1861 held the gloomy opinion that in spite of Newfoundland's 'long and tedious history,' as far as he could tell the 'original character' of the colony as a fishing station remained intact, 'unchanged by those marks of advancement and civilization which are obvious in the progress of other countries.'[65] Historians, for their part, hardly noticed the people's actual circumstances, so intent were they on elaborating upon the mythic sorrows of the country's distant past or envisioning her glorious future. When Bonnycastle saw the 'labouring poor' around St John's going into the woods for fuel in winter 'with scarcely any other than their ordinary clothing on,' he noted this as evidence of Newfoundland's salubrious climate.[66] A local writer who tried to comprehend the disasters of the period 1846–54 was Stephen March, in his book *The Present Condition of Newfoundland, with Suggestions for Improving its Industrial and Commercial Resources* (1854). March was an outport member of the House of Assembly who had seen at first hand the distress of the people of Trinity Bay and had been genuinely appalled. He was a mesmerized optimist, and what puzzled him was how Newfoundland, which he described variously as 'Nature's Great Post Office,' the 'Guardian Angel of the Coasts of the Continent,' an 'important link in the mighty chain of fraternity which shall girdle the globe,' and '*the great dock-yard of the North*,' could be reduced to her present straitened circumstances. He offered a number of reasons for the country's decline, among them the stubbornness of the Newfoundland mother, who tended to give way to 'a good deal of sobbing and crying when Jack goes to the ice or Labrador' and who certainly would not allow her children to travel to foreign countries to take part in what March conceived to be the lucrative activity of carrying freight. March had a number of other suggestions to get the country moving again, proposing shipbuilding, emigration, and building stone fences. 'Newfoundland has suffered more in her agricultural interests from the want of the stone wall fence than from any other cause,' he warned; adding, 'It will never prosper without it!' Having seen many grown men 'lounging on the beach, or hauling sticks to boil the kettle, or walking to the Government meal depot for provisions, or sleeping, or smoking in their punts,' March was concerned that the 'accumulated misfortunes' of the past eight years had 'crushed their spirit.' Work was the answer. Carrying freight and building barrels. Chapter VII of his book was entitled 'Oak Staves' and began: 'Let not the reader ridicule the title of this chapter.'[67] Oak staves! The oak tree is not native to Newfoundland.

'BOOMING NEWFOUNDLAND': CHARLES PEDLEY, MOSES HARVEY, PHILIP TOCQUE, AND D.W. PROWSE

From the coming of Responsible Government in 1855 until the end of the century, Newfoundland slowly changed from an 'embittered little Ireland,'[68] torn by sectarian strife, into a country that tried to realize her North American potential, and politics became dominated by four major issues: the opening up of the west and north coasts to settlers and industrialists; the confederation issue; the attempt to gain equity and some measure of control in the marketing of fish; and the assertion of Newfoundland's rights in the tortured French Shore question. The period saw a determined effort to seek alternatives to the fishery and to achieve a more stable economy based on a diversity of agricultural and industrial activities. The key to such a diversified economy, in the view of the dominant political figure of the time, William Whiteway (Premier, 1878–85, 1889–94, 1895–7), was the railroad, which would make the reported rich agricultural lands in the west and the mining regions of the north accessible to would-be farmers and entrepreneurs. Hopes for the success of northern and western enterprise had been fuelled by the exaggerated reports from Alexander Murray's and J.P. Howley's first series of geological surveys of Newfoundland (1864–80).[69] Newfoundland now also became aware of her strategic position as a kind of halfway house between Europe and the United States, an awareness sharpened by the landing of the transatlantic telegraph cable at Heart's Content in 1866. Increasing numbers of literary tourists and adventurers (to be discussed in the following chapter) were bringing the colony to the attention of the world in books and periodical articles. Local historians responded to this increased international attention, the growing sense of political independence, and the drive to develop the country's resources, by adopting a tactic described by Prowse as 'booming Newfoundland and making her attractions known.'[70] There was, perhaps, only one significant historical work from the period that stood apart from this activity of 'booming,' and, though it was limited and flawed, it deserves attention. It was Charles Pedley's neglected *History of Newfoundland* (1863).

Pedley (1820–72) had arrived in Newfoundland from County Durham with his wife and four sons in 1857, to become minister of the Congregational Church in St John's.[71] He quickly became well known as a lecturer, and when he was informed by the governor of the day, Sir Alexander Bannerman, that a collection of local records was available which could provide the basis for a history of the colony, Pedley set to work to comb what are now known as the Colonial Secretary's Letter Books for new information about his adopted country. The book that resulted was the earliest comprehensive scholarly history of Newfoundland. Pedley did not manage to incorporate his new information into a connected historical narrative, and he complained of the 'weariness' he felt at having to confront 'the multiplicity ... of affairs which devolved personally on the governor.' Newfoundland history, to him, was a series of minor transactions when compared with events in the European arena, and while he plodded through the records of the governors in St John's, his eye was on Napoleon and the Duke of Wellington. And yet he did amass facts carefully, filling out to some extent the virtually unknown period from 1660 to 1800, and shying away from suspect authorities. In many respects, Pedley was a sound historian.

He gave an excellent assessment of King William's Act, and though we can perceive in some sentences about 'poor planters' living 'at the mercy of the adventurers and merchants' the influence of Reeves, he evidently did not feel comfortable with the fictions of the nationalists and did not state that settlement or agriculture had been illegal in Newfoundland. (He came close: colonization, he noted, had been 'discouraged,' and to obtain land for agriculture was 'almost prohibited.'[72]) His eighth chapter was an attempt to explain why, up to 1800, Newfoundland, 'in the midst of growing communities of men,' remained 'isolated not only in respect to foreign states and peoples, but as a member of the great British family.' His first reason – and elementary but important concession in Newfoundland historiography – was geographical; namely, 'the fact that the country did not present to settlers those attractions in the qualities of its soil and climate, which invited them in the regions further west.' This directly challenged the argument of the nationalists that it 'was not the sterility of the soil or the severity of the climate, but it was her vast inexhaustible wealth, not her poverty but her riches, that so long prevented the settlement of Newfoundland.'[73] Pedley went on to note other reasons 'of a more special character,' the whole discussion being a fine analysis of the causes of the retardation of Newfoundland prior to the nineteenth century. The example of Pedley's caution and attentiveness to sources had no immediate effect upon Newfoundland historians. In 1866 William Wilson's *Newfoundland and its Missionaries* contained an angry denunciation of the 'foolish and wicked law' which had led to the 'prohibition of emigration' and caused settlers to be 'innocently expelled,' and by the end of the century imaginary wrongs had become entrenched in the colony's literature, appearing in common texts in chapters with such titles as 'Tyranny by Act of Parliament' and 'Oppression of the Weak.'[74]

The most prolific and relentless 'boomer' of Newfoundland in the second half of the nineteenth century was Moses Harvey (1820–1901), an Irishman of Scottish descent who was educated in Belfast and ordained as a minister in the Presbyterian church in 1844.[75] He became minister of the St Andrew's Free Presbyterian Church in St John's in 1852. On arriving in the capital, he set about busying himself in the intellectual and cultural life of the city, and became a prominent lecturer on biblical and other subjects.[76] After twenty-six years of service to his church, his voice, according to Prowse,[77] failed him, and in 1878 he retired from the active ministry and was given a life annuity by his congregation. Harvey was a writer with wide interests, great industry, and impressive ability. His first book of general interest was *Lectures, Literary and Biographical* (1864), the kind of rambling miscellany of essays of which Victorians were fond, covering such topics as 'Wit and Humour,' 'Edmund Burke and Oliver Goldsmith,' and 'The Poetry of Geology.' Harvey was a true product of his age, and in essays such as 'Human Progress – Is it real?' – later expanded into a book entitled *Where are We and Whither Tending?* (1886) – he declared his belief in the prevailing Victorian orthodoxy: that science, education, and technology were leading the world forward to higher levels in virtue and happiness, 'winning better and better conditions for the human race.'[78] 'I hold that human progress is a glorious reality,' he declared'; adding, rather lamely, that 'as yet it is largely a matter of faith rather than of experience.' He had a particular faith in the steamship and locomotive, which seemed to him to be 'throwing open the whole world, and drawing the nations into mutual acquaintance and incipient brotherhood.'[79] In the late 1860s Harvey started applying his principles to his adopted country, and began what might be interpreted in retrospect as a massive publicity campaign on behalf of the colony. In pamphlets, periodical articles, newspaper columns, speeches, and books, he indefatigably brought the wondrous potential of Newfoundland to the attention of outsiders. During the last quarter of the century, for example, he computed that he had written the 'appalling quantity' of nine hundred columns in the *Montreal Gazette* alone.[80] Bonnycastle was merely a precursor of Harvey, sent before to prepare the way. Nor did any subsequent writer, including, perhaps, the industrious native publicist P.T. McGrath (1868–1928),[81] match Harvey's enthusiasm or prodigious output as a propagandist.

While there was in Harvey an effervescence and driving energy that set him apart from other nineteenth century publicists, his dreams for Newfoundland were the same as those of men like Morris and Bonnycastle, and his books and articles were really endless iterations of one theme: the potential of Newfoundland, despite the misfortunes of her past, to provide an abundant future for her people. A supporter of Whiteway, he was convinced that the coming of the railway (for which a survey was conducted in 1875 with the help of Sandford Fleming, with actual construction starting in 1881), the strategic position of the island, the copper mines at Bett's Cove, Tilt Cove, and other places in the north, and the agricultural potential of the interior and west, would combine to ensure Newfoundland's greatness. He was also a supporter of union with Canada, and was not reluctant, in 1869, on the eve of an election in which a confederate party was soundly defeated, to predict that it would soon come about:

Happily for herself, Newfoundland is at length convinced that her interest lies in joining the Dominion of Canada and in all probability, the union will be consummated in a few months. Then her great natural resources will be turned to account. The railroad projected by Mr. Sandford Fleming will cross the island from St. John's to St. George's Bay, linking us with the Intercolonial line, and making St. John's the great port of communication between the Old World and the New, being within five days steaming of the Irish shores. The risk of crossing the Atlantic will thus be immensely diminished, and the bulk of the passengers, and fine goods' traffic will, in all probability, be attracted to this route, as well as all mail matter. The railroad will open up the Island for settlement. On the western side the formations are wholly different from those of the eastern and northern. There a carboniferous region is found, where coal and marble beds are known to be extensive; while fine timber and a fertile soil present inviting attractions to the agriculturist. Specimens of marble equal to the finest Italian have been obtained in that region. The Dominion will find Newfoundland one of her finest provinces, requiring only capital, skill and energy to render it a prosperous and wealthy country. Taking into account her splendid position between the Old World and the New, – her magnificent harbours – her inexhaustible fisheries – her rich minerals – her coal, and marble beds and heavily timbered fertile lands in the west, it is difficult to name any country possessed of such a combination of natural advantages. At present, her condition is one of depression and misery of the extremest type. An Island as large as Ireland is inhabited by 130,000 people, of whom a very large proportion are at this moment in the lowest depths of poverty – in fact bordering on starvation. Joined to a wealthier, more progressive community, whose interest will lie in developing her material resources and elevating her naturally fine, intelligent people in the scale of being, a brighter future opens before her.[82]

The passage illustrates well Harvey's bubbling rhetoric and his disarming ability to maintain a progressivist stance even when confronted by the abject poverty of those he called the 'toiling masses.' The absurd idea of Newfoundland serving as a transportation link between Europe and America he picked up from Sandford Fleming. But Harvey himsel was in truth an inveterate surmiser and diviner, and a tireless promoter of dubious schemes for the colony's development. Nothing was more typical of him than to turn away from the sordid present and look forward to the 'good time coming.' Looking around the area of copper deposits in Notre Dame Bay, for example, he envisioned a future 'when a vast mining and farming population will overspread these solitudes, and the smoke from the furnaces and workshops and mines will darken the air, and the hills will be re-echoing with the blows of the miners, and the harbours crowded with shipping; when railways will connect this region with the capital, and with the fine farming and mining lands of the West; and a vast mining interest, pouring wealth into the country, and furnishing remunerative employment to thousands, will have grown to vast dimensions here, and overshadowed our diminished fisheries on which we are now chiefly dependent.'[83] Such flourishes as these were literary echoes of the high hopes being expressed by local politicians in the late 1870s and 1880s, hopes which some more realistic commentators pronounced to be 'all clap-trap and nonsense.'[84] In another prophetic mood Harvey predicted that the shores of Grand Lake – which are today virtually as rugged and uncultivated as when he saw them in 1878 – would soon 'be filled with a busy, prosperous population' and covered with 'smiling cornfields and meadows.'[85] Among his other prognostications were that Newfoundland's copper would make her 'a new Cornwall' or 'the Chili of North America,' that the population of the island 'a century hence' would be 'at least two millions' (this in 1870), that the transshipment of goods and passengers would one day make St John's 'one of the most important places on this side the Atlantic,' and that a recurrrence of the fire that destroyed St John's in 1846 'may be regarded as impossible.'[86] Time, alas, would reveal him as a forecaster of doubtful ability, but Harvey's motives were sincere and his love for the land and people genuine. The people he praised, extravagantly as we would expect, as 'men of bone and muscle who can fearlessly "lay their hands on ocean's mane" and wrestle with the Atlantic's billows.'[87]

By instinct an amateur scientist rather than a historian, Harvey nevertheless wrote numerous articles on the history of the island and in 1883 combined with the English scholar Joseph Hatton to produce a weighty tome called *Newfoundland: its History, its Present Condition, and its Prospects in the Future*. This was followed by a number of shorter historical textbooks for the schools, one on the occasion of Queen Victoria's Diamond Jubilee (1897) and another at the end of the century. Harvey was much more inclined to adumbrate the future prospects of Newfoundland than to investigage her past history, and as a consequence his historical writing was founded on no new research and had no significance, except in so far as it repeated and further entrenched the myths begun by Reeves and Morris. His chief contribution to Newfoundland may have been as a popularizer and disseminator of scientific knowledge and as a journalist. He became well known for his detailed description of the giant squid (or, as he preferred to call it, the 'devil fish'),[88] and his essays also illuminated the geology of the island. Harvey's numerous publications, with their burning message about the country's resources, possibly had effects upon generations of Newfoundlanders that are hard to calculate.

Whereas Harvey was an eager participant in the life of the colony he was advertising abroad, the Newfoundland-born writer Philip Tocque (1814–99) chose to celebrate her wonders from afar. Tocque was born in Carbonear and spent his early life as a clerk, teacher, and justice of the peace. Around 1850 he left the colony for good, and after studying at a divinity school in Connecticut, took orders in the Episcopal church. He subsequently made a few brief visits to his homeland. His first book, *Wandering Thoughts or Solitary Hours* (1846), was a collection of essays on a variety of topics, a few of which related to Newfoundland. The book was noteworthy, however, for its condemnation of the seal fishery as 'a nursery for moral and spiritual evils. It has a tendency to harden the heart and render it insensible to the finer feelings of human nature. It is a constant scene of bloodshed and slaughter. Here you behold a heap of seals which have only received a slight dart from the gaff, writhing, and crimsoning the ice with their blood – rolling from side to side in dying agonies. There you see another lot, while the last spark of life is not yet extinguished, being stripped of their skin and fat; their startings and heavings making the unpractised hand shrink with horror to touch them.' Thus Tocque went further than his predecessor Jukes by associating the seal fishery with moral turpitude. His was the prologue to many such sentimental observations. Tocque also wrote a tearful lamentation over the fate of the Beothucks:

The poor Indians were hunted like wolves by those merciless and unfeeling barbarians, the white men, till at last, of all this noble race, at one time a powerful tribe, scarce a trace is left behind. No canoe is now seen gliding noiselessly over the lakes, no war-song breaks upon the ear. If we go to the River Exploits, no sound of the Indian is heard breaking the silence of these gloomy solitudes. If we visit that beautiful sheet of water, Red Indian Lake (their last retreat), no smoke is seen curling from their wigwams, no footstep is traced, all is barrenness and naked desolation. Where then are the red men? They are gone, they have passed away forever, and are now in the far-off land of the Great Spirit.[89]

Throughout the nineteenth century the fate of the Beothucks also became obscured by such lugubrious and apocryphal tut-tutting over the tribe's last days – another feature of the growing entanglement of the colony's history with sentiment. The first novel set in Newfoundland, *Ottawah, the Last Chief of the Red Indians* (1847), concerned itself nominally with the Beothucks, although there was no knowledge of their language or customs displayed in it, and wailing over the disappearance of the Indians was commonplace in the writing of tourists.[90] But Tocque's comments remained unequalled until 1875, when they were surpassed by Moses Harvey's macabre rumination on a Beothuck skull.[91]

After a visit to his home in 1876, Tocque next wrote *Newfoundland, As It Was and As It Is in 1877* (1878), a book that combined features of a history and a gazeteer. In his preface he remarked that he 'made this book out of myself, out of my life,' and that when he wanted to know the history of the Newfoundland people, 'I had but to interrogate my memory.' This meant, among other things, that he did little original historical research, and he therefore repeated the distortions he found in Morris, Wilson, and others. Tocque had an eye for scenery, but his descriptions ('nought is heard to disturb the solitude save now and then the notes of the ptarmigan') tended to be mawkish. He gave the exact dimensions of the 'coal field' in western Newfoundland ('thirty miles long and ten broad, situated only eight miles from the sea'), stressed the agricultural potential of the island, noting that the west coast was destined to become 'the granary of Newfoundland,' and, as evidence that the climate was the 'healthiest' in the world, pointed out, in an unlucky phrase, that 'consumption, so common on the American Continent, is hardly known there.'[92] This latter theme was enlarged on in Tocque's last book, *Kaleidoscope Echoes* (1895), in an essay entitled 'Newfoundland as a Health Resort,' a piece containing much unwittingly humorous commentary on the island. 'In Newfoundland we have a bracing climate,' he wrote, 'with no trace of malaria. Sunstrokes are entirely unknown.' He went on to indicate the attractions of Hermitage Bay, St George's Bay, and Bay of Islands, 'all of which are delightful places for the tourist and invalid to visit.' In a later essay he added to the statistics already recorded about the 'coal field' on the west coast the supplementary information that it was three and one half feet in thickness. But to ridicule *Kaleidoscope Echoes* is ungracious. It was, in fact, a melancholy, brooding book by a gifted man who had left his home for 'wealth, pleasure, and fame,' and discovered in old age that such ambitions were 'broken cisterns that hold no water.' Returning to Carbonear on his last visit, he found it to be 'the village of the dead, where my forefathers dwell.' Few of his early associates were living, but 'In the grey-haired, wrinkled, old ladies, I found the once blooming and handsome belles of the place – the companions of my youth.' Seeing these and other gloomy signs, he knew that 'the winter of life is upon me.'[93] In *Kaleidoscope Echoes* we see the appearance of a poignant theme of twentieth-century New-foundland writing: the outharbour man as émigré, lost in another country or city, and longing for home.

In 1895, three years after the destruction of St John's in yet another catastrophic fire, and during another period of uncertainty and misery in the colony caused by the bank crash in St John's in December 1894, D.W. Prowse (1834–1914) published his magisterial volume, *A History of Newfoundland from the English, Colonial, and Foreign Records*. Prowse was born in Port de Grave and was educated at a private school in St John's and at the Collegiate School in Liverpool. Called to the bar in 1859, he became a member of the House of Assembly and, in 1869, judge of the Central District Court. His book was hailed on its appearance as the most comprehensive history of the island, and no comparable work has appeared in the twentieth century to challenge its dominant position in Newfoundland historiography. The *History*, however, despite its impressive scholarship and Prowse's own superb gifts as a writer, was rather the culmination of nineteenth-century historical views than a new approach. Prowse amassed more data and examined more documents than any previous historian, but he had no new ideas. On the contrary, he enveloped the history of the country more thoroughly than ever in a cloud of misunderstanding, by combining his genuine scholarship with sentimental editorializing. His picture of the colony's history during the sixteenth century, for example, parallels Victorian images of 'merrie England.' He praised 'the doughty deeds of the old Devon sailors,' the 'proud beef-eating Englishmen' who 'left their little ports to reap the harvest of the seas' and eventually, as 'born hunters, restless roaming spirits, like the Daniel Boones and Kit Carsons of western fame,' stayed on to settle the new country. There were 'many mute inglorious Nelsons amongst these Devonian skippers,' he noted. St John's itself, in 1583, was 'an important free port' where 'a large international trade was carried on' and which was, 'then, and now, famous for its hospitality.' Prowse enlarged on the festive occasions in the old Newfoundland ports:

But they were merry souls amidst all the dangers of the seas, wars, pirates, and rovers. Each week the Admiral of the port retired, and at every change the new official gave a feast to all. The cheap and generous wines of Europe would then be freely circulated, and the sombre woods of the little port be enlivened, perchance, by the chanson of the French or the rattling of the castanets and lively airs on the Spanish guitar. If it was a Basque port the fun would be fast and furious – there would be the national Gaita (the bagpipes) and song, dance, and single-stick with broken heads, to enliven the feast.[94]

There was a thick layer of such contrived emotion throughout Prowse's book. It was displayed nowhere to better effect than in his sorrow over the 'barbarous' edict designed to drive Newfoundlanders out of their 'substantial, comfortable wooden homes' in the 1670s:

Englishmen accustomed to their own highly cultivated land, the labour of many generations, can hardly understand the strong ties of affection which bound the Newfoundlanders to their rugged homes. Their little gardens and fields were rude and rough compared with English culture, but they were the work of their own hands; the apple trees and small bushes brought from the old country, tended with loving care, had developed and blossomed and borne fruit, the admiration and wonder of the little settlement. To be driven from home and the smiling fields and gardens ... was a terrible wrench at their heart strings, a separation that seemed like death.

The poet has sung to us of the sorrows of Evangeline and of the evictions from Grand Pré. The Acadians were not in a more miserable plight than the poor Newfoundland settlers during that long period from 1675 to 1677, while the terrible edict hung over their heads.

Though 'a Devonian myself,' Prowse could not help but cry out against such monstrous abuses, although, to his credit, he did not claim that anybody had actually been evicted. He went on to adopt the views of Reeves and Morris and to declaim against the 'monopolists' and fishing admirals. (Like Morris, he had to recant somewhat in his assaults against the merchants, pointing out that 'occasional large profits are a necessity in such an exceedingly risky business.') It was the old cant of the patriots and 'boomers' parroted once more. When Prowse moved on to the nineteenth century, his account, though lively and amusing, became more anecdotal than analytical, and was filled with the comings and goings of governors, judges, and politicians in St John's, and with imperial ranting. Prowse did not often dwell on the condition of the mass of the population. Indeed, he was inclined throughout his book to patronize 'the simple outharbour people,' whom he viewed as credulous and ignorant.[95] His later chapters, in essence, recounted the activities of the country's urban élite, of which Prowse himself was fully a part. His book enshrined as historical truth a twisted and sentimental view of the colony's past.

Thanks partly to historians like Prowse and 'boomers' like Harvey, Newfoundland would enter the twentieth century believing herself to have been in the past the sport of 'historic misfortune,' and 'the patient Griselda of the Empire,'[96] but looking forward to a new age of civilization and prosperity.

5   The lure of the north

FICTION AND TRAVEL
LITERATURE / 1850–1905

A STRANGE COUNTRY IN THE WATERS'[1]

In the second half of the nineteenth century Newfoundland and Labrador became an object of scientific, romantic, and humanitarian interest among foreign writers. No doubt this was partly the result of the energetic promotional activity of local writers such as Moses Harvey, but perhaps the modest international curiosity about the colony would have developed anyway in an era of imperial and economic expansion, when intercontinental travel was becoming commonplace and the reading public's appetite in England and America for travel literature was keen. Again, with the rapid advance of the comparatively new sciences of geography, geology, and biology, it was inevitable that an unmapped wilderness such as Labrador would attract the attention of inquirers, especially in an age noted for daring Arctic and Antarctic exploration. Thus the new interest in Newfoundland and Labrador was in part a feature of a larger scientific and literary curiosity about the North, and the writers discussed in this chapter are to be linked with contemporary figures like Robert Peary, Jack London, and Robert Service. Newfoundland during this period was, in addition, at the centre of heated and complicated fishery disputes between Britain and her two rivals France and America, disputes that made the mother country belatedly aware of the value of her 'oldest colony' and that prompted British authors to write numerous articles on 'the first-born' of her overseas possessions and to take notice of its many 'tribulations.'[2] Authors with an interest in colonial matters now called attention to 'the sorrows of Newfoundland' and expressed the hope that though 'she has suffered much,' 'her spirit, we love to think, is indomitable.'[3] But while the increased British attention to Newfoundland might have been expected, of particular interest in this period was the involvement of American writers with the colony. It may not be an exaggeration to say that the island and Labrador became in some sense an imaginative outpost of the eastern United States, with authors recreating in this sparsely populated and primitive territory an image of their own diminishing frontier.

Apart from these general considerations, there were particular features of the colony that brought literary and artistic visitors to its shores and inspired others to write about it. The island had the appeal of singularity. An ancient possession of Britain situated near the North American continent, it was yet so different from both, so undeniably 'foreign,' that it seemed an oddity of history and geography, with the 'fishiest' of capital cities and outports that ranked among 'the queerest places in the world.'[4] The enduringly primeval quality of the coastline puzzled observers. There was 'something curiously fascinating,' one writer noted, 'in a coast so long a familiar unit in the world's history, and yet even now containing upon its face such scanty impress of human life.'[5] A writer in 1892 lamented that 'No English Homer has yet arisen to tell the tale of Newfoundland, shrouded in mystery and romance, the daring invasion and vicissitudes of these exhaustless fisheries, the battle of life in that seething cauldron of the North Atlantic ... where the swelling billows never rest.'[6] It was just this mixture of strangeness, antiquity, and turbulent action that brought Newfoundland to the attention of authors of adventure stories. R.M. Ballantyne's *The Crew of the Water Wagtail: A Story of Newfoundland* (1889) and Joseph Hatton's *Under the Great Seal* (1893) were tales about the early English fishery and settlement in the colony. As if to illustrate how widely Moses Harvey's influence was felt abroad, the former related a frightening encounter with a 'devil-fish' while the latter dwelt on tyrannical fishing admirals, helpless colonists, and other aspects of the sentimental history of the island that Harvey had helped to propagate.[7] Other storytellers were attracted by the drama and possibilities for romance inherent in the New England bank fishery, and also in the nineteenth-century Gloucester herring fishery around the south and west coasts of the island. Kirk Munroe's *Dorymates: A Tale of the Fishing Banks* (1889), Kipling's *Captains Courageous* (1897), and the stories of James B. Connolly (1868–1957) belong in this genre, with Connolly's work capturing the excitement of the herring fishery along the west coast of 'wild Newf'undland.'[8] Nor was Labrador left out of this yarning, being represented by C.A. Stephens's *Left on Labrador* (1872), and W.A. Stearns's *Wrecked on*

Labrador (1888), among others. All these works were, in essence, romances for younger readers, with the setting often functioning as a conveniently remote territory in which to locate improbable adventures. Newfoundland and Labrador continued to serve as a backdrop to such escapist fiction well into the twentieth century, in, for example, the Billy Topsail stories of Norman Duncan, T.G. Roberts's *Brothers of Peril: A Story of Old Newfoundland* (1905), *The Red Feathers* (1907), *A Captain of Raleigh's* (1911), *The Harbor Master* (1912), and other tales, and the various performances of the Newfoundland-born novelists, Anastasia M. English (1864–1959) and Erle R. Spencer (1897–1937).[9] Another noteworthy local specimen of this kind of writing was J.A. O'Reilly's *The Last Sentinel of Castle Hill* (1916).

In this period, painters too began to sense the appeal of Newfoundland and Labrador, and their activities were recorded in a number of literary works, including L.L. Noble's highly romantic *After Icebergs with a Painter* (1861), in which it is observed, not for the first or last time, that 'Here on these bleak and barren shores, so rocky, rough and savage, is a rich and delicate splendor that amazes.'[10] This was one of a great number of books and magazines displaying Newfoundland scenes pictorially, the most distinguished being two twentieth-century works, J.G. Millais's beautifully illustrated *Newfoundland and its Untrodden Ways* (1907) and Rockwell Kent's *N by E* (1930). Millais's book described his experiences hunting caribou in the interior of the island, an activity that drew a parade of sportsmen to the colony throughout the nineteenth century and resulted in numerous books and articles.[11] Another phenomenon that focused the attention of the world on Newfoundland was the effort to lay an Atlantic cable between Europe and America after 1855. This produced yet another flurry of comments on the colony.[12] In addition to all these incitements to authors, Newfoundland supplied what had become, or was about to become, subjects that seemed to invite perennial displays of literary sentiment: periodic conflagrations and other calamities, the unfortunate fate of the Beothucks, and the slaughter of seals. A writer in *Chambers's Journal* for 29 January 1887, for example, took note of recent reports that 'hundreds' of Newfoundlanders had starved to death and that 'their bodies had been savagely devoured by troops of hungry Polar bears.' This was by no means a typical item, but the island and Labrador did offer plenty of opportunities for the chronicler of catastrophe. The topic of seals, already clouded by emotional excess in the writing of Jukes and Tocque, evoked an even more exaggerated response in 1889 from a talented visitor to Newfoundland, Lady Edith Blake, wife of Governor H.A. Blake. Her essay entitled 'On Seals and Savages' bemoaned the fate of the 'unhappy' seal cubs, who are pictured as 'frolicsome and playful,' and watched over 'tenderly' by the 'mother.' Lady Blake noted the 'brutalising and degrading' effects of the hunt on the 'filthy and foul-smelling men' who killed them. [13] But the colony's leading attraction to writers in the closing decades of the century was, without doubt, the territory of Labrador which, as Charles G.D. Roberts wrote in 1891, offered 'strange landscapes, and wonderful cataracts, and all the charm of the mysterious unknown.' [14] After 1892, when Wilfred Grenfell (1865–1940) began his lifelong connection with the northern regions of the colony, that attraction grew even stronger, and Grenfell's medical and missionary heroics came to embody for many writers the glamour of Labrador.

The story of Grenfell's life and long service to the people of Newfoundland has been narrated in various biographies, and his own voluminous *œuvre* provides ample illumination of his character and motives. [15] What led him to establish and maintain his medical mission in the northern extremities of the colony was an undeniable sense of dedication, together with a love of risk-taking and athletic adventure and a powerful need for recognition. In his childhood he had loved books like Charles Kingsley's *Westward Ho!* (1855), which featured some of the 'red-blooded men' of Devon who had early ventured to North America and whom he numbered among his ancestors. [16] In 1885, while a medical student in London, he wandered one evening into an evangelical meeting conducted by the American preacher D.L. Moody, and learned that Christ required of men 'real hard service.' He determined to do surgery 'as Christ would do it,' for he was convinced that 'when Christ made doors and windows in Nazareth, they did not jam and misfit.' [17] Seven years later he sailed for Newfoundland to assess the need for medical services in the north, arriving in St John's just in time to see the city burn to the ground. He returned to the colony in 1893 with two doctors and ten nurses, and established at Battle Harbour the first hospital of the Labrador Medical Mission, founding a service that continues to this day.

Grenfell himself never spent a single winter on the Labrador coast, but his life was nevertheless consumed with the advancement of his mission. Much of his time was spent in travelling and making speeches, and his numerous publications should be seen as part of this activity of enlightened self-advertisement. His first book, *Vikings of Today, or Life and Medical Work among the Fishermen of Labrador*

(1895) – a title facing a photograph of the doctor and his crew aboard the hospital ship *Princess May*, unfortunately leaving it doubtful whether Grenfell and his associates, or the fishermen, merit the designation of 'Vikings' – illustrates the essential ingredients of most of Grenfell's works: accounts of the geology, people, flora, and fauna of Labrador, mostly derived from previous scientific accounts but given a distinctive flavour by an emphasis upon the extreme and idiosyncratic; grim, detailed anecdotes of disease among the fishermen and Eskimos, combined with examples of the enormous benefits derived from even the simplest medical treatment; effusive testimonials to the heroism and efficacy of Grenfell's efforts; and narratives of his own brushes with death on the Labrador coast, told with British aplomb. To go to the book for an exact account of conditions on the Labrador coast in 1895 would be unwise, for it was rhetoric rather than plain description, designed to catch the eye and win the support of readers. He was out to persuade as well as inform. Throughout *Vikings of Today* we nevertheless feel the force of Grenfell's highly individual personality and sense his supreme confidence in the rightness and ultimate success of his mission. And while he was labouring on behalf of the people, healing the sick, preaching the Word, and championing the wronged, he was also, one feels, enjoying himself. He once told the Canadian Club in Toronto that he would be glad to see any of its members in Labrador 'to have a leg off,' and on another occasion he bemused one of the many writers drawn to the north by his shining example with this comment on his experiences: 'It's been jolly good fun!'[18]

TOURISTS AND OTHER OBSERVERS: THE LITERARY 'NEWFOUNDLANDER'

Accounts of the Newfoundland people in late-nineteenth-century literature were as varied as the motives and intelligences of the writers describing them. We have seen how local historians depicted them as 'hardy' Newfoundlanders, loyal to England and wonderfully hospitable. A similar tendency to manufacture an image of the people to accord with a particular thesis or viewpoint was noticeable in other writers. If, for example, a visitor wished to teach his American audience a lesson in proper dietary and living habits, he might dwell on the 'health and longevity' of Newfoundlanders: 'No race of people that I have ever seen shows more healthy and vigorous stamina, and the natural morality which accompanies this condition. They are nourished by the pure, vital blood, unmixed with any of those morbid elements which so often poison the life of our physically and spiritually intemperate American people.'[19] On the other hand, a medical missionary like Grenfell who was looking for money and moral support from readers, would tend to emphasize the hardship and disease he witnessed in the outports. In White Bay, Grenfell noted that 'the number of cases of tubercle, anaemia, and dyspepsia, of beri-beri and scurvy, all largely attributable to poverty of diet, is very great; and the relative poverty, even compared with that of the countries which I have been privileged to visit, is piteous.'[20] Some observers found in Newfoundlanders a degree of ignorance 'hardly to be credited,' calling them 'simple-minded' and deficient in 'energy' and 'self-reliance,'[21] while others noted 'a studied independent bearing' among the people and pronounced them 'quick-witted,' 'shrewd and intelligent.'[22] The majority of comments on the people's mental capacities tended to be disparaging, and a visitor in 1888 was surprised to find that local fishermen 'are not the fools they are *too often* taken for.'[23] Lady Blake, however, summarized the prevailing view when she commented in 1889 that in Newfoundland, 'as usually in fishing populations, the intellectual faculties are decidedly in abeyance.'[24] Different commentators may be cited to indicate that inhabitants of the colony were subservient, and hostile, to authority, habitually lazy and hardworking, and excitable and dully submissive. There was even disagreement about the size of Newfoundlanders, with one writer describing them as 'large boned and powerfully built' and another noting that in one community people were 'stunted and ill-favoured.'[25]

Just as there was a variety of views about the people, so too one notices conflicting opinions about the general conditions of life in the outports. Comments on the barbarousness of life along the coastline were common, one of the most extreme being that of a touring musician in 1876, who wrote that the 'state of things' in the 'remoter villages' on the seaboard 'is far more woful than the condition of the South Sea Islanders.'[26] The Earl of Dunraven, however, on a hunting expedition in the 1870s, found at least in the outports along the French Shore 'a delightfully primitive state of society.'[27]

It is not hard to pinpoint the sources of so much disagreement on the nature of life in Newfoundland among casual observers, for opinions would naturally vary depending not only on the character and views of the onlookers, but also on the particular part of Newfoundland they saw, and in what year they saw it. But the chief source of so much hostile comment was without doubt superciliousness. Surprisingly, this was most noticeable in the observations of military personnel. Lieutenant-Colonel R.B. McCrea's *Lost Amid the Fogs* (1869), an entertaining and occasionally penetrating account of Newfoundland, was vitiated by just this sensation felt by the author of being in a little place, a 'fish-kettle,' ruled by a 'ridiculously small' parliamentary government. The bloody political riot in St John's in May 1861 McCrea described as a 'storm in the fish-kettle.' Before he left the colony for a more important part in 'the great drama of life,' McCrea nevertheless regretted being taken 'away from scenes we had now learnt to love so well.'[28]

One noteworthy feature of this bulk of occasional writing on Newfoundland was the growing recognition we can see in it of the uniqueness of the Newfoundland people. Missionaries in particular, having become intimate with the people's ways, were struck by what Moses Harvey called their 'peculiarities.'[29] 'From many causes,' the SPG missionary Julian Moreton wrote in 1863, 'the people generally are much altered in temper and bearing from the class in England to which they belong.' Moreton tried gamely to understand what he termed the 'stronge imperturbable habit' of his parishioners at Greenspond. They appeared to him 'unaccustomed to move at other men's bidding' and were 'hardly to be excited to action unless impelled by their own perception of need.' He wondered too at the odd 'tone of mind' that allowed men to 'enter your house unasked to light their pipes at your kitchen fire, and perhaps sit down to smoke and spit.' Moreton was so impressed by the individuality of his parishioners that he made a study of the 'words and phrases peculiar to Newfoundland' to try to understand the people more fully. He confessed, however, that he was 'too dull' to perceive the meaning of some of their proverbs, and his attitude towards those he served was one of mild bewilderment.[30] We sometimes notice a similar perplexity in J.G. Mountain's and F.E.J. Lloyd's accounts of their missionary activities for the SPG in the colony. Mountain was stationed at Harbour Breton in Fortune Bay from 1847 to 1854, while Lloyd served on the Great Northern Peninsula from 1882 to 1884. Lloyd, like Moreton, was struck by the differences between Newfoundlanders in his parish and the stock of English farm labourers from which they had sprung. 'Transplantation to a country where there was absolutely nothing to be obtained but by their own individual exertions,' he wrote, 'transformed these country bumpkins into carpenters, boat-builders, netters, foresters, fishermen, coopers, blacksmiths, and sawyers.'[31] As early as 1794 the seaman Aaron Thomas had remarked that 'the Natives' of Newfoundland, whether of

British or Irish ancestry, spoke English in 'a manner peculiar to themselves,'[32] and increasingly, as the nineteenth century wore on, es-
sayists and journalists noticed – sometimes merely for the purpose of
ridicule – the distinctive accents, idiom, songs, and proverbs of
Newfoundlanders. Before the century ended Lady Blake had made
quite an intelligent attempt to understand the origins of their folklore,
while George Patterson, having observed the people 'using English
words in a sense different from what I had ever heard elsewhere,' had
begun the scholarly study of Newfoundland dialect.[33] But even in
more general accounts, disparaging or otherwise, there was now
usually a recognition of the people's separate identity:

the inhabitants of St. John's and of the outports – as all the other towns and
settlements are called – and of the island in general, are a splendid set of tall,
strong, active, healthy-looking men. Accustomed from childhood to brave the
hardships of a most rigorous climate, drawing their sustenance from the
teeming but treacherous bosom of a storm-vexed ocean, that rages in vain
forever round a rugged, reef-bound coast; navigating their frail and ill-found
schooners amid tempest, ice, and fog, the Newfoundlanders have developed
into one of the finest seafaring populations on the face of the globe. Nowhere
can better mariners be found than among the hardy, adventurous, self-reliant
men who ply their precarious calling along the dangerous shores of their native island, or on the wintry coast of the neighboring mainland of Labrador.[34]

The bombast and adolescent vocabulary notwithstanding, there is in
the words of this onlooker in the 1870s an implicit perception of
nationhood, a perception made the more interesting in the way it
embraced both St John's residents and the people of the outports.

   With outsiders so pointedly proclaiming the distinctiveness of
Newfoundlanders, it was to be expected that local writers would begin
articulating a national self-consciousness. One of the earliest and most
eloquent statements by a Newfoundlander on the subject of local
identity was triggered by the international quarrel over the colony's
Bait Act of 1886. The Bait Act, passed by the House of Assembly and
the Legislative Council, empowered the government to prohibit the
sale of bait to French fishermen. This was a measure of great potential
benefit to Newfoundlanders, who thought they were being priced out
of the international market by the subsidized French fishery. In 1887,
responding to pressure from French diplomats, Britain refused to give
its sanction to the act, whereupon the local legislature immediately
passed a second Bait Act in response to 'awakened ... public senti-

ment.'[35] This, after much lobbying and certain qualifications, was eventually approved by the Mother of Parliaments, but not before the incident had angered the local press and raised questions about the extent of Newfoundland's control over its own affairs.[36] It was not an idle exaggeration to picture the Newfoundlander in this revealing episode as a 'victim' of an 'Olympic contest' between Britain and France, 'driven by a foreigner whom he detests out of his own waters' and 'finding all hope of aid rendered vain by the diplomatic interests of the Government in England.' That at any rate was Richard Howley's response to the episode in a long article in the journal *Month* in 1887. 'The poor Newfoundlander,' he stated, 'is at the apex of the hot fire,' and Howley's purpose in writing his paper was 'to introduce him and his industry, and win for him if possible a little public sympathy.' After presenting his analysis of the cod fishery, Howley turned his attention to the Newfoundland fisherman:

For nearly half a century there has been no immigration (sufficient to give any notable impress to the population) to the colony of Newfoundland. Its people therefore stand revealed, among the inhabitants of the American Continent and its islands, as a special type, and a production of their own clime, its constituents and influences. It were untrue to say that they retain no marks of their race, and their descent from the vigorous British stock whence they derive. Nevertheless the brand of a new life and a new land is already set upon them, and the Newfoundlander is as distinct in mental character, in certain points of physique, and tricks of speech, as any separated race can be from the parent source. Southern Ireland and Western England supplied the main tide of the blood of the present islander. He is a large, often a gigantic, man, with heavy bones well clothed with flesh and muscle, but coarse in the joints, cheek bones, and other prominent parts of his structure. He has, usually, a kindly blue-grey eye with the sailor gleam – a sort of reflection of the sea sheen – upon it. He has a rolling gait, walking everywhere as though on deck. He speaks down in his throat with an indistinct far-off utterance. He avoids dental sounds, and all his th's are d's. His tongue is decidedly lazy, or perhaps too well employed in turning his 'quid,' or holding it in position, to bother about the minor business of articulation. He is a long and strong eater of pork, salt beef, fish, and hard biscuit. His favourite beverage is tea, usually sweetened with molasses. ... The Newfoundland fisherman undoubtedly drinks hard, at times of a less harmless liquid. Rum, and rum only, straight from the West Indies in Spanish and native bottoms, is his beloved invigorator. He is not however a persistent drinker, ... but he drinks thoroughly when about it. He becomes noisy but not usually quarrelsome. No country is more free from acts of crime or violence than Newfoundland. Yet with all his soft 'slobbishness' of temperament the Newfoundlander is not a safe animal to exasperate. Like the dog of the country he will bear any amount of teazing and tantalizing from a kind master or a trusty friend, but is a decidedly ugly customer for a recognized foe to deal with. The schools of the country are few and indifferent outside of the two chief towns, and the fisherboy has scant time to devote to them. He is therefore, in our modern sense, ignorant. Yet he can, as a rule, read and write, and no man, after all, is really ignorant who knows his particular calling so thoroughly and extensively, and loves it as well as the Newfoundlander. Draw those loose lines together. Form a figure clothed in heavy pilot cloth, when ashore and unemployed; in canvass trousers, reeky and oily, and guernsey shirt with fur cap or sou'-wester when at sea; behold a brown, weather-beaten face, smooth, except for the thick muff of hair that grows up from and around the throat, and peaks out from the chin, and you have the Newfoundland fisherman as he is, a healthy, hardy, patient, and somewhat stubborn sea-dog.

Howley (1836–1912), perhaps the most brilliant member of a distinguished literary family, was a Roman Catholic priest and a native of St John's. He concluded his essay by stating that the Newfoundlander did not consider his country from the international or strategic viewpoint. 'He rightly looks upon Newfoundland as his very own, for pretty much the same good reasons that the cod regards the banks as his proper realm, viz., because it is his race resort, his feeding ground, and his home.'[37]

Howley's defiant essay was the precursor of a number of similar attempts to delineate the Newfoundlander around the end of the nineteenth century, the most notable being P.T. McGrath's paper on 'The Fisherfolk of Newfoundland' in 1904. McGrath went a little further than Howley and claimed that Newfoundlanders 'for sheer daring and absolute endurance have no equal in the world to-day.'[38] Like Howley, McGrath was a native of St John's – a point that should be noticed. Prowse too wrote in a similar vein in 1900, claiming that 'In all their works and ways Newfoundlanders are wholly unlike either Canadians or Americans.[39] But while it is easy to dismiss such portraits as urban, literary, and sentimental, they do nevertheless illuminate a truth about Newfoundland. Despite its near anarchic condition over the centuries, and despite the lack of a common historical or political struggle in the distant past which could have united the people, the colony was becoming a nation and to some extent beginning to sense that it was one. The hardy Newfoundlander along the

'loose lines' drawn by Howley might not exist, but that the Newfoundlander was in some way 'a special type' could not be doubted.

R.T.S. LOWELL AND NORMAN DUNCAN

The first two foreigners to see in Newfoundlanders, not just material
for anecdote, but the inspiration for imaginative literature, were
R.T.S. Lowell, an American missionary, and Norman Duncan, a
Canadian on assignment for an American magazine. Lowell (1816–91)
was the older brother by three years of the poet James Russell Lowell.
A Harvard graduate, he was ordained a minister of the Episcopal
church in 1843, in which year he also became the third resident SPG
missionary at St Matthew's Anglican Church in Bay Roberts, a thriving fishing community in Conception Bay. Lowell stayed in Newfoundland through the bitter winter of 1846, and left the colony in 1847
to become, in later years, a headmaster, poet, and professor. After his
departure he raised money in Massachusetts for the purchase of
supplies of 'Indian meal' to be sent to Newfoundland.[40] In 1858 he
published a novel based upon his experiences in the colony, *The New
Priest in Conception Bay*, prefacing the book with the remark that
'These Figures, of gentle, simple, sad, and merry, were drawn, (not in
a Day), upon the Walls of a House of Exile. – Will the great World care
for them?' (He later conceded that his 'exile' had, however, been a
'willing' one.[41]) As it turned out, the great world did not in fact care
greatly for his efforts, and the book, though a *succès d'estime* in
America,[42] passed into virtual oblivion after a revised edition of 1889.
It was the first novel to be based upon actual experience of life in
Newfoundland.

The New Priest in Conception Bay* was a book filled with the religious preoccupations of its time and some of the more tiresome man-
nerisms of Victorian fiction. Its principal theme was Protestant-
Catholic rivalry, with Anglicans everywhere getting the upper hand
while the treacherous Romans, hunting for souls, connive, cheat, and
inevitably fail. The plot, unravelling with an almost intolerable slowness, centres upon the mysterious disappearance of Lucy Barbury, a
lovely Anglican of eighteen years, who is thought to have been ab-
ducted by nuns and a Jesuit, helped by local Roman Catholics. Instead, as we learn some hundreds of pages into the book, she had
managed to escape her captors and find her way onto a ship bound for
Europe. The book describes the agitation in 'Peterport' (Lowell's name
for Bay Roberts) during her absence. Further heightening the religious

tension is the appearance of a 'new priest' named Ignatius Debree, who has some kind of mysterious connection with another newcomer to Peterport, Mrs Barré. A cunning Jesuit named Nicholas Crampton is also implicated in the intrigue and odd goings on. All three are highly unlikely residents of a Newfoundland outport, but it was not to be expected that a member of the Lowell family would make ordinary Newfoundlanders the principal characters in his book. The common folk nevertheless play an important part in the novel, for Newfoundland in Lowell's work is no mere backdrop for the action but a setting that is almost as fully realized and as important to the plot as Wessex is in the novels of Hardy. Lowell's gifts of observation and description were such that if he had been less obsessed with his religious theme he might have written a classic novel.

What the book captured was the living voice of the people of Bay Roberts and vicinity in the middle of the nineteenth century. Lowell's skill at duplicating in print the accents he heard in and around his parish has never been equalled. A recent study by a linguist has revealed the novelist's subtle understanding of the differences among the dialects of the various races and classes in his area.[43] But Lowell is to be credited with more than technical virtuosity in recording dialects. He saw beyond accent to attitude and mannerism. In a chapter that is an especially rich display of accents, we listen in to the fisherman Jesse Barbury's effort to explain in court, before an impatient and self-important magistrate fingering a law book, the local Anglican minister, the constable, and some other neighbours, exactly what he had seen on the day of Lucy Barbury's disappearance:

The witness being now encouraged to go on, (all difficulties being taken out of the way,) proceeded as follows, the magistrate ostensibly neglecting to listen, and studiously, with much flutter of leaves, comparing one place with another in his great book.

'I was aw'y over, t'other side, a-jiggin squids, I was; and Izik Maffen was along wi' I; and I says to un, "Izik," I says, "'ee knows Willum Tomes," I says, "surely." "Is, sure," 'e says, "I does," to me, agen. "Well, Izik," I says, "did 'ee hear, now, that 'e 've alossed 'e's cow?" I says.'

The magistrate officially cleared his throat of some irritation; the Minister wiped his face with his handkerchief, a circumstance that seemed to have an encouraging effect upon the witness. He went on: –

'So Izik 'e says to I agen, "No, sure," 'e says, "did un, then, Jesse?" "Is, sure," I says, "'e've alossed she, surely." With that 'e up an' says to I, "A loss is a loss, Jesse," 'e says. "That's true," I says.'

This moral reflection brought the Minister's handkerchief suddenly to his face again. The constable received the saying with less self-control, though it was as true as any sentence of the Philosophers. William Frank, who was further off, commented: 'Wull, wisdom is a great thing; it's no use!' – Jesse continued.

'"Izik," I says to un, agen, "Izik," I says, "do 'ee think, now, would n' the squids do better a little furderer up?" I says. With that we takes an' rows up tow'rds Riverhead, a bit. Wull, after bidin' there a spurt, I axes Izik what 'e thowt sech a cow as that might be worth. I says' –

'You must remember, Mr. Barbury,' interposed the Stipendiary, 'that the time of a magistrate is valuable, not to speak of the time of the others that are here.'

'Be 'e, now, sir?' said the poor fellow, getting abashed, 'so 'e must be, surely, that's a clear case. That's a'most all I've agot to s'y, sir.'[44]

In Jesse's leisurely, roundabout way of approaching a subject, and in his persistence in sticking to such homely topics as squids and cows, we note the infallible marks of real speech. Moreover, through Jesse's words the entire milieu of the fisherman is perceived and summoned up, and while there is an overriding aristocratic condescension here as everywhere in Lowell's book, there is also a sympathetic understanding of common life. This is also apparent in the depiction of another brilliantly conceived minor character, Mrs Bridget Calloran. Later in the chapter involving Jesse, there are other indications of Lowell's shrewd insight into the fishermen's ways. When the magistrate's inquiry ends and the suspected kidnappers are set free, the deference of the individual fisherman gives way to a somewhat menacing collective disdain for erring authority and contempt for official pomposity. There is no mob scene, just public ridicule of the magistrate's incompetence. Lowell is probably glancing at the volatile Newfoundland electorate, stirred by racial and religious bigotries which erupted into violence on a number of occasions in the nineteenth century.

While certain chapters in Lowell's book bring ordinary people to centre stage, generally in the novel they remain in the background, gossiping, commenting, simmering, conveying by their presence the slowness and uniformity of rural life and pointing up by contrast the melodrama in the main plot. Lowell also makes use of the physical attributes of the island to provide background and create atmosphere. He responded with great sensitivity and lyrical power to the primordial, startling, and, to him, appalling beauty of the Newfoundland seascape, and he also described the terrain inland, with its trackless scrub, low, stunted spruce, and tricky marshes. Once again, a comparison with Hardy is suggested. Lowell is the only novelist ever to depict this rough hinterland that lies behind so many Newfoundland communities and intrudes upon so much of human activity in them. His occasional descriptions of the land, sea, and sky show a close familiarity with the stern face of nature in Newfoundland, where, as he wrote in 1847,

> ... drifting, bitter sleet and blinding snow
> All man's poor work o'erwhelm![45]

Despite the evident warmth in Lowell's portrayal of Newfoundlanders, an impression corroborated in one of his published poems on the island in which he tells fishermen that he wrote his novel 'for love of you,'[46] his attitude towards them is tinged somewhat by patrician snobbery and American chauvinism. At one point he called Newfoundland speech, which he took so much pains to transcribe, 'the coarse dialect of the island,' and it is possible to see in some of his observations signs of an impatience with his pastoral role of 'directing the consciences of fishwives.' The harshest criticism of the colony in his book is made by an American character, Elnathan Bangs, who makes unflattering comparisons between Newfoundlanders and his own people. To Bangs, Newfoundlanders were 'slaves' to the merchants, and needed 'a little teachin' ... 'pon a good many things.'[47] Throughout the book Bangs represents Yankee know-how, and in his observations we perhaps see Lowell's true assessment of Newfoundlanders as a rather odd race, open-hearted, and a trifle simpleminded. We have to wait until 1900 to find a writer of fiction who would probe deeply into the experience of life in Newfoundland.

Norman Duncan was born in Brantford, Ontario, in 1871, attended the University of Toronto, and in 1895 went to the United States to begin a career in journalism. After publishing *The Soul of the Street* (1900), a book of stories based on legends he heard in the Syrian quarter of New York, he went, in the summer of 1900, to Newfoundland to write articles for *McClure's Magazine*, a journal that specialized in geographical adventure. Though bound for St Anthony to interview Grenfell, Duncan, who was troubled by seasickness, was relieved to pass from 'that waste of grasping waves' in Notre Dame Bay to the temporary 'sanctuary' of the harbour at Exploits Island, where he planned to catch another boat headed north.[48] The stopover changed his life. At Exploits he met the family of the local merchant, Jabez Manuel, and decided to spend the whole summer with them and other residents of the community. For most of the summers between 1901 and 1906, and again in 1910, Duncan returned to Newfoundland to visit the Manuel family and, for part of one summer at least, to travel with Grenfell along the Labrador coast.[49] He stayed in close contact with the Manuel family until his death in 1916. Outport life in what Duncan called 'the real Newfoundland'[50] – the coast between Cape St John and Cape Bauld, apparently the only part of the island he knew – became the subject of his finest book, a collection of stories entitled *The Way of the Sea* (1903), and the inspiration of much of his later work. Duncan was a prolific and popular writer, and his books on Newfoundland form a substantial body of work that deserves attention. He wrote not just fiction but as well a few superb essays on aspects of life in Newfoundland, among them an account of the migratory Labrador fishery which captures, in a truly astonishing way, the drama and adventure in that now almost forgotten part of Newfoundland's history. His essays were collected in a book called *Dr. Grenfell's Parish* (1905), yet another attempt to publicize the 'indefatigable, devoted, heroic' efforts of the good doctor.[51] Two of Duncan's novels, *Dr. Luke of the Labrador* (1904) – a book obviously inspired, once again, by Grenfell[52] – and *The Cruise of the Shining Light* (1907), were in essence adventure stories for young readers, but they have a degree of authenticity which sets them apart from similar romances about the colony. Indeed everything Duncan wrote, even in his last years when his life was darkened by alcoholism, shows the stamp of original literary genius. But he was at his best in his earliest stories about Newfoundland, when he was still close to the sound and smell of the northern ocean.

Duncan was the first writer of fiction to make ordinary Newfoundlanders the leading characters in his stories and to see in their routine, everyday activities a fit subject for literature. What he saw and celebrated in the colony was a kind of drama. He came to Newfoundland from the settled, urban, comfortable life of a New England intellectual, the sheltered worlds of academe and journalism in which 'fellows with muscles of dough and desires all fed fat' sat around in clubs discussing 'new philosophies.'[53] A small man physically, never having been, as Grenfell noted with a touch of condescension, 'a fighter or an athlete,' he had not before been at sea and regarded ocean travel with some apprehension.[54] Having these qualities, he was astounded by the mode of life in the northern Newfoundland outports. Instead of the rich farmlands he had seen on the Niagara Peninsula and in the eastern United States, here was an appalling bleakness. The 'ice and wind and rain and fires of unnumbered years,' he wrote, 'have stripped the coast to its unsightly ribs. The untracked wilderness, of a growth scraggly and stunted, crowds the cottages to the verge of the sea.'[55] Soil was so scarce in some outports that it was hard to find a place for the dead to rot in decency.[56] Then there were the treacherous Arctic ice-floes, the fog, and cold to contend with: the cold, which 'fills the uttermost parts of the universe,' is 'unwavering and eternal,' 'infinite in its evil power and patience.' But most awesome to Duncan was the eternally young, tameless, niggardly ocean: '... as it was in the beginning, it is now, and shall ever be – mighty, savage, dread, infinitely treacherous and hateful, yielding only that which is wrested from it, snarling, raging, snatching lives, spoiling souls of their graces.'[57]

And yet here, on this grim edge of the North American continent, to Duncan's enduring amazement, human life went on. It did not thrive, to be sure, but what a wonder that it existed at all! Duncan never ceased to marvel at the people's tenacity. The inhabitants of northern Newfoundland, he exclaimed, 'abide in the shadow of mystery.' They 'who live in the North – in the shadow of its frown – within reach of its marauding forces ... maintain the sovereignty of the race to the edge of the uninhabitable.' Duncan's men and women endure on the perilous brink of the earth's darkest places, a kind of heroism that merited the dignity of prolonged scrutiny.

In Duncan's work outport life is seen as great adventure, as unwitting epic. There was to him something sublime in the way mere fishermen day after day pitted their puny strength against the vast, capricious, and incomprehensible forces of the north, something mysterious in their attachment to a land and sea that made the getting of daily bread a deadly gamble. Though he thought he saw the limitations of Newfoundland life, the isolation, superstitiousness, and narrow views that had to be found among a people 'left behind and forgotten,'[58] and the tendency of such a precarious society to periodic if not chronic disaster, yet he also saw the life of the outporter as of a different order from his own. It offered greater opportunities for the display of courage, for living life on a grander scale. In one of his finest stories, 'The Strength of Men,' he pictured a sealing schooner caught in moving ice and being driven towards a fearsome shoal. The crew eventually must take to the ice, lose their load of seals, and risk death from exposure, but before they leave the doomed ship one of them speculates about which edge of the shoal she will hit. A heated argument breaks out, and the men continue it for some time, proud of their seamanship and fond of a dispute even in the jaws of death. This was one of the qualities Duncan admired in the ordinary Newfoundlanders he met: the ability to maintain humour and homely attitudes while surrounded by peril. In the same story, which looks at times as if it might become a socialist tract on the exploitation of sealers and the hardships they have to endure, we see Duncan side-step political philosophy to attempt a greater subtlety. Saul Nash, the story's hero, struggles for fifteen hours to stay alive on an ice-pan, and survives despite being tossed around in a choppy sea and struck by clumps of ice. In his last paragraph Duncan wonders about the effects of the experience upon Saul:

A crooked shoulder, which healed of itself, and a broad scar, which slants from the tip of his nose far up into his hair, tell him that the fight was hard. But what matter – all this? Notwithstanding all, when next the sea baited its trap with swarming herds, he set forth with John, his brother, to the hunt; for the world which lies hidden in the wide beyond has some strange need of seal-fat, and stands ready to pay, as of course. It pays gold to the man at the counter in Saint John's; and for what the world pays a dollar the outport warrior gets a pound of reeking pork. But what matter? What matter – all this toil and peril? What matter when the pork lies steaming on the table and yellow duff is in plenty in the dish? What matter when, beholding it, the blue eyes of the lads and little maids flash merrily? What matter when the strength of a man provides so bounteously that his children may pass their plates for more? What matter – when there comes a night wherein a man may rest? What matter – in the end? Ease is a shame; and, for truth, old age holds nothing for any man save a seat in a corner and the sound of voices drifting in.[59]

The passage shows Duncan at his best, narrowly missing adolescent excess, but rising surely above it to perceive and celebrate the instincts of common men. As for the political attitudes hinted at here and elsewhere in *The Way of the Sea*, Duncan never developed them into a consistent philosophy. The only opinion he expressed on the political scene in Newfoundland was to the effect that the government in St John's neglected the remoter outports and Labrador.

The stories in *The Way of the Sea* are all, at one level, analyses of the particular features of outport life that struck Duncan as memorable. 'The Raging of the Sea' shows Job Luff's skill at bringing his old punt, loaded with fish, safely to harbour in a storm, a skill which he triumphantly displays until, indulging in a tiny moment of exultation and pride, he takes his eye off the waves ahead of him and brings on disaster. Duncan's theme is the need for perpetual vigilance in a setting where danger constantly threatens. 'The Breath of the North' celebrates Eleazar Manuel's unerring instinct, which guides him home through fog and cold to Ragged Harbour, just before the onset of a savage storm. In 'The Love of the Maid,' a nineteen-year-old girl marries a craggy, aging fisherman named Elihu Gale rather than young Jim Rideout, choosing, at a time of near famine, economic security over the prompting of 'love-sighs.' The result is the flowering of love in Elihu's heart and general good to the community, while Jim Rideout, who 'had no heart for a tragedy,' falls in love with 'another maid.' Elihu's practical bride resembles Arabella in Hardy's *Jude the Obscure*, and the same deep rustic wisdom lies behind both portraits. Especially sensitive in its insight into the character of outport fishermen is the last story in the collection, 'The Fruits of Toil,' which is arguably the finest piece of fiction ever written about oldtime Newfoundland. The story is about Solomon Stride, a young fisherman of Ragged Harbour, who starts a life of fishing in the vigour of his early manhood, gets nearly $350 worth of twine on credit from the merchant, Luke Dart, knits his own trap, builds his own house, and tells his young bridge, Priscilla: ' 'Twill be a gran' season for fish this year. ... Us'll pay un all up this year.' But that first season is ruined by Arctic ice, Solomon's trap is badly damaged, and the fish have gone offshore before he can get it back in the water. He now goes further into debt, but next spring we find him again talking to his wife: 'Priscilla, dear, they be a fine sign o' fish down the coast. 'Twill be a gran' season, I'm thinkin'.' 'Sure, b'y,' Priscilla agreed, ' 'twill be a gran' cotch o' fish you'll have this year.' But in that year the fish failed utterly. For the next thirteen years Solomon, 'in plenitude and quality of strength – in the full eager power of brawn – ... was as great as the men of any time, a towering glory to the whole race, here hidden.' But his catches were meagre. Thirty more years pass, and on thousands of other occasions he matched himself 'against the restless might of the sea.' With every spring comes the dawn of faint hope; with every summer, just enough or too little. At the end, wearied and wrecked with toil, he is still in debt, and his labour, daring, and dogged persistence have made nothing happen. On the night he dies, a storm arises and, as if sounding a note of triumph, 'the sea, like a lusty youth, raged furiously.' Solomon Stride has been overmatched.[60]

'The Fruits of Toil' was intended, probably, as a kind of allegory of the experience of life in outport Newfoundland. What stirred Duncan was the frailty of human strength and desire, however heroic, when contrasted with the eternal vigour of the imperturbable ocean. But he did not dismiss Solomon's efforts, even if they added not a jot nor a tittle to the progress of human civilization, as trivial. Solomon endured, year in and year out, in a setting where to subsist was a sort of triumph. He did not despair, because there was something in the promise of every spring to keep hope alive. He did not become brutalized, though he had to act brutally, hunting and killing to live. Surrounded by blind and capricious forces, he did not become dumbly fatalistic, although Duncan knew that there had to be an element of impassiveness at least in the character of men whose lives depended on elements over which they had no control.[61] The task of driving on his own life from year to year, Solomon performed himself, using the gifts of brawn and brain. There was dignity in all these things. The fruit of his toil was his own persistence. And yet, for all his thousands of laborious days, at the end hardly a sign of his existence remained on earth.

Duncan's insights in this exquisite story may be confirmed by any visitor to the remote outharbours of Newfoundland. For perhaps it would be hard to find a place in the world in which greater effort has been expended with so little remaining to show for it. In outport Newfoundland, as Duncan saw, one generation could not tame the country for the benefit of the next, and thus all generations were really pioneers, in the sense that they had to confront the same wildness. While there was indeed what the geographers call 'a discontinuous strip of cultural fabric' along parts of the coast, such a strip was made by clearing away scrub and geological debris rather than by building any permanent structures, and many structures that were raised were built in the knowledge that they would not last. And so with so much effort directed at the sea, which shows no mark of human labour and savagely reduces the subtlest contrivances of man to garbage on beaches, at times the long history of ordinary Newfoundlanders seems as evanescent as Solomon Stride's battle for a living in Ragged Harbour. Surrounded by a northern ocean that forever refuses to be companionable, Newfoundland is a region, like Hardy's Egdon Heath, where human enterprise with 'pickaxe, plough, or spade' is less noticeable than 'the very finger-touches of the last geological change.'[62]

Duncan's deficiencies as a writer, too conspicuous to need discussion, are sentimentality and a liking for melodrama. His achievement was to embody the ancient ways of the Newfoundland people in living literature. He reproduced their eccentricities of speech (not as efficiently, however, as Lowell), explored their superstitions, revelled in the odd nomenclature they attached to the coast and the offshore fishing grounds, investigated their peculiarly intimate acquaintance with God, questioned their children (with whom he had a particular empathy), and pondered on the harmony of their lives. After *The Way of the Sea*, his vision of Newfoundland and Labrador become tinged more and more with romance, and he was one of the earliest writers to propagate a view of the colony that was close to primitivistic nonsense. Duncan was quite capable of writing that in Labrador there are 'no brick walls, no unnatural need or circumstance, no confusing inventions, no gasping haste, no specious distractions, no clamour of wheel and heartless voices, to blind the soul, to pervert its pure desires, to deaden its fears, to deafen its ears to the sweeter calls – to shut it in, to shrivel it: to sicken it in every part.' This he wrote in *Dr. Luke of the Labrador*.[63] But in *The Way of the Sea* and certain of his essays he conjures up the real life of Newfoundland, its attractive features along with its cruelties and limitations. What made Newfoundland life an appealing subject to Duncan in his early books was just this enigmatic quality, which gave to even casual encounters the aura of mystery. He found it hard to understand why Newfoundlanders could not only inhabit, but 'strangely love,' their bleak and barren home.[64] One day he visited a small settlement, not far from Conche, on the Great Northern Peninsula, and met an old man named Uncle Zeb who was in the last stage of consumption. A haunting interview ensued, which illustrated well what led Duncan to make Newfoundland his own imaginative homeland:

''Tis a fine harbour t' fish from, zur,' he gasped. 'They be none better. Leastways, so they tells me – them that's cruised about a deal. Sure, I've never seen another. 'Tis t' Conch I've wanted t' go since I were a young feller. I'll see un yet, zur – sure, an' I will.'

'You are eighty-three?' said I.

'I be the oldest man t' the harbour, zur. I marries the maids an' the young fellers when they's no parson about.'

'You have fished out of this harbour for seventy-six years?' said I, in vain trying to comprehend the deprivation and dull toil of that long life – trying to account for the childlike smile which had continued to the end of it.

'Ay, zur,' said Uncle Zeb. 'But, sure, they be plenty o' time t' see Conch yet. Me father were ninety when he died. I be only eighty-three.'

Uncle Zeb tottered up the hill. Soon the dusk swallowed his old hulk. I never saw him again.[65]

THE LABRADOR INTERIOR: LEONIDAS HUBBARD

As indicated earlier, such journeys as Duncan's form a part of the history of northern adventure, and before turning to the escapade of Leonidas Hubbard, it is necessary to glance at his predecessors in Labrador exploration. In 1831 the Hudson's Bay Company established Fort Chimo on the Koksoak River near Ungava Bay, with the intention of extending the fur trade to the Labrador peninsula. In 1837 John McLean, a Scot employed by the company, was assigned to the fort and instructed to establish communication between it and another new post, Fort Smith (North West River), on Lake Melville. McLean, accompanied by Donald Henderson, Henry Hay, and two Indian guides, set out overland for Fort Smith on 2 January 1837, reaching their destination, after enduring great hardship, on 16 February. In the year following this spectacular journey, McLean went by canoe up the George River, accompanied by 'ten able men' and an Indian guide, in an attempt to open up a canoe route between Ungava Bay and Hamilton Inlet. After over a month of excruciating labour during which the men were incessantly tortured by mosquitoes, McLean reached the newly established Fort Nascopie on Pettiskapau Lake on 16 August, 'half starved, half naked, and half devoured.' One day later he nevertheless set out for the coast, but soon found that his passage down the Hamilton River was blocked by 'a mighty cataract':

About six miles above the fall the river suddenly contracts, from a width of from four hundred to six hundred yards, to about one hundred yards; then rushing along in a continuous foaming rapid, finally contracts to a breadth of about fifty yards, ere it precipitates itself over the rock which forms the fall; when, still roaring and foaming, it continues its maddened course for about a distance of thirty miles, pent up between walls of rock that rise sometimes to the height of three hundred feet on either side. This stupendous fall exceeds in height the Falls of Niagara, but bears no comparison to that sublime object in any other respect, being nearly hidden from the view by an abrupt angle which the rocks form immediately beneath it. If not seen, however, it is felt; such is the extraordinary force with which it tumbles into the abyss underneath, that we felt the solid rock shake under our feet, as we stood two hundred feet above the gulf. A dense cloud of vapour, which can be seen at a great distance in clear weather, hangs over the spot.[66]

McLean was thus the first white man to see the Grand Falls (later renamed the Hamilton, and still later the Churchill Falls), and the first on record to cross the Labrador peninsula. Moreover, though he failed in 1838 to reach Hamilton Inlet by way of the Hamilton River, in 1841, acting on the advice of an Indian, he succeeded in finding a canoe route around the falls along a chain of small lakes, thereby making the interior of Labrador accessible to enterprise and exploration. McLean's book describing his experiences, *Notes of a Twenty-five Years' Service in the Hudson's Bay Company* (1849), was a landmark in the history of exploration and one cause of the aroused scientific curiosity about Labrador in the later decades of the century.

Another impetus to the scientific investigation of Labrador was the well-publicized visit of the great naturalist John James Audubon to the north shore of the Gulf of St Lawrence in the summer of 1833. Audubon was searching for material for his *Birds of America* (1827–38), and brought back twenty-three large sketches of birds, together with numerous bird skins and a collection of marine animals and plants. 'All – all is wonderfully grand, wild – aye, and terrific,' he wrote in his journal, after commenting on the excitement of coming upon an 'unexpected Bunting' and of seeing 'in every fissure a Guillemot, a Cormorant, or some other wild bird.'[67] 'Did I wish to write a Novel,' he told his wife in a letter from Bradore Bay, 'I would doubtless entitle it "Tales of Labrador."'[68] It is not surprising that in the second half of the century Labrador became recognized by North American naturalists as 'a virgin field to the investigator,' and by students of anthropology as 'a kind of Pompeii of the New World' where native Indians and Eskimos could be seen 'in a state far more primitive than in any other part of the continent of North America.'[69] After 1860 scientific expeditions and summer excursions by students and professors became a feature of life along the coast. The American scientist A.S. Packard was an eager participant in two such summer cruises in 1860 and 1864, which are described in his valuable book, *The Labrador Coast* (1891). The work conveys well the 'nameless charm' of the north and the elation Packard felt on encountering the 'new world' that opened before his eyes in the numerous harbours of Labrador.[70] Other expeditions of importance were conducted in June of 1861 by H.Y. Hind, a professor of chemistry and biology at Trinity College, Toronto, and in 1875, 1880–1, and 1882 by the American botanist W.A. Stearns. Hind led a party of twelve men up the Moisie River, which flows into the Gulf of St Lawrence near Sept Iles. His purpose was to follow a Montagnai canoe route from Hamilton Inlet to the Gulf. He turned back after proceeding 120 miles inland, where, at a height above sea level of 2240 feet, he saw the edge of the Labrador plateau:

> The whole country appeared to consist of a succession of low mountains, few of them exceeding in height the one which formed our point of view. I counted twenty-two large lakes, besides numerous small sheets of water, which evidently merged into swamps, and are probably more or less connected in the spring of the year. A countless number of erratics were scattered in every direction, best seen, however, towards the south and west in the burnt country. The hill-sides appeared to be covered with them, and many were of very large dimensions. ... Long and anxiously I looked round in every direction to see if I could distinguish any signs of animal life, but without success. No sound was audible except the sighing of the wind. A marshy lake lay at the foot of the hill, which we had ascended with the greatest caution on the opposite side, but no waterfowl were visible or even fish seen to rise. Not a bird, or butterfly, or beetle appeared to inhabit this desolate wilderness.[71]

Hind's two-volume work describing his brief expedition, *Explorations in the Interior of the Labrador Peninsula* (1863), remained for decades 'the standard authority' on Labrador, and Stearns too produced a weighty and plodding account of his activities on the coast.[72] Hind's book illustrated the formidable barriers facing explorers of the Labrador interior: barely navigable rivers, falling from the high central plateau and compelling numerous portages, a shortage of game, and torturing flies.

While such expeditions as Packard's and Hind's were of great interest and significance, the principal attraction to geographers in Labrador was the cataract that McLean saw in 1838. During the fifty years after McLean's visit, apparently only one other white man, another employee of the Hudson's Bay Company, saw the spectacle, which as years passed seemed to enter the realm of legend. In the report of a scientific expedition in 1860, it was noted that '*voyageurs* affirm that the fall is 1000 feet high' and that 'at the verge the precipice vibrates fearfully.'[73] In 1887 the first attempt was made to reach the falls by going upstream on the Hamilton River. Randle F. Holme, a twenty-three-year-old Oxford graduate in law and an amateur geographer, started up the river with two companions on 24 August in a fisherman's punt. This boat proved to be the main impediment on the journey, for to haul it over the rapids on the Hamilton was too much for three men to accomplish. On 11 September, after reaching Lake Winokapau, about 150 miles upstream, Holme decided to turn back.

In his account of his expedition he speculated 'that there is no other fall in the world ... of so great height with such volume of water, 'thereby stimulating renewed curiosity about the dimensions of the falls.[74] One newspaper report in 1891 placed its height at 1500 feet.[75] Holme's effort was followed by another unsuccessful expedition in 1890, led by J.G. Alwyn Creighton, who tried to reach the falls by way of the St Augustin River.[76] In the summer of 1891, two separate American expeditions headed up the Hamilton River, one consisting of four students from Bowdoin College in Maine, and the other a more elaborate excursion led by a lawyer and a professor, H.G. Bryant and C.A. Kenaston. Two of the 'Bowdoin boys,' Austin Cary and Dennis Cole, reached the falls on 13 August. Cary's physical condition was such that he immediately rolled up in his blanket and slept, but his companion, who had developed his physique at Bowdoin by 'throwing the shot and hammer and running,' advanced further 'to see more of a region new to human eyes':

Cole pressed forward into the strange and unknown country three or four miles, and then, for a final view of the location, climbed the highest tree he could find and from its top surveyed the waste of land and river. He stood thus exalted near the center of the vast peninsula of Labrador. Four hundred and fifty miles to the east lay the wide expanse of Hamilton Inlet. Four hundred and fifty miles to the north lay Cape Chudleigh ... Only six hundred miles due south the granite chapel of Bowdoin College points heavenward both its uplifted hands. Four hundred and fifty miles to the west rolled the waves of the great inland ocean, Hudson's Bay ... Cole, with his mind and imagination filled with these facts, involuntarily took his knife and carved his name and the expedition on the upper part of the tree which formed his outlook. It might be his monument as the Inland Sea was that of Hudson.[77]

The name Bowdoin Canyon survives on maps to attest to this improbable collegiate adventure on the Hamilton River. After staying at the site of the falls for twenty-four hours, the two adventurers returned to their boat a little downstream, only to find that it had been destroyed by fire in their absence. They pluckily returned to the coast by foot and on rafts, passing, but not meeting, the expedition of Bryant and Kenaston, which was proceeding upstream at a more professorial pace, in yet another important episode in Labrador exploration. On 2 September they also reached the falls which, being measured, turned out to be 316 feet in height. In October the *New York Tribune* carried a story on the Bryant and Kenaston expedition, written, with his usual flair, by the ubiquitous Moses Harvey. Harvey was impressed by the great age of the falls. 'For unknown myriads of years,' he wrote, 'its deep, thunderous diapason has been resounding through this grim wilderness.' But even the optimist Harvey predicted that it would be 'a long time' before the falls became 'a resort for ordinary tourists.'[78]

Between 1892 and 1895, A.P. Low of the Geological Survey of Canada conducted extensive explorations in southern Labrador, mapping the entire length of the Hamilton together with the complicated system of lakes and rivers that form the headwaters of the river. One of the lakes partially explored by Low was Lake Michikimau, a huge body of water on the interior plateau linked to Grand Lake by the Naskaupi River and close to the headwaters of the George River, which flows into Ungava Bay. A glance at the elaborate maps of Labrador published by Low in 1896 reveals that one of the largest portions of Labrador that yet remained obscure was the area lying north and west of Hamilton Inlet. McLean had passed through this region on his winter journey of 1838, pronouncing it to be 'the roughest country I ever travelled' and recording the opinion of his Indian guides that to go from Lake Michikamau to Hamilton Inlet by way of the 'North River' (the Naskaupi) was to invite 'inevitable starvation,' since 'no game could be found by the way, and we would have, therefore, to depend solely on our own provisions.' McLean also learned that the Naskaupi River was 'deemed to be impracticable for any kind of craft.'[79] After McLean's journey no white man attempted to cross the territory until 1875–6 when a Roman Catholic missionary, Père Lacasse, was reported to have crossed from North West River to Ungava Bay in two successive summers.[80] However, by the end of the century there was no trustworthy map available even of Grand Lake, the long northwest extension of Lake Melville. On Low's map this lake was pictured as longer and narrower than it should be. At the western end of the lake Low, who drew this portion of his map from hearsay, tentatively sketched a single river which, some miles inland, divided into two branches. One of these branches, christened by Low 'North West River,' led westward to Lake Michikamau; the other, the 'Nascaupee River,' flowed from Seal Lake in the north. It is hardly necessary to say that Low's map was a gross oversimplification of the complex system of lakes and rivers northwest of Lake Melville. To name just one error, a fateful one in the story of the Hubbard expedition of 1903, there are not one, but five, rivers flowing into Grand Lake, only one of which leads directly to Lake Michikamau.

The young American, Leonidas Hubbard Jr. (1872–1903), was a

writer for the magazine *Outing* when, in 1901–2, he conceived a plan to lead an expedition up the Naskaupi to Lake Michikamau, and then proceed onwards to the George River and Ungava Bay. His motives in making the expedition were scientific and romantic. By going up the Naskaupi rather than the now well-travelled route along the Hamilton, he was deliberately plunging 'into a region where no footsteps would be found to guide him,' and over which 'still brooded the fascinating twilight of the mysterious unknown.' He had already visited the Labrador peninsula once, on a minor excursion north of Lake St John, but this was not sufficient to satisfy his 'longing to make discoveries.' He explained the appeal of Labrador to his friend Dillon Wallace (1863–1939), a lawyer whom he persuaded to join him on the new expedition: '"It's always the way, Wallace," he said; "when a fellow starts on a long trail, he's never willing to quit. It'll be the same with you if you go with me to Labrador. You'll say each trip will be the last, but when you come home you'll hear the voice of the wilderness calling you to return, and it will lure you away again and again."'[81]

In addition to this boyish desire to do a 'big thing' in 'the vast solitudes of desolate Labrador,'[82] Hubbard also wished to observe the annual migration of the caribou herds across the George River and describe the hunting habits of the Naskaupi Indians. Accordingly, on 15 July 1903, Hubbard, Wallace, and a half-breed Cree Indian from James Bay named George Elson, set out by canoe from the North West River post of the Hudson's Bay Company and proceeded westward into Grand Lake. In the early afternoon of 16 July they reached what they thought was the mouth of the river depicted on Low's map, and headed inland. This was the disastrous blunder that doomed the expedition to failure and made the record of their journey, Wallace's book *The Lure of the Labrador Wild* (1905), one of the most poignant documents in the literature of exploration. The river they had found was not the Naskaupi, but the much smaller, unnavigable Susan River. Had they located the Naskaupi, as Hubbard's wife, Mina, and Wallace himself, proved in two separate expeditions in 1905, they would probably have been able to accomplish their plan without great difficulty.[83]

This tragic mistake was compounded by other errors of judgment and accidents. The 15th of July was obviously late to begin a Labrador expedition of the magnitude of the one they attempted. However, it should be noted that they had intended to start earlier but had run into delays caused by faulty information and irregular boat schedules between Newfoundland and Labrador. In any event, they were late leaving for the interior and knew they had to make haste. This need for haste was no doubt partly responsible for their missing the mouth of the Naskaupi. Another mistake was believing they could live off the land. Here chance again played a role, for it seems that 1903 was an especially meagre year for hunters on the Labrador, and a piece of equipment that could have warded off hunger, a gill net, was unavailable at the Hudson's Bay Company posts at Rigolet and North West River. They made still another blunder: Wallace and Hubbard took with them one pair of moccasins each – those they had on their feet. After only a few days on the Susan River, much of the time spent in the water dragging their heavily laden canoe around rocks and over shoals, or on the river bank portaging through rough undergrowth, these moccasins started to deteriorate, and after two weeks the bottoms were beginning to wear through. Their feet became sore, Hubbard's toe-nails began to fall off, and he had to resort to various contrivances, none of them effective, to protect his feet against the rocks and underbrush. Lacking adhesive plaster, he was obliged to bandage his sore feet with electricians' tape. The condition of the men's feet continued to plague them throughout their journey, perhaps even to a greater extent than Wallace was willing to admit. To name just one more item in this catalogue of blunders, they delayed turning back to the coast until the season was too far advanced. They might have learned from McLean's book that in the Labrador interior there was 'no time to be lost in vain regrets' and that any prolonged delay in travelling had to be rectified by an 'instant decision' to head for safety.[84]

The three men dragged, pushed, and carried their canoe and equipment up the narrow, deep valley of the Susan for two solid weeks, wading and tumbling in the water, scraping through thick bushes, and portaging around impassable shoals. All this at a season when the wilderness of Labrador can be intolerably hot, and when mosquitoes and black flies are hardly to be endured. Even after they emerged from the 'cursed' Susan valley, they still had more long portages and disappointments ahead of them, and not even the occasional recitations Hubbard gave from Kipling could protect their spirits for long from the monotonous drudgery of enforced labour. As time passed and the three men plodded on, the days began to get shorter, the nights colder, the weather stormier – and they themselves inevitably grew weaker. The wilderness beat them down, amply corroborating the grim testimony supplied by McLean in 1838. After a month of grinding work, they were still less than halfway to Lake Michikamau and the three men were 'ragged and almost barefooted.'

Hubbard was the weakest, having shrunk to little more than 'a walking skeleton' and now becoming troubled by attacks of depression and
diarrhoea.[85] But the most distressing feature of the expedition was the
men's inability to kill game. Incredibly, they were able to shoot only
one caribou on their whole trip, and there was a similar scarcity of
edible birds. Only Elson seemed to be fully aware of what might be in
store for them if they were forced to come back from Lake Michikamau
instead of going on to Ungava Bay. He refused to throw away the
fly-infested and decaying caribou skin, indicating that it might eventually have to serve for food.

Wallace's daily record of the journey indicates vividly the effects of
prolonged isolation and continual hunger upon even seasoned
woodsmen. All three of the men, but especially Hubbard, became
obsessed with food. Night after night, Wallace and Hubbard talked
about the food they were served at home, or the food they would eat at
various New York restaurants when they returned. Conversations
which started out by picturing some new exploration to be undertaken
after the present one had been completed, sooner or later got around to
what food they would take on their planned trip. All thought, culture,
endeavour, and energy were set aside in favour of wondering what
would go in their stomachs tomorrow. Thoughts about the beauty of
the Labrador landscape were also driven out of their heads. 'It is
difficult,' Wallace wrote, 'to be receptive to beauty when one has had
only a little watered pea meal for breakfast after a long train of lean and
hungry days.'[86] *The Lure of the Labrador Wild* presents the spectacle of
three men slowly starving, turning in upon themselves psychologi-
cally, indulging in fantasies about past comforts, and growing more
and more sentimental in their relationships with one another. The
connection between Hubbard and Wallace became particularly loving, but in fact after 19 September, four days following the decision to
turn back, all three men 'quit rolling in blankets and made bed to keep
warm'[87] But while there was much illustration of weakness in the
book, there were also moments of inspiration and triumph. An especially poignant development was the growing maturity we see in
Hubbard himself, who late in the journey came to regret his tomfool
desire to be thought a hero. 'What does glory and all that amount to,
after all?' he asked Wallace; adding, 'I've let my work and my ambition
bother me too much.'[88]

Miraculously, considering the nature of the terrain they had to
pass over, they almost made it to Lake Michikamau. But they did not
reach it; Elson and Hubbard only saw it from a distance, on 9 Sep-

tember. With characteristic boyishness, Hubbard recorded the event in his diary: 'September 9th – BIG DAY ... we went on across the mountain top and looked west. *There was* MICHIKAMAU! And that's what made it a BIG DAY.'[89] On 15 September they decided to turn back from Windbound Lake after trying unsuccessfully to find a way to advance further by canoe, but a bitter and unlucky wind prevented them from leaving the lake until the 21st. Then at last they started back, picking up and eating the bones and other decaying garbage they had thrown aside on their way to Lake Michikamau, trying their best to make haste. They killed and ate whatever animals they came upon, including porcupines and whiskey jacks. The weather relentlessly followed and caught them, and Hubbard gave up the struggle and was left behind in his tent on 18 October in the valley of the Susan River, while the two others desperately floundered towards Grand Lake. Hubbard perished in his tent; the two stronger men survived, by the skin of their teeth.

The overpowering impression left by Wallace's book is of the rawness, the brutal inhospitableness, of the Labrador wilderness. How quickly, faced with it, the idealism and hope of Hubbard are destroyed. How quickly he and his companions must become grimly materialistic and cunning in order to survive. How inappropriate Hubbard's dreams of glory appear in the context of the heartless subarctic tundra. The painful printed record survives to illustrate the difficulty of breeding, out of the spit of the sea, the labour of men, and the jagged edges of grim landscapes, the frail literary flower of romance.

6 *Emigrant muse*

E.J. PRATT AND NEWFOUNDLAND / 1882–1907

In 1869 a general election was fought in Newfoundland on the issue of whether or not the colony should become a Canadian province. The confederate party, led by F.B.T. Carter, was defeated by a large majority, and with the exception of the brief negotiations of 1895, when the Newfoundland government was desperately seeking a way out of a financial crisis, there was no serious consideration given to union with Canada until the 1940s. With the decision of 1869 behind her, Newfoundland set out on a course of national self-assertion. We have noted the efforts of her political leaders to diversify and stabilize the local economy. A similar patriotic spirit was noticeable in their activities in the international arena. In 1854 and again in 1871 Newfoundland had allowed the mother country to negotiate on her behalf in treaty discussions with the United States, but she now began to insist on having her own voice in such negotiations. In the 1880s and 1890s Newfoundland took steps to try and consolidate her hold on her own territory – no easy matter in view of the extensive treaty rights on large portions of her coast possessed by the French and Americans – to gain an advantage or at least an influence in the crucial international marketing of salt fish, and, in the imperial context, to win equal standing with other self-governing colonies, notably Canada, within the Empire. This was a period of aroused nationalism and widespread expectations of imminent wealth in the colony – expectations fuelled by rhetoric about the benefits arising from the transinsular railway and by the vision of a prospering Canada across the Gulf of St Lawrence. 'We have begun the onward march of progress,' Ambrose Shea announced in the House of Assembly in 1882. Continuing, he glanced significantly at the progress evident elsewhere in North America: 'we are determined to use all our efforts to help the country keep pace with her neighbours in that march. We have a country, capable of holding and maintaining an immense population by mining, fishing, lumbering, and above all by agriculture.'[2] The speech expressed the nineteenth century's most enduring fantasy about Newfoundland, the idea that the country was a treasure house of riches which, once unlocked, would provide boundless wealth and opportunity for a vast population. Picturing pie in the sky rather than counting loaves on the table is a tradition of some antiquity in Newfoundland politics and literature. However, far from pressing onward in the great march envisioned by Shea, one populous and important part of the island, the north side of Conception Bay, was about to enter a long period of decline and would experience an actual drop in population between 1884 and 1901.[3] It was on this fading shore that the poet E.J. Pratt was born, in the same year that Shea proclaimed the dawn of a new age in the country's legislature.

Pratt spent his boyhood and early manhood in a Newfoundland teased by a dream of wealth but embittered, time and again, by the reality of failure. The hopes raised by the building of the railroad and Whiteway's various other development schemes proved groundless; indeed, the drain on the public purse during the heady years of rail construction probably contributed to the precarious financial position of the colony throughout the 1890s.[4] The railroad was completed between St John's and Port aux Basques in 1897, with the first train crossing the island in June 1898. At this point public exasperation with the whole enterprise was so intense that the government of the day, led by Sir James Winter, decided to hand over ownership and operation of the line to a private company for a cash settlement of a million dollars.[5] But the railroad was not the only shattered hope of the period. The plan to locate and exploit the 'hidden resources' of the interior and western portions of the colony was another chimera, and the copper deposits in the north were by no means as extensive as men like Moses Harvey had anticipated.[6] Such resource development as would occur in Newfoundland was destined to take place slowly, the two most notable successes around the end of the nineteenth century being the beginning of large-scale iron ore mining on Bell Island in 1895 and the start of construction on a paper mill at Grand Falls in 1905. Despite the hopes of many writers and politicians, the fate of the colony was still dependent on an occupation which many had reason to associate with poverty: fishing. Not surprisingly, it was in this traditional economic activity that the colony's chance for prosperity and security really lay.

The latter decades of the century brought increased competition from foreign countries, principally France and Norway, in the international market for fish, and a general tendency of fish prices to decline. The situation was exacerbated by the actual presence of French and American fishing ships along the still disputed French Shore and the south coast. In the circumstances, it was perhaps to be expected that Newfoundland should try to protect her fishery through diplomatic manœuvring. The passions aroused by the Bait Acts of 1886 and 1887, designed to deny the French access to local bait supplies, have been alluded to. The attempt to limit the French fishery failed, and Newfoundland's position in the market was not improved. In 1890, and again in 1900, Robert Bond (Premier, 1900–9) tried to negotiate separate reciprocity agreements with United States administrations, agreements which would have given Newfoundland exporters unrestricted access to the lucrative American market.[7] Had either attempt been successful, it is probable that the whole course of Newfoundland history would have been changed. The first agreement was disallowed by Britain after she received vigorous protests from Canada; the second, which Bond had been permitted by Britain to negotiate, was undermined by the influential American Senator, Henry Cabot Lodge, the spokesman in Congress for the New England fishing interests. Both failed agreements were succeeded by hostile international posturing on the part of Newfoundland, directed, in turn, at the Canadian and American fisheries. Neither was effective. Newfoundland's bitter experience in these complicated transactions was to learn that it held a second-class status as a British colony. Imperial policy was to place Canada's interests first, and there is evidence showing that the policy was founded, at least partly, on contempt for what was thought to be the 'blundering stupidity' of politicians in 'a Trans-Atlantic Ireland of a lower type.'[8]

One recent historian has persuasively argued that after the defeat of the Bond government in 1909 Newfoundland came to accept the 'limitations imposed by size, poverty and geographical position,' and never again tried 'to achieve a position of imperial importance.'[9] Certainly, the Whitewayite bubble of dramatic progress had burst, though Whiteway himself, as late as 1897, was claiming that 'We have emerged from the shadow, the crisis is over, and signs of prosperity are on every hand.'[10] Throughout the last decade of the century the colony staggered from one crisis to another, with all branches of the fishery in decline, the public debt mounting ominously, and the spectre of bankruptcy looming ahead. The destruction of St John's by fire in July 1892 may actually have postponed a financial crisis by bringing money in the form of insurance settlements into the colony,[11] but in December 1894 the Commercial and Union Banks in St John's failed, and several mercantile houses followed them into bankruptcy. The bank crash appalled Newfoundlanders and seared their memories for generations. In 1898 the colony was dealt a third blow when forty-eight sealers from the *Greenland* were frozen to death at the ice-fields. These were events to make the most ardent Newfoundlander doubtful about the future prospects of his country. The youthful E.J. Pratt was an eyewitness of the fire and he was at the docks in St John's when the still frozen bodies of the sealers were landed. Many years later, as he looked back on his life in the 1890s, what stood out were the calamities. 'I remember the big fire at St. John's,' he wrote, 'the bank crash, the Greenland disaster on the ice-floes, the homecoming of the ship and the great memorial services.'[12]

One effect of the economic uncertainty in the latter part of the nineteenth century was emigration. The rate of population growth on the island declined steadily between 1869 and 1901, and at the end of the century the population was virtually stagnant.[13] While few detailed statistics are available, it appears that the main body of emigrants came from Conception Bay, where the economy had been in decline since the middle of the 1800s. By 1910 there were over five thousand Newfoundlanders living in the United States; a decade later, this number had almost tripled, and there were Newfoundlanders living in every state of the union.[14] Another possible contributing cause of emigration around the end of the century was the spread of tuberculosis 'mainly among those who are in the prime of life.'[15] In 1901 the number of adult deaths from this 'most malignant and dreadful of all scourges'[16] stood at 654, but by 1906, amid growing alarm, the figure had increased to 933. The number would drop to 692 by the end of the decade, but it would take another fifty years for TB to be beaten. Another dream of the nineteenth century, that the colony would one day become a 'health resort' for foreign invalids, was laid to rest, and another element of uncertainty and peril was added to Newfoundland life to complicate further her enigmatic future.

GROWTH OF A NATIVE LITERATURE

Sparring with foreign nations over fisheries questions and anxiety about possible French territorial claims on the treaty shore brought the twentieth century in on a wave of surging nationalism. The period 1895–1915 was remarkably productive of patriotic and scholarly writing. Moses Harvey, it is true, died in 1901, but the two other prominent literati of the 1890s, D.W. Prowse and P.T. McGrath, continued to publish well into the next century. The latter's most sustained work was *Newfoundland in 1911* (1911), a book that carried on the 'booming' tradition of earlier decades. Two of Richard Howley's brothers were now also well established in local literature. The Roman Catholic Archbishop M.F. Howley (1843–1914), author of the pioneering *Ecclesiastical History of Newfoundland* (1888) and an early student of the country's places names, was an important scholar and minor poet of the period, and J.P. Howley (1847–1918) added significantly to the store of published scientific and historical information about the colony. The culmination of J.P. Howley's efforts was *The Beothucks or Red Indians of Newfoundland* (1915), a compilation of authentic reports on the Beothucks which remains a standard source work for historians. The Bermudian W.G. Gosling (1863–1930) came to Newfoundland in 1881 and soon played an active role in the island's intellectual and political life. Gosling's two major additions to Newfoundland literature were the imposing *Labrador: its Discovery, Exploration, and Development* (1910) and *The Life of Sir Humphrey Gilbert* (1911). P.K. Devine (1859–1950), a pioneer in the study of Newfoundland folklore, H.W. Le Messurier, H.F. Shortis, J.O. Fraser, and J.A. O'Reilly were other authors with topographical and antiquarian interests who were now helping to foster a sense of local identity in Newfoundland. Altogether, as one observer commented, the country could now boast of having 'a dozen or more graceful and easy writers' of prose.[17] Except for Harvey, Gosling, and Fraser, all these writers were native Newfoundlanders – an impressive show of scholarly talent which subsequent generations would be hard pressed to equal. To admit one non-resident to this select circle of scholars, the Englishman J.D. Rogers' *Newfoundland, Historical and Geographical* (1911) was a witty and penetrating study of the colony which recognized as a fundamental premise her 'apartness' from the rest of British America.[18]

Newfoundland in 1900 had a literary intelligentsia, composed principally of St John's residents with ties to the business and governing élite. The periodical in which many of them published their work was the *Newfoundland Quarterly*, which was founded by the printer John J. Evans (1861–1944) in July 1901, and is still in existence.[19] This was one of two ambitious magazines concentrating on Newfoundland to be started at the turn of the century. The other, *The*

Newfoundland Magazine, edited by the New Brunswick novelist T.G. Roberts who lived in Newfoundland from 1899 to 1902, proved to be ephemeral. To read the early numbers of the *Quarterly*, which Evans tried to make 'a faithful reflex of the best and highest thoughts and aspirations in our Colonial life,' is to witness the emergence of a fledgling literary tradition. Surprisingly, it did not feature discussions of imperial questions but concentrated instead on local phenomena. Evans apparently did not fear the charge that his work was 'Peculiar, Provincial, Insular, [and] Local.'[20] Prowse's numerous historical articles and M.F. Howley's long series on 'Newfoundland's Name-Lore' between 1901 and 1914 provided a core of scholarly work with popular interest which set a standard for other writers. The dominant theme in the *Quarterly* was local history, but there were also excursions into biography, humour, poetry, and story-telling. J.P. Howley wrote optimistic pieces suggesting the building of a canal through the Isthmus of Avalon or pondering the 'future outlook' of the Grand Lake.[21] The *Quarterly* was charged with patriotic feeling. It seemed to challenge writers to respond to the themes offered by the country's past and the possibilities of her future. 'Where are our men of letters?' a correspondent asked in 1902, after expressing his confidence in the ability of Newfoundland's 'sons and daughters' to take their place in the 'March of the Intellect.' By 1909 the magazine had aroused hopes for the creation of 'a national literature,' and J.A. O'Reilly felt called upon to issue a word of caution. Though 'a certain number of really brilliant writers' had emerged in Newfoundland, he wrote, he felt convinced that 'the period in which we live is departing from classical culture.' O'Reilly called for 'National Education' and grumpily suggested that 'A scribbling mania is not necessarily a taste for literature.'[22]

What was happening in Newfoundland around the turn of the last century resembled, to some extent, movements in the cultural history of Ireland in the middle and late 1800s. A fund of historical and topographical information was being provided for creative writers to draw upon, and Newfoundland itself was seen increasingly as a sufficient motif for literature. Not unexpectedly, we now see an outburst of versifying. Isabella Rogerson, M.F. Howley, F.B. Wood, and R.G. McDonald produced substantial volumes of verse between 1898 and 1908, inspired, at least in part, by life in Newfoundland.[23] The title of McDonald's volume, *From the Isle of Avalon* (1908), showed that he preferred euphony to accuracy. In 1901 the British governor Sir Cavendish Boyle even turned poetic and wrote the stirring 'Ode to Newfoundland.' The country now had plenty of poets but, alas, little real poetry. J.A. O'Reilly noted the deficiency in verses penned in 1902:

The Harp of Caledonia rung
When Scott with wizard note hath sung;
Old Tara's Harp was, as of yore,
Unstrung by gifted Thomas Moore.
But who shall venture to command
The tuneful harp of Newfoundland?[24]

E.J. PRATT'S LIFE IN NEWFOUNDLAND

Whereas the intellectual activity described in preceding paragraphs emerged from a mercantile and urban milieu, E.J. Pratt's background was rural and ecclesiastical. He was born in Western Bay, the third son of John Pratt, a Methodist minister from Yorkshire who had come to Newfoundland in 1873 at the age of thirty-four, and in 1877 married Fanny Knight, a Newfoundlander. The life of the Pratt family was shaped by the father's career as an itinerant preacher in a succession of outport 'charges.' After the poet's birth in Western Bay, the family moved to Bonavista, and there followed in turn stays in Cupids, Blackhead, Brigus, Fortune, and Grand Bank. These outharbour travels were relieved by a period between 1892 and 1895 when John Pratt was minister at the Cochrane Street Methodist Church in St John's – the only period, according to a report by a member of the family, when he earned a salary of a thousand dollars per year.[25] A childhood passed in this migratory fashion might well have prevented the poet, a sensitive, sickly boy, from developing an attachment to any one place, and could instead have fostered especially strong ties with his family. There is much in Pratt's work to support this interpretation of his earliest years. Two personal poems about his childhood, 'To Angelina, an old Nurse,' and 'Magic in Everything,' were in essence sentimental family anecdotes, and he claimed in manhood that his father and mother had 'ever been the sustaining forces of my life.'[26] In addition, the mature Pratt showed little or no interest in the communities in which he had passed his boyhood, not even in Cupids, the oldest Newfoundland settlement, or in Blackhead, with its ancient Methodist associations. Life as a preacher's son brought him close to the 'edge [of] human grief' in the outports, and there stayed with him throughout his life vivid recollections of his father's reluctance to carry the sorrowful news of fishing disasters to widows and orphans.[27] Pratt would write later of the 'horror' of the huge tolls taken by collisions and storms and of other 'grosser human calamities.'[28] If the economic conditions in which the Pratt family lived were 'hard,'[29] those of the people John Pratt served were harsher and infinitely more perilous.

In 1897 E.J. Pratt became an apprentice at a draper's shop in St John's, an interlude lasting three years. He then returned to school for two years at the Methodist College in St John's, in order to complete his Matriculation. During his stay at the college a gifted teacher made him aware of the wonders of science, and an event occurred which to him always remained 'one of the big moments of existence.' He was allowed to go to the House of Assembly to see Guglielmo Marconi in person. It was, Pratt thought, 'like coming into the presence of a Deity.' On the day following this epiphany, 16 December 1901, it was revealed to the world that Marconi had received the first transatlantic wireless message on Signal Hill near St John's. 'Those of us who remember the announcement,' Pratt wrote thirty-five years later, 'may recall the sense of conquest over nature that visited the hearts of men.'[30] In his response to the episode we can see a wide-eyed rustic pondering the wonders of modernity and, perhaps, intimations of a desire to escape from the oppressive natural environment of Newfoundland. We also see the makings of the 'out-and-out hero-worshipper' that Pratt would later become.[31] From 1902 to 1904 Pratt taught school in Moreton's Harbour, a small community on New World Island in Notre Dame Bay, where, it is reported, he was 'often discouraged, homesick and worried about the illness of his father.'[32] John Pratt died of an undiagnosed but painful and prolonged illness in the bitterly cold March of 1904, and one of the poet's two strongest ties to the colony was broken. In the same year Pratt began a probationary period of study and preparation for the Methodist ministry, serving during the following three years in two Conception Bay charges: the Clarke's Beach–Cupids charge and the Bell Island–Portugal Cove–Pouch Cove charge. As a young Methodist probationer with intellectual ability and ambition, it was natural that he would hope eventually to study at the Methodist college of the University of Toronto, Victoria College. The opportunity to achieve this goal came while he was serving on the Bell Island charge, apparently in 1907. In years to come the story of how he raised the necessary money to get out of Newfoundland (a story no doubt embellished and exaggerated somewhat to satisfy listeners' desire for a tall tale) would become part of the Pratt mystique. He was fond of telling it himself on public occasions such as university convocations:

Now Father LeBel [President of Assumption University] asked me to relate an incident in connection with my departure from Nfld and its bearing upon Higher Education. He said that Father Dwyer had written him to get the story which I told at St. Thomas University in Houston, Texas, some five years ago. Well, it is not much of a story but some people found it humorous. I was a probationer for the Methodist Church and the pay was practically zero. I wanted to come up to Toronto University but how could I do it on a stipend which no more than paid for my board and lodging. I was staying with a friend, a Mr. X, who helped me to solve my problem in this way. His father-in-law, so he alleged, had been cured of tuberculosis by a potion which he manufactured himself out of spruce tops, wild cherry bark and the rind of fir trees plus sarsaparilla. Such a concoction was not on the market, so when I was staying at the Bell Island Mines I used to go out under cover of night with a huge bag and pluck the spruce tops [and] the cherry bark, and during the day in the intervals between my clerical ministrations such as getting up my sermons and visiting my parishioners, I boiled the stuff in a huge vat, brought it down to a vile concentrate, got hold of several gross of bottles on credit, and had a newspaper plant make cartons for the bottles – four sided bottles. I made up the instructions which were printed in English, French and Italian. I knew a little French but no Italian so I got an Italian grocer to do that job for me for ten cents.

On the fourth side was printed in large letters – Universal Lung Healer, and the theory was that the contents would cure not only lung trouble but all the most diverse diseases. I bought the sarsaparilla, put a tablespoonful in each bottle and added a small but powerful tincture of Barbadoes rum, *of course* to keep the concoction from freezing. I then made a tour of the island and sold several gross. That was the summer time. I knew that the stuff couldn't do any harm, and I knew the solution of cherry bark was at least drinkable. I made enough money to get to Toronto. No one was killed, though complaints came in to my brother who acted in my interest after my departure that the u.l.h. froze with the first frost and broke the bottles. Apparently there wasn't enough Barbadoes in it. The only ill effect was a stream of blasphemy that came from the dealers. I had a long time trying to soothe my conscience with the rum, but the good old conscience healed up after a time. It was the only thing that did heal, and that gentlemen, was my introduction to Higher Education.[33]

And so Pratt left Newfoundland in 1907, at the age of twenty-five, to go 'in quest of the Humanities'[34] and begin his lifelong academic association with Victoria College. He had never before been off the island. Though he would return for short visits in the years ahead, from 1907 until his death in 1964 Toronto would remain his actual and intellectual home.

Pratt's first published poem on Newfoundland was *Rachel* (1917), a long narrative which was begun after a visit to his home in 1916. Though it is flawed and immature, showing too openly the influence of Pratt's undergraduate reading in the English Romantic poets, yet it is in fact his most sustained study of Newfoundland life and offers clues to fundamental attitudes. It is an attempt to depict in detail the development of a fisherman's son from boyhood to early manhood in an outport. After a perfunctory opening description of the outport (called a 'village'), we learn that the boy's father,

> A gallant seaman in the prime of life,
> Inured to rigorous blasts, scornful of fear
> And Death's white hazards in the sweeping waves,

had been drowned while his son was yet an infant. The boy, Henry Lee, is reared by the widow, Rachel, herself orphaned by an earlier sea disaster, who finds to her dismay that as her son grows older his spirit manifests 'Impetuous cravings for the restless sea.' Soon he is venturing onto the inshore fishing grounds, under the tutelage of 'some old weather-beaten salt' selected by Rachel for his cautiousness. But Henry is not content to be an ordinary fisherman:

> Far away
> The Atlantic thralled his soul with mystery,
> Beckoned him on, and called him by his name.
> The sagas of the Gulf of Labrador,
> The stories of the Banks, the travel lore
> Of Ocean tracts, and European marts
> Had cast their spell upon him.

(The non-existent 'Gulf of Labrador' is an indication of Pratt's occasional carelessness with facts in his poems about Newfoundland. In one of his poems in *Newfoundland Verse* (1923) an old salt illustrates an argument by referring to the habits of the skunk – there are no skunks on the island.[35]) Henry Lee's blood is fired when he hears the 'high recital of heroic deeds' from 'A thousand years of British seamanship.'

This long tradition

> Of valorous action, gave to Newfoundland,
> Whose heritage it was, ancestral pride.
> This he accepted as his birthright, – his,
> Never to be relinquished.

There were still other deeds that stirred him, deeds 'Not charactered indeed by History's pen,' but illustrated in

> ... conduct nearer home
> Which though of lesser magnitude, still bore
> The deep and sovereign stamp of chivalry.
> It was the common mould of men, – the love
> That warmed the cramp of penury, and rained
> Its benedictions on a sailor's home.[36]

Soon Henry is chafing against the restrictions on the life of an inshore fisherman. These 'nearer fishing grounds' were meant, in his view, for the aged, not for 'youth and life's full prime' and his own first full summer of fishing was offshore on the 'Banks.' Returning with less than an average catch, he joins the crew of a trader bound for Portugal. This ship is lost in a storm, and Rachel, on hearing the news of her son's death, drifts into insanity and dies.

Such is the plot of *Rachel*. Whatever may be said of the poem as, simply, a sea story, as a 'sea story of Newfoundland,' to quote Pratt's subtitle, it may be viewed as revealing a great deal about his retrospective poetic response to his homeland. The Newfoundland we see in *Rachel* is a Newfoundland glamorized, a fictitious 'Elizabethan'[37] Newfoundland, lumbered with the stock imagery and themes of Victorian sea romances, and honoured, more in flattery than in truth, with a large share in the traditions of the English sea dogs. Henry and Rachel are characters from British literature rather than Newfoundland life, and while Pratt pays lip service to the heroism inherent in the 'common mould of men,' it is hard to see evidence of an intelligent interest in such men in the poem. In fact, there is hardly any observation even of the land and sea that summons up the real Newfoundland. Pratt's eye was not drawn, as was Hardy's, simply to depict commonness; it tended to make commonness uncommon by ascribing to it storybook heroics. This habit of huffing and puffing about the heroism of Newfoundlanders stayed with him throughout his life.

'Newfoundland,' he would tell audiences, 'has always been for me the place of great deeds which have been traditionally the texture of its sea-faring life. The people are accustomed to taking chances – great gambles, if you like, with the highest stake of all, life itself. There is always something profoundly moving and dramatic in decisions where the odds are against you, where the issue is fought out on high ground, where the end is noble, where the battle is joined with the wind and the stars against you, and especially when the risk is taken on behalf of the lives of others.'[38] Such boasting about Newfoundland – so patently contrived when one realizes how easily he broke his ties with the colony once he got the chance to leave for Ontario – can be found in poetry written long after the derivative *Rachel*. In the poem 'Newfoundland,' the title poem for *Newfoundland Verse*, we can sense the same kind of strutting poetic mentality that was apparent in the earlier work:

> Here the tides flow,
> And here they ebb;
> Not with that dull, unsinewed tread of waters
> Held under bonds to move
> Around unpeopled shores –
> Moon-driven through a timeless circuit
> Of invasion and retreat;
> But with a lusty stroke of life
> Pounding at stubborn gates,
> That they might run
> Within the sluices of men's hearts[39]

– lines which prompt the retort that the tides ebb and flow in Newfoundland in much the same manner as they do elsewhere in the North Atlantic. The uniqueness of Newfoundland is not demonstrated by this kind of braggadocio.

In an interview in 1955, Pratt recalled that as the child of a Methodist minister in Newfoundland he had been 'always close to death.' He added that what then seemed significant to him about his first poem, *Rachel*, was its theme: 'the loss of an only son at sea.'[40] The poem is indeed preoccupied with death, and the same shadow of tragedy which darkened his memories of his earliest years also dominates in *Newfoundland Verse* and the Newfoundland inspired poems in *Many Moods* (1932). Some of the poems in these volumes have as much embarrassing editorializing about heroes as is found in *Rachel*, but the essential vision of Newfoundland life contained in them is spare and bleak. Pratt's outharbour men and women are typically victims of the brutal forces in their hard world. Rachel, her son, father, and husband have their counterparts in the sealers in 'The Ice-Floes' and 'The Toll of the Bells,' the victims of the *Florizel* disaster, the sorrowing woman in 'Erosion,' and the terrified family in 'The Ground Swell.' The list of sufferers is long. Pratt's Newfoundland poems form a sombre chronicle of human defeat, displaying a gloomy but intense interest in the impassive forces of nature which unite to dwarf and destroy men. He was strangely attracted and awed by such phenomena as the 'paleolithic' face of the iceberg, the cold viciousness of the shark, the stealthy sea, the moan of the groundswell, and the stark features of a granite cliff. A Pratt seascape accentuates the ominous and non-human:

> Swift has the darkness settled on the deep;
> A moment past, and lurid streaks of day
> Were casting fitful splendours on the waves.
> Retiring, they have left the graying sea
> Mantled in gloom. With slow and labored hands
> The crawling waters tumble round the shore,
> Or swung upon the pivot of the tides
> Against the frontal basement of the cliffs,
> They shudder and recoil. Black fissured crags
> That hugely range along the tortuous coast,
> The eternal bulwarks of the earth's domain,
> Loom silent, and with sides encased with mail
> Of streaming basalt intercept the sea.[41]

This passage is from his unpublished closet drama *Clay*, written around 1918, which is set 'on the rocky shore of an island in the Atlantic.'[42] A similar dreary setting appears in *The Iron Door* (1927). Pratt conceived of cliffs and snarling seas with the terror of a boyish nightmare, and such images may indeed be based on recollections of his childhood experiences around the harsh coastline of Conception Bay.

When one considers the entire body of Pratt's Newfoundland poems – not a large portion of his *œuvre* – what stands out are these images of horror and grief and the persistent theme of tragedy. The overwhelming impression given is that Newfoundland was a good place to escape from. After *Rachel* he attempted no further lengthy analyses of Newfoundland life. *Newfoundland Verse* was more of an experiment with poetic technique than a rumination upon Newfoundland, with the poet testing his theory that 'poetry blossomed more healthily out of the concrete than out of abstractions.'[43] In this exercise, and in *Many Moods* as well, Newfoundland functioned as little more than a convenient stock of images and illuminations for an aspiring imagist poet to draw upon, and Pratt did not attempt, much less achieve, a comprehensive statement about his homeland. This is not to belittle what he did write. In such poems as 'The Ground Swell' and 'Erosion' he does indeed succeed in summoning up much that is horrid and spare and dark about the milieu of Newfoundland, and in the latter poem especially, so daringly stripped of detail that it seems almost a study in geology rather than human suffering – or even a poetic experiment with metaphor – he yet seems to give us all that we need to know about pain:

> It took the sea a thousand years,
> A thousand years to trace
> The granite features of this cliff,
> In crag and scarp and base.
>
> It took the sea an hour one night,
> An hour of storm to place
> The sculpture of these granite seams
> Upon a woman's face.[44]

In 'Sea-Gulls' too he succeeds brilliantly, conjuring up the wonder in a common sight. And there are other brief lyrical masterpieces. Whatever Pratt may have failed to do, he was, without question, Newfoundland's finest poet. And yet it is still surprising to see what is left out of his poems on Newfoundland. While there are, indeed, references to such heroes as Cabot, Grenfell, and Gilbert in his work, really his poetry showed no interest in Newfoundland history. He evidently had no interest in exploring the distinctive traditions and habits of speech of his people. There was nothing in his poems that showed a genuine curiosity about the outport way of life, no fingering of outharbour contrivances, no examination of the mechanics of fishing and sealing, no investigation of how the people adjusted to the demands of their harsh environment, no detailed studies of individual fishermen. The 'drama of the sled and dory'[45] is alluded to but not examined. One critic has recently argued that the poems of Pratt are influenced by the

Newfoundland ballad, but her arguments are unconvincing and it takes overworked scholarly ingenuity to discover from his work that he was curious about the people's lore, songs, or culture.[46] He does indeed refer to 'culture' in 'Newfoundland Seamen':

> This is their culture, this – their master passion
> Of giving shelter and sharing bread,
> Of answering rocket signals in the fashion
> Of losing life to save it.[47]

But this is just more of the romancing and strutting we saw in *Rachel*. Pratt could not conceive of culture without the element of heroism, and he had no poetic interest in humdrum reality. Nor was he in the slightest degree interested in the nascent literary movement associated with the *Newfoundland Quarterly* or in any of the printed literature. Pratt's Newfoundland is seen in retrospect, simplified into images of cruelty and fear, reduced to the hard and fixed outlines to which memory often reduces the distant past. It is a Newfoundland jettisoned, and half remembered.

Pratt in his maturity was obviously making an attempt to move beyond what two Canadian critics have called 'the lesser inspirations of Newfoundland'[48] in order to become, 'apparently quite deliberately,'[49] Canada's national poet. This meant throwing off parochial concerns to take on bigger themes: the Canadian Pacific Railway rather than Newfoundland's narrow gauge line, Brébeuf rather than Coughlan or Jens Haven, the Iroquois rather than the Beothucks. It also meant developing a new language. Late in life, Pratt professed to have an interest in Newfoundland dialect, and would claim that the 'sailors' he had known as a young man had 'a native eloquence, a fervent, if rough, type of speech.'[50] He would illustrate this richness of speech to his audiences by telling stories in the dialect: '"Any arn [herring] dis marn?" Answer – "No dere aint any arn dis marn. Might as well be no arn as arn, cause if dere are any arn, dere nar a bit big."'[51] 'That's the pure McCoy,' he would say after relating the anecdote. There is in fact no interest in Newfoundland speech shown in Pratt's poetry. Indeed, it is not an exaggeration to say that the language we see in *Rachel* is a learned language, taken from English poets rather than real life, almost as foreign as English was to Scottish poets like James Thomson and Robert Burns. Pratt rarely used a dialect word from Newfoundland in his poems, and when he did, as in 'The Ice-Floes,' he placed the word in inverted commas to distinguish it from the standard English context.[52] Pratt's poetic language was a genteel distillation from other poets and from educated speech in central Canada, whereas in his own speech he never lost his Newfoundland dialect.[53] Thus his literary language represents his almost complete dissociation from the culture into which he was born.

When Pratt became famous he grew fond of parading his Newfoundland background before the many audiences he addressed. It somehow became an ornament to be displayed rather than a limitation to be overcome. On these occasions he would sometimes talk of the influence Newfoundland had on his life and work: 'Those first twenty-odd years of my life gave me a wealth of experience which will never be completely drained. In fact, it crops out in my work in the most unexpected places, in subjects which might at first glance appear to be outside of the area. It is like an idiom or an accent from which one could not and would not if he could, dissociate himself. Such subjects as storms, marine disasters, rescues, sacrifices, all the way down from the heroic to the sharing of bread and the little nameless unremembered acts of kindness and of love – these seem to be the natural subjects for the thoughts and expression of Newfoundlanders.'[54] 'A man cannot get far from his heritage,' he would say, noting that 'the sea has a way of despatching a wave to wash the doorstep or spray the sills.'[55] Such statements have a human interest, but it is apparent that they cannot be defended on looking through the Canadian and imperial poetry he left behind. There, no significant Newfoundland influence is evident. It is poppycock to see in Pratt's later poetic musings on man's relationship with nature distinct traces of his island upbringing, for such a theme is universal. Pratt succeeded in discarding, to the extent that it could be discarded, his ancestral claim on the Newfoundland experience. Although one commentator has stated that much of his later work is merely 'grist for the critic's mill' and 'irrelevant for common folk,'[56] it nevertheless seems apparent that Pratt did achieve his ambition of becomine a fine Canadian poet. What he would have become if he had, like W.B. Yeats, turned his great talents upon the materials supplied by his own people, must be left to conjecture.

MARGARET DULEY'S FICTION / 1936–42

'NOT BY FISH ALONE': NEWFOUNDLAND, 1909–34

It has been suggested that the defeat of the Bond government in 1909 signalled the end of Newfoundland's international posturing and her acceptance of a second-class status within the British imperial family. Perhaps this was so. Although it would take another quarter of a century before the actual loss of self-government would occur, it is not hard to find signs of a slackening national will in the years following the First World War. The war itself fostered a sense of local identity, and immediately afterwards Newfoundland officially assumed the title of 'Dominion'; but the following decade brought such economic adversity that any pretension to international status was dampened. Newfoundland did not share the aspirations of those dominions which, in the 1920s, wanted equivalent status with England within the Empire. Indeed, the Prime Minister of Newfoundland stated in 1927 that his government 'had not asked for, nor did they wish, a status of equality with the mother country,' since such a request might prove a barrier to getting help from Britain in the event that New-foundlanders had 'difficulty in governing themselves.'[1] Such was the political mood of the times. But however short Newfoundland may have been in international influence and visible natural resources, she never lacked hope in some imagined future prosperity. Between 1909 and 1930 the country continued to pursue this elusive prosperity. Bond's initiatives in securing reciprocity agreements with the Ameri-cans having failed, governments now set about to implement a policy which had in fact been clearly enunciated by a committee of the House of Assembly as early as 1880. 'No material increase of means is to be looked for from our fisheries,' the House had been assured, and 'we

must direct our attention to the growing requirements of the country.'² Newfoundland would pin her hopes in the next century as well,
not on fish, but on her other resources. As one observer noted in 1911
during the heady days following construction of the paper mill in
Grand Falls, 'the people must realise the necessity of not living by fish
alone.'³

Though Newfoundland did at last fail to diversify her economy to
such an extent that she could withstand the pressures of the 1920s and
early 1930s, yet she did score two remarkable successes in the interlude prior to the coming of Commission Government. These were the
building of the huge paper mill at Corner Brook in 1923–5, and the
commencement of lead and zinc mining at Buchans in 1928. With the
Bell Island mine and the Grand Falls mill already in operation, Newfoundland was by 1930 more dependent upon the export of minerals
and forest products than she was on the export of fish.⁴ All four of
these large industries came into existence through investment of
foreign capital, and thus a pattern of primary resource development
was established that continues to our own day. These successful
enterprises, in combination with the award of Labrador to Newfoundland in the British Privy Council decision of 1927, aroused anew
the people's hopes for an industrial future and spread across the island
some of the amenities of urban life which had previously been available only in certain parts of the Avalon Peninsula.⁵ And even the
schemes that failed to get off the ground – and there were many of
them, including imagined factories to manufacture guano, explosives,
cereal, peat fuel, glue, and fertilizer – had about them an aura of
excitement and glamour.⁶ Newfoundland had been given a taste of
North American prosperity during the First World War, and in the
post-war period increasing opportunities for travel abroad, films,
tourist traffic, and communications between Newfoundland immi-
grants in Canada and the United States and their families back home,
further contributed to making the North American way of life desira-
ble.⁷ In a shrewd analysis of the Newfoundland people written in
1930, J.R. Smallwood observed in 'St. John's, Bell Island, Grand Falls,
Buchans and Corner Brook, and similar other large places, a distinct
Americanization trend.' Owing to a number of 'non-insular factors,'
he wrote, 'Newfoundlanders are gradually coming to higher conceptions of living. Having them, they will gradually begin to demand
realization of them.' 'Soon,' he added ominously, 'wants will become
needs.'⁸ A similar perception occurred to an English observer, J.L.
Paton, in 1933. 'Coming into our island,' he noted, 'are American

magazines, the radio, American Sunday papers and American movies, subtly instilling a sense of new wants and ideas which outrun the native simplicity of the people.'[9]

In Newfoundland in the second and third decades of this century the most advanced opinion favoured industrial experiment and enterprise. 'Today,' Smallwood wrote in 1930, 'the symbol of the national ideal is a hydro-electric power station rather than a codfish.'[10] In retrospect, it can be argued that Newfoundland ought to have turned more energetically to developing her obvious resources in the ocean. However, recent history had shown that there could be no major breakthrough in that industry unless the country could win some favoured position in the international marketing of salt cod. Not even the efforts of W.F. Coaker's militant Fishermen's Protective Union (founded in 1908) could achieve this objective. It was hard for a small nation to gain such an advantage at the best of times. Given the at first haphazard and then intensely competitive trade conditions in southern Europe in the post-war period, Newfoundland could not hope to have any control over markets. She was at the mercy of forces 'certainly uncomprehended, and perhaps incomprehensible, and which were the consequence of causes outside [her] influence.'[11] An attempt in 1920–1 by Coaker, then minister of marine and fisheries, to impose uniform regulations on Newfoundland exporters of salt cod was a complete failure. One historian has argued that the collapse of these regulations 'marked the end of Newfoundland's pre-eminence as a fishing country.'[12] In 1920–3 the country suffered a severe recession, and throughout the 1920s Newfoundland's position as a fish exporter stagnated in the face of stiff European competition. While Corner Brook and Buchans grew into modern communities, the outports declined, with emigration draining away many of their most energetic young people. 'Thousands of fishermen have quit the fishery in recent years,' Smallwood commented in 1930; adding, 'those of them who could be absorbed by the new land industries or their satellites remain in the country, and the others have emigrated to the mainland of America.'[13] By 1931 there were fifty thousand Newfoundland-born men and women living in the United States and Canada.[14]

In describing the 'new Newfoundland' of 1930, Smallwood probably caught the prevailing mood of the day. The 'new' Newfoundland, the country that was moving 'into the full noonday of enlightenment, development and prosperity,'[15] was urban and industrial; the outport, he implied, was old and outmoded. There is a similar attitude, though touched with regret and bitterness, in Captain Bob Bartlett's autobiography, *The Log of Bob Bartlett* (1928). Bartlett was born in Brigus, Conception Bay, in 1875, when that community was a thriving centre of fishing and commerce. But in fact, according to Bartlett, Brigus had reached its 'crest,' its 'Golden Age,' some fifteen or twenty years before he was born. In 1928 the town was 'scarce an echo of its proud yesterdays,' and to illustrate this decline Bartlett gave statistics showing the drop in the number of seals killed in Newfoundland between 1830 and 1923:

That dwindling column on the right tells the whole story of Newfoundland's terrible and downgrade slide in the last one hundred years; it explains the poverty of her people and the misery of some of the finest mariners that ever sailed the sea.

The New Englanders were wiser. When they saw their whale fishery slowly going to pot the ship owners began to quit it and invested their money in other things, such as cotton, woolens, boot and shoe factories, and so forth. ... I sometimes visit Salem, Newburyport, New Bedford, New London and Stonington. Notwithstanding the great changes which have taken place I can still see identically the same types of homes, furniture, etc., as those in Newfoundland, even to the china, old four posters, rugs, pictures, front doors and brass knockers. For the same sort of men who manned and owned the New Bedford and Nantucket whalers manned and owned the sealing vessels of old times in Newfoundland. But I also see fine houses on splendid estates which prove my point that the Yankee mariners knew how to change trades when forced to.

We Bartletts of the present generation feel the change keenly because we have endured its worse phase. My own father had thousands of acres of land. Today it isn't worth the space it would occupy on a blueprint.[16]

We now know that the decline in the economy of Brigus and similar Conception Bay communities in the second half of the nineteenth century was due to causes which Bartlett did not understand, causes much more complex than simple human unwillingness to change jobs.[17] But the main point is that he saw outharbour life as decayed and backward. Viewing the outports in the early 1930s would merely have confirmed his gloomy views, for in 1929 the world entered the Depression, the bottom fell out of the international market on which Newfoundland depended, and the country, far from finding herself 'in the front rank of the great small nations of the world,'[18] was brought to her knees within five years. In 1934 Newfoundland surrendered Responsible Government in favour of rule by a Commission appointed by Britain. As might have been expected, in the period 1929–34 it was the outport that was hardest hit. J.R. Smallwood, who knew the outports well, commented simply: 'You could smell the poverty.'[19]

AN URBAN PERSPECTIVE

If life in the outports seemed to men like Bartlett and Smallwood to be limited and poverty-stricken, it can easily be imagined what habitués of the best society in St John's thought of it. By the end of the nineteenth century the capital city's dominance over the social and economic life of the country was complete. Whatever 'leisured classes'[20] Newfoundland could boast of possessing were located in St John's East in close proximity to the elegant home of the governor. It was into this world of privilege that Margaret Duley was born in 1894. Her father was a prosperous tradesman, the English-born jeweller Thomas J. Duley, and her mother was Tryphena C. Soper, who came from a merchant family in Carbonear. 'It was a cultured family,' a biographer of Margaret Duley has written, 'appreciative of the arts.'[21] Margaret Duley grew up enjoying the amenities and the company of 'the élite of St. John's,'[22] mixing with sons and daughers of the city's 'merchant-princes,' the owners of the old trading and shipping companies whom she later described as 'the country's bone and blood.'[23] She was educated at the Methodist College in St John's, and in 1913 enrolled in the Royal Academy of Drama and Elocution in London, England, where she intended to train as an actress. When the war broke out she returned home, but not before the delights of British culture had made a deep impression upon her. For many years afterwards, London and all that it represented had an important place in her life. 'She was very British,' writes Margaret-Ann Maher, 'had a strong British accent, and referred to the boat which travelled to London every two weeks as the "Home Boat."' During the war one of her brothers was killed and another seriously wounded. The effects of these tragedies upon her have not been explored. They were possibly profound. From 1918 until she began serious writing in the 1930s, her life was devoted to travel, to her family, to attending 'parties, many of which were at Government House,'[24] and to local feminist agitation. To judge from the literary allusions in her novels, she must also have read widely. No sign of a literary ambition occurs, however, until the Depression years, when her father's jewellery business went into decline. Margaret Duley began writing fiction apparently to help make a living, and the subject to which she first turned for literary inspiration was, somewhat unexpectedly, the Newfoundland outport. There was little in her education and background to suggest that she had any knowledge of the outports, much less a sympathy for them. She knew the outports in the vicinity of St John's of course, but only as a summer visitor would know them. She had also visited Labrador as a passenger on a coastal steamship, the S.S. *Kyle*. It was while she was leaning on the deck of the *Kyle*, one summer day in Labrador, that the inspiration came to her to write her first novel. 'A gull hovered in front of her,' she recalled in 1956, 'and she experienced eyes like yellow ice, the symbol of the pitiless heart of the north.'[25] Out of this experience came *The Eyes of the Gull*, published in 1936.

The book expresses perfectly the disdainful attitude towards the outports that we would expect from a coddled sophisticate in St John's East. It tells the story of Isabel Pyke, aged 29, trapped in an outport from birth, who experiences a summer of sensual love and philosophical uplift with an artist named Peter Keen, who comes to her community to paint for a few months. Keen may have been modelled on Rockwell Kent, who lived in Brigus during the First World War and was deported for alleged espionage.[26] Apart from his artistic proclivities, Isabel's lover has the other attractions and possessions of a rich adventurer: a servant, a love of wine and literature, a certain world-weariness, and radical ideas about freedom and amorous experiment. 'For myself,' he says at one point, 'I believe most strongly that nothing lasts, everything changes, and no one note is struck forever.' Hearing such cosmopolitan ideas, Isabel is entranced. She has been 'in spiritual rebellion' to 'savage, bitter, and chill' Newfoundland all her life, and has never before accepted a lover. The nearby villagers who have been the only available supply of husbands and lovers for her and other women have too many obvious deficiencies. They 'don't wash enough,' and have 'slack shoulders' and 'leather' faces. They would make her 'fat and ugly,' and would condemn her to a life of 'working from daylight to dark.' Moreover, they would keep her perpetually pregnant, giving her children who would turn out to be 'inert slatterns ... with smeared mouths.'[27] Repressed for three decades by the narrow and stifling outport, Isabel now awakens to a world of sense and culture. This lasts until the end of the summer, when her artist goes his own way and leaves her alone and desperate. Although he has repeatedly encouraged her to seek freedom, and given her enough money to get to Andalusia in Spain – the locale of many of her girlish fantasies – she cannot muster the strength to break away from her surroundings and dies in frustration, melancholy, and lunacy.

The Eyes of the Gull is not far above the level of mere romance, and perhaps there is little point in prolonged analysis. However, the values enforced in it are deeply revealing. To judge by this book, the quality of love-making is determined by latitude, the Spanish variety being more than acceptable, Newfoundland's of a decidedly lower cull. The poppycock of Peter Keen's ideas, adolescent nonsense really, is embraced as profundity. He gets off scot-free after meddling in Isabel's life and muddling her values for a summer, and neither he nor the novelist seems to think that he bears some responsibility for her future. Newfoundland life, glimpsed only occasionally as background, is not explored, although the landscape surrounding the outport is seen in its stark and appalling beauty. The outport itself is merely 'a huddle of whitewashed houses' sucked at by the sea. The occupations of the people, their method of adapting to a difficult environment, their religious values and family loyalties, are not seen as possessing any intrinsic worth. 'I don't know anything. How could I learn anything in this place?' Isabel asks, ignoring the inheritance of gradually accumulated skills and attitudes needed for maintaining life in such a milieu. The brutal forces of nature that surround her make her inarticulate and submissive. At one point, after a minor quarrel Isabel knows she has caused, Peter Keen asks her why she did not take the initiative and say she was sorry. '"Peter," she answers, "I never thought of it. I thought there was nothing to do but wait." He laughed for a moment then sobered quickly. "Isabel you mustn't have such acceptance. It's all wrong! You must help yourself – reach out." "Peter," she said unhappily, "It must be the place, the wind, and the sea. They do what they like and we accept it."' This attitude, which Duley sees as stupified stolidity of character, is ultimately what Isabel is unable to overcome, and Peter eventually realizes that he was wrong to think she could ever change for the better. 'I very stupidly tried to transfer some of my own ideas to you,' he tells Isabel, 'without realizing that your life was fixed in very limited surroundings with only the grim variations of nature to give you any sense of change.' It is Peter who is seen as having the good life and the correct attitudes. It is life on the outside that has value. We are given a glimpse of exactly what that life consists of when Isabel contrives to spend a day and a night with her lover. They 'eat strange and fascinating looking dishes' cooked by the servant, sip wine, read Tennyson and Keats, and whisper 'nebulous things' to one another.[28] The good life, to the author of this book, appears to be one of genteel laziness and self-indulgence.

In *Cold Pastoral* (1939), Duley's second novel, we begin with a setting similar to that in *The Eyes of the Gull*. Mary Immaculate Keilly, a child recognized as especially gifted and beautiful, is growing up in a tiny Newfoundland community for which the author feels the same sickened loathing that is noticeable in the earlier book. There is in the description of this cove, however, a far greater attention to squalid detail, showing the writer's combined fascination and horror as she is drawn closer to the realities of outharbour life. We find Mary Immaculate refusing to go look at the broken body of a cow that has fallen off a cliff onto the landwash; also, she is offended by 'the strong suck of the sea' and by the 'sea's offal,' finding it 'impossible to touch the slime of cod or press spawn from the body of a caplin.' The smells, spurting blood and guts, and buzzing flies associated with fishing, all frighten her. She dislikes the fishy taste of local chicken, and notes the ugliness of her father's hands, which are 'calloused, cracked, blunted at the finger tips, scarred with lines and twine and splitting knives.' Even her mother, with her 'oily' hair, 'scorched' face, 'sagging' flesh, rotting teeth, and swollen red hands, is seen by the young girl as repulsive. About half way through the novel, we get this picture of Mary Immaculate's mother on a visit to St John's:

Josephine advanced under their eyes, and nothing about her suggested ordeal. Her shoes were dusty, her nose shiny, but her walk suffused serenity. Days filled with work, and leisure given to prayer, gave her an equality beyond the standards of man. Frequently called to mind the greatness of God and her own nothingness, she trusted the humility of others. She wore a brown knitted skirt, a cardigan coat over a wool-lace jumper. The newness of the suit was evinced in the startling whiteness of skin suddenly exposed against a red neck. Hair had been washed and frizzed by some agency and lay bunched under a toque of the same wool as her suit. Hands in cotton gloves clasped a cheap bag. Josephine had come to town! Molasses-brown eyes stared with frank interest, while full lips smiled away from teeth holding black-edged cavities. ... Scrubbed as she was, Josephine held a secret cling of dishwater and cooking ...[29]

In this Josephine is allowed some dignity, but the note of mocking irony directed at the 'bay noddy' is unmistakable. It looks as if Mary is destined for a life like Josephine's or Isabel Pyke's, until one day at the age of twelve she runs alone into the woods behind her settlement, gets lost and frost-bitten, becomes the object of a lengthy search that receives international attention, and ends up in a St John's hospital, something of a celebrity, with a great deal of money contributed by concerned onlookers. Her doctor, Philip Fitz Henry, recognizes that Mary has special qualities, and arranges to have her adopted by his own family – which is, as the name indicates, of the very finest St John's stock. So to her own and her mother's delight, Mary escapes from the outport quite early in the novel, and the rest of the book shows her coming of age in the world outside, at first in the upper echelons of St John's society, and, much later, in London.

Mary is now, by a lucky chance, fully a part of the world that Isabel Pyke desired. The outharbour girl is shown adapting to her new life. She loses her uncivilized accent, learns to respond to affection with gracious touches rather than with the bay's 'inarticulate grunts,' and is slowly moulded into a young lady. She starts calling Lady Fitz Henry 'mater,' and keeps the homely 'mom' for her jettisoned mother. Her Roman Catholicism becomes weaker. The 'welter of folklore' in which she grew up gives way to 'sanity.' By the age of eighteen she can speak and read French, is a zealous pianist, and can skate, swim, and play tennis, golf, and bridge. This process continues at length, rather tediously for the reader perhaps, but with no apparent disapproval by the novelist, until far into the novel, when we begin to doubt whether what is happening to the heroine is really desirable after all. There seems to be a change of heart on the part of the writer herself, who wants to depart from her original conception of the character's development. We hear Mary described now by disinterested outsiders as an 'awful young snob' and a 'prig.' The whole Fitz Henry family is described as 'prigs.' A subtle questioning begins of the whole set of values and kind of behaviour which had hitherto been thought praiseworthy. The phrase 'fisherman's daughter' reappears in the novel, and is used to explain Mary's distinctiveness. 'We've never seen Mary,' Philip's brother David says of her; 'She comes of people who have lived generations in predatory fight with nature.' This is stated emphatically as if it had meaning; what that meaning is, what coming from people who have been engaged in 'predatory fight with nature' really signifies, is not indicated. A disaster involving a young man who loves her sends Mary to London, and after her initial excitement over the wonders of the city, she begins to see even it, the centre of British civilization, with 'balanced eyes.' She knows at the end of the novel that 'If she stayed [in London] long enough she would begin to feel pinched. This need be no more, this could be so much less, than the Cove. There people stood foursquare to natural peril. Here people cowered under man's unnatural threats.'[30] This comment at the end of *Cold Pastoral* is the only direct statement in the book that her earlier life, in the cove among people long abandoned, has a validity. Even though we are prepared for it by the suggestions pointed to earlier, it is still a devastating comment, torpedoing all that had been implied earlier about the values of sophisticated society, and qualifying the romantic ending of the book: Mary's anticipated marriage to the doctor who had treated her years earlier, Philip Fitz Henry. This conventional ending possibly does violence to the subtle disentanglement of the heroine from the urban values represented by the doctor and his family.

Cold Pastoral, a deeply flawed novel, is also a significant work in Margaret Duley's career as a writer. We see in it a partial retreat from snobbishness, and an eventual reconciliation, though it is stated rather than achieved, with the country that she eventually acclaimed as 'a magnificent and dramatic background for fiction.' The meaning of that phrase should be noted carefully: Newfoundland in her first two books remains primarily background to what is her principal interest, depicting an unfolding feminine consciousness. In the end, in her final novel *Novelty on Earth* (1942), that interest takes precedence over all others, and the Newfoundland background disappears. But in *Cold Pastoral* we see her beginning to overcome her lingering distaste for the cramped lives and harsh conditions that she thought she saw in the outports in the 1920s and 1930s. Though that distaste never completely left her, her 'compulsion'[31] to describe Newfoundland, to understand it, and to express its meaning to the world outside, led her beyond the superficialities of *Cold Pastoral* to a third and much more important novel. This was *Highway to Valour*, which appeared in 1941.

HIGHWAY TO VALOUR

Duley's third novel is dedicated to Newfoundland, 'a country which the author loves and hates.' The phrase indicates that whatever truce Duley arrived at in her imaginative and social quarrel with her homeland was an uneasy one. Her attitude would always be ambivalent. Nevertheless, in *Highway to Valour* she works her way towards acceptance and insight. The book describes the odyssey of a refined young outport Newfoundlander, a merchant's daughter named Mageila Michelet, through a variety of sufferings to a final situation of equanimity. The initial setting is like those in the earlier novels, and there is a similar conflict between the heroine's sensitive nature and the harsh environment in which she comes to maturity. But whereas that environment is seen in the earlier books primarily as destructive and confining, here it is finally perceived quite differently. This is a book of intuition and inquiry rather than one expressing fixed social attitudes. From the very beginning we notice a changed attitude towards common life, a compassionate interest in those who had once been rejected as smelly and ugly. Here, for example, Mageila enters the kitchen of an ordinary outport home. She has come to cure the toothache of a child, for as the seventh daughter of a seventh daugher she has the power to heal. Having lingered on the landwash, she is late for her appointment:

Almost at once she was welcomed by a thin-faced woman with a sunken mouth, spare shoulders, and a body stout below the waist. ...
  'Mrs. Butler, I'm so sorry –'
  'Oh, Miss Mageila, dear, 'tis of no consequence. Bertie has been at it that long now.'
  Smiling widely, Mrs. Butler revealed false teeth like curves of pearl buttons.
  'Come in now, Miss, and take a chair.'
  Mageila knew prosperity was relative. Her family would be considered poverty-stricken by some standards of living, but to this they represented wealth. The kitchen was scrubbed and warm with the perilous comfort of a hand-to-mouth existence. There was a wood-stove, a pile of kindling, a box of twigs, a table covered with white oil-cloth, wooden chairs, three-cornered shelves, cluttered with household utensils, and a wide settle on which lay a bundled-up baby pawing the air with fat curled hands. On a chair beside it sat Bertie Butler, a six-year-old boy with eyes made small from weeping. From the circle of a black stocking tied round his head, his face peered out peaked and shadowed with childish grief.[32]

It is hard to find a false note in this description. Margaret Duley's eye for significant detail was sure once she learned where to look, and her ability to create atmosphere shows the certain touch of a novelist. We may note too the contrast between this sympathetic depiction of a youngster's suffering, summing up so much of what was wrong with oldtime Newfoundland, and the picture of uncouth urchins in *The Eyes of the Gull*. The author has now tried to enter the lives of these people, whereas previously she had stood aloof and passed judgment. There is a new alertness here to the texture and meaning of life in outport Newfoundland.

Bertie's toothache, incurable by all available agencies save magic, shows man's vulnerability and helplessness. Standing in opposition to even Mageila's power to cure, and to all human life, is the violent face of nature, symbolized early in the novel by a vicious tidal wave which, immediately after Bertie falls asleep, sweeps over the community of Feather-the-Nest causing enormous destruction of life and property. (The tidal wave was no stroke of fancy, for a real one had hit the south coast of Newfoundland in 1929, with similar results.) This is the contest which is the theme of *Highway to Valour* – the fury of a hard and unpredictable nature, in compatititon with men and women trying to live alongside it, 'a war between people and place, with the strength of both contending forever.'

The tidal wave kills Mageila's family. Horrified and sickened with despair, hatred, and fear, appalled more and more by the comfortless land and treacherous ocean, she has still other horrors to face and more pain to try and relieve. The tidal wave disaster gives her a glimpse into her future, and she can see that 'she would be let off from nothing.' Wherever she looks she sees the rawness of nature and the scars of calamity: her friend Mrs Slater's deformed back, misshaped through decades of labour; the antlered heads of two stags, who fought, got entangled and interlocked, then starved to death; a malodorous whaling station on the Labrador coast, with 'a mass of bleeding flesh on the platform in front of the factory'; and still other horrid images. The prolonged journey to Labrador which Mageila undertakes in the book (and which is elaborately described) is seen as a healing encounter with raw, brutal nature. To Trevor Morgan, the Englishman who loves Mageila, the land is 'too rough, too elemental,' and the people too 'tightened up.' 'You Newfoundlanders,' he exclaims to her, 'So full of acceptance! ... You are all terribly accepting. It's wrong.' But what happens to Mageila is not seen as stifling or debasing. Through suffering, she becomes reconciled; having initially feared the sea, she eventually comes to know that her fear is unworthy and decides that she will not 'grovel away from her heritage.'[33] We leave her at the end a moral victor over both her lover and her surroundings. Avoiding the cheap ending of romances, Duley leaves her alone, dedicated to a life of medical service in remote Newfoundland, and characterized by a mysterious self-possession.

In Mageila's triumph and in her refusal to forsake her heritage, Margaret Duley is asserting the value of the traditional way of life in Newfoundland. Given her élitist background and her open hostility to the outport in *The Eyes of the Gull*, this is surely a stunning reversal of attitude. But there is more in her book than nationalistic assertion. There is also probing into the Newfoundland character. Mageila's responses to her environment contain illuminations of an entire people's manner of thinking. They are illuminations rather than definitions, for Mageila's character in the end remains elusive, and Duley side-steps the peril of racial formula. But tentative insights nevertheless are sprinkled throughout the book, as in this rumination by Trevor Morgan as he travels on the coastal steamer:

After staring glassily at rain he became alert, seeing it lessen and show signs of clearing, and when the ship anchored in one of its comfortless places he avoided the accommodation-ladder. Instead he stepped brisly astern and found a member of the crew jigging cod for the *Assou*'s table, with another standing by to split and clean. Interested and diverted, he watched and then asked for a line. With the civility of the Newfoundlander the seaman stopped jigging to show him how to hold the line between the fingers, how to jig and haul in. It was not difficult; and after the excitement of the first catch he found cod could be hooked in the side, the belly, the eye – anywhere but the place good fish should be hooked – and when the line was hauled in they flopped, gasping and dying. So much drab death repulsed him, making him see it as a symbol of his surroundings. Acceptance? Inertia? It was the quality he had seen in the patients waiting to enter the mission-hospital [in St Anthony]. It was in the risked lives whether the sea was open or shut.

It was in Mageila. She had no right to be so brooding, so uncomplaining over devastation. She should protest, cry woman's tears, and make some sucker of a man pay for her losses. He was turning on her mentally when he remembered to ask himself how much he protested systems, traditions, and backgrounds. Everything was out of focus, cock-eyed, he thought, frowning at gaping cod-fish mouths.

He was still standing when he became conscious of the blood-spattered deck, the slimy feel of his hands, and the fact that he was overlooked. Glancing up towards the after-deck, he saw Captain Dilke [Mageila's grandfather] and Mageila – the former laughing out loud, as if the sight of an English official jigging cod-fish held plenty of humour.

'Bloody decks, Mr. Morgan?' inquired Captain Dilke.[34]

The bewildered observations about Mageila and her countrymen are offered in a scene that is funny and ironic. They are not Margaret Duley's suggestions, but her character's. Still, they combine with other similar insights to form a rich imaginative rendering of the country and her people. And if her inferences and intuitions about the national character of Newfoundlanders are, in the end, unsatisfactory, they are nevertheless more acceptable than the facile postulations of some later writers. Newfoundland may not be fully understood in her book; but it is acknowledged and confronted. Duley is at least writing on a serious theme, in a serious way, trying to offer an integrated vision of the relationship between land, sea, and people.

That vision, to Duley's credit, is not sentimental or effusively patriotic. We can see the influence of her reading in sentimental Victorian fiction; but her style and attitudes are, finally, her own. She sees Newfoundland as a place hard to love and easy to hate. Men were 'pinched between rock and sea,' with the sea spitting at them and sometimes daring to 'cross the road to lick at their doors.' Life along the coast 'seemed a continuation of putting out, of balancing in a threatened boat and seeing caverned cliffs with no more refuge than a bird-ledge for a gull.' This is, in essence, Norman Duncan's perception of Newfoundland too; but Duley's response to the stark images of her uncomfortable home is more tremulous and shocked. It is as if she emerged from a cocoon of sophistication to see her rough country for the first time. She seems to wrench herself towards acceptance of what can no longer be concealed by the pantomime of romance, but her woman's eye does not cease to be appalled by the truths that press in upon her:

Between sea and settlement she walked slowly, feeling the soundlessness of snow underfoot. ... There were so few people around that she walked alone, coldly bathed in the dwindling glare of the western sky. Marvelling again at the stillness, she savoured the relaxation of a Newfoundlander perpetually tightened from the torment of wind. Now she felt herself walking softly like an Indian, moccasin-clad, easy in body, unblown and unpuckered. Occasionally she paused, knowing she was seeing stark beauty bathed in red. A streak of sunset on snow made her think of blood on white fleece. Her narrow world had brought her close to the slaying-knife, the axe, and the barbed hook striking at the fruit of the sea. Blood, blood, she thought unhappily, visualizing the beauty of the slain lamb and the proud strut of the rooster laid low on the block; but she bad herself look at them, firmly knowing such things must be.[35]

It is in such moments as these, such exact replications of Newfound-land's moods and images, that we can see Duley's uniqueness as a novelist. Perhaps nobody has conveyed more sharply in words what it feels like to live on this ancient rock. As R.L. Nathan wrote in the

Saturday Review of Literature, the novel 'brings us as close as the written word can to an immediate knowledge of Newfoundland.' He added, in subtle praise of Duley's language, that 'Time has not dulled the force of Anglo-Saxon imagery; it lies there still in our language fount to be used. Miss Duley's novels of Newfoundland is rich in this primal, poetic perception. It is bright and fresh in colour, sound, sensation, like a child's world newly experienced, free of stale impressions.'[36] Like Prospero's strange isle, Newfoundland too has its own special atmosphere, its own 'noises,'[37] and Duley evokes that atmosphere with extraordinary skill.

It has been suggested earlier that in *Highway to Valour* Duley is making a claim for the value of Newfoundland's traditional way of life. There is also in the book an open distaste for the life of privilege that is seen as desirable in *The Eyes of the Gull*. Mageila, like Mary Immaculate in *Cold Pastoral*, eventually goes to live with a wealthy St John's family, where she is employed as a tutor. Her employer, Mrs Kirke, is world-weary, 'saturated with disillusion,' involved in a sham and hopeless marriage. She tells Mageila that there 'should be a way to abolish privilege in case it enervates a generation.'[38] Her husband is a drunk and drug addict, decayed into premature senility by his filthy habits. The whole upper caste of society of which the Kirke family forms a part is perceived as decadent, and the outport girl Mageila brings into it freshness and energy. However, it is not just the élite of St John's that has lost its appeal. The attractions of London and Europe are also growing faint. News of Hitler intrudes even into the small communities of Newfoundland. The shadow of war is falling over the world.

A sense of foreboding about what was taking place in Europe was no doubt partly responsible for leading Margaret Duley, in *Highway to Valour*, to take a fresh look at the country to which she belonged. In doing so, she became the first local writer of significance to see that the country could inspire a national literature. As an essay she wrote in 1956 makes clear, she tried to do for Newfoundland, on a modest scale and not in any organized, political way, what W.B. Yeats had done for Ireland – claim for it a status as an imaginative resource for writers, a place worth looking at for itself, with a presence, a power unlike that of all other countries.[39] The cool reception which her novels received in Newfoundland showed that the country was not ready to respond to her challenge.[40] Having gone through hard times, the people were concerned with economic rather than cultural matters. The tradition of local writing and scholarship which had flourished in the period

1890–1915 had withered, and Duley was left in the 1930s with few intellectual peers to encourage her work.

A university college had, indeed, been founded in St John's in 1925, but it set about imitating the model of an English public school and was almost totally indifferent to Newfoundland studies. Newfoundland history, for example, was not taught at the institution until the academic year 1943–4, when a course was offered by the Scottish-born scholar, A.M. Fraser. The first president of the college was an English schoolmaster, J.L. Paton. On the eve of the loss of Responsible Government in 1934, Paton, then resident in England, gave a public lecture on Newfoundland. Newfoundlanders, he said, 'strike me always as big children, moved by fairy tales and often superstitious, ... and led by the nose by designing men.' They are, however, he continued, 'law-abiding and deeply God-fearing.' Paton heartily approved of the coming of the Commission Government, and asked British authorities to get to 'know' the Newfoundlander, 'the big, simple-minded, brave, big-hearted fellow who lives so close to nature and sees something more in water than two parts of hydrogen and one of oxygen.'[41] Paton's views were similar to those of Lord Amulree, whose royal commission report to British authorities in 1933 recommended the suspension of self-government. While the Newfoundland people 'lose no opportunity of demonstrating their loyalty and devotion to the Throne and to the Empire,' Amulree wrote, they exhibit a 'child-like simplicity' and the 'years of adversity have sapped physical stamina and moral courage.' Still, the commissioner had 'no doubt that the people of Newfoundland are potentially fine material.'[42] Paton's and Amulree's opinions show little improvement over those of the old governor Thomas Cochrane, who in 1831 described Newfoundlanders as 'merely children of a larger growth.'[43]

'I am a lonely American in this dismal little British colony,' Rockwell Kent wrote from Newfoundland in 1915; adding, 'The thought of the land is stupefied by dogma – the dogma of British virtue, British heroism, sea power, loyalty, and all that pile of trash that seems to be a part of the pretension of empire.'[44] In the twenty years that followed Newfoundland moved slowly towards material progress, but in 1933 she remained under the yoke of British influence. Margaret Duley, as her work indicates, broke away from this yoke to discover and proclaim the uniqueness of her people. But the people themselves were slow to change. Duley's novels appeared in print in the period following the country's surrender of sovereignty, a time unfavourable to nationalist self-assertion. The thinking of men like J.L. Paton had won the day. The achievement of one of Newfoundland's finest writers went unrecognized, and she died in obscurity in 1968.

8   Visions and revisions

SOME WRITERS IN THE NEW
NEWFOUNDLAND

THE WAR AND ITS AFTERMATH, 1939–49

By 1941 Newfoundland had spent seven years under the rule of a Commission appointed by Great Britain and responsible to the Dominions Office in London. The period of seven years, one journalist in St John's noted drily, 'has been sufficiently long to give this new experiment in administration a thorough test.' In his opinion, which echoed 'the general view in local circles,' the results of the Commission's activities had 'not justified the change' from Responsible Government.[1] In fact, we can now see that the Commission really achieved more than might have been expected from cautious British civil servants sent out to look after a fractious and backward colony. They were not just a custodial government. They introduced bureaucratic efficiencies, tried to eliminate political patronage, and extended the minimal public services offered by previous governments. In such areas as public health, labour relations, education, and co-operatives, they made significant and imaginative improvements in the country. But despite interesting agricultural experiments and efforts to improve the organization of the fisheries, they did little initially to improve the economy or eliminate poverty in the outports. In the winter of 1938 a staggering total of 85,000 out of a population of 290,000 were living on government relief at the rate of six cents per day[2] – a dole rate that humiliated an impoverished people and stayed in their memories years afterwards when monied ignorance was trying to convince them not to enter the Canadian confederation. Yet in spite of the poverty of the years 1938–40, Newfoundland was on the eve of a period of great prosperity, the result of the country's strategic position in the North Atlantic. What the Commission could not accomplish was brought about by war and the accident of geography.

Following the collapse on the Western Front in the spring of 1940, the importance of Newfoundland's position quickly became apparent to North American governments. Canadian troops made their appearance on the island in June. But it was not until the following year that Newfoundlanders began to realize the important role they were to play in the war. On 25 January 1941, a few months after Churchill agreed to give America ninety-nine-year leases on territory in Newfoundland on which to build military bases, us marines landed in Argentia in Placentia Bay, the chosen site of a huge naval base. It was the first movement of American troops overseas in the Second World War. More spectacularly, on 29 January the American transport ship *Edmund B. Alexander* arrived in St John's and docked on the south side of the harbour. She was 668 feet long – the largest ship ever to have passed through the Narrows – and she carried, in addition to her crew of two hundred, one thousand regular troops of the us Army and two thousand tons of construction material for the proposed new base near the village of Quidi Vidi on the outskirts of the city.[3] A school holiday was declared to let children view the massive ship, and hundreds of citizens flocked to the waterfront. The arrival of the *Alexander* and her human cargo in what had been, prior to 1941, a sleepy little seaport, was the prologue to a new age. To illustrate the impact of the war on Newfoundland, it may be useful to cite a few statistics. In 1936 a committee charged with drawing up a 'Defence Scheme' for Newfoundland discovered that there was just one aircraft on the island, a two-passenger plane owned by the government; but between 1940 and 1945, almost five thousand planes passed through Gander and Goose Bay on their way overseas, making Newfoundland an important link in a 'new age of mass Atlantic flying.'[4] In 1936 Newfoundland was described as 'entirely undefended'; seven years later there were six thousand Canadian and ten thousand American servicemen garrisoned on bases across the island and at Goose Bay in Labrador. In addition, there were also now on the island British airmen serving in the Atlantic Ferry Command, the Newfoundland militia, Canadian naval personnel engaged in convoy duty in St John's, and Canadian airmen serving at Torbay, Gander, Goose Bay, and RCAF headquarters in St John's. By 1944 the capital city had been transformed into the 'principal western base and turn-around port for ships flying the white ensign,' with a rough total of about sixty destroyers, frigates, and corvettes operating from her crowded harbour, now 'a hornet's nest' of activity.[5] St John's, Gander, and Goose Bay remained crucial links between North America and Britain throughout the war. Thus Newfoundland was pulled out of obscurity into unexpected international prominence. Other statistics show the opportunities now available to ordinary Newfoundlanders looking for work. The outports sent a flood of job hunters to the bases as soon as construction started. Shortly after work began at Argentia, for example, an observer noted that 'train after train brings gangs of men, unregistered for work, and trusting to obtain employment.'[6] At the peak of the war effort in Newfoundland, some twenty thousand men were working on construction projects. Thousands of others were emigrating to the United States and Canada, where jobs were plentiful. The Canadian Department of Labour actively recruited workers on the island, and between June 1943 and August 1944 approximately 4500 Newfoundlanders moved to Canada and the United States to take jobs. The available work was mostly menial labour, 'pick and shovel'[7] jobs in mines and on farms, and work as stevedores on the docks in Halifax. But there was ready money in it, whereas the fishery was associated with dependence and poverty. For the first time, a salaried mode of life was made available to great numbers of men who had known only the vagaries of the seasonal pattern of life in the outports.

Statistics alone, however, do not tell the full story of the effect of the war on Newfoundland. The war made visible, and to some extent accessible, the North American way of life, with all its extravagance, speed, confidence, and vulgarity. Almost overnight, American know-how and technology built bases that duplicated services available in the big cities. American and Canadian radio blasted over the airwaves, and American cars, movies, games, and accents were everywhere. Famous visitors descended on St John's almost, it seemed, every week. U-boats prowled outside St John's harbour and in Conception Bay, bringing the country into the thick of the war. In the fall of 1942 two submarine attacks were made on ore carriers at Bell Island, and a ferry, the S.S. *Caribou*, was sunk in the Gulf of St Lawrence. The blackout and rationing also contributed a note of urgency. Wartime excess pervaded the atmosphere. 'There would appear to be something in the atmosphere of war,' the sober *Evening Telegram* commented, 'that is conducive to a stronger desire for pleasure.'[8] Margaret Duley summed up the wartime mood of St John's in this way:

East, west, north and south there were men, as well as a whole floating population on the harbour. It was both Bedlam and Babel, with the unfortunate civilian lost between uniformed men. The streets thundered and broke down under the weight of army-vehicles. Mechanical equipment made loud snorting noises. It was exciting, but wild and disorganized, with the strangers carrying all before them. When the blackout fell, people were unhappily aware that every law was being broken. Quiet householders began to find soldiers and sailors everywhere; sitting on their doorsteps, dating in their gardens, and maybe jacknifing in their doorways as they took a little nap.

St. John's had become a Mecca for women. The older girls persuaded their parents it was time to leave school. The maids gave notice because they could make better money elsewhere, and stay out later at night. Every girl had a 'fellah,' even those who had never had a date in their lives. Some thought that the sentry-box was a peaceful place for a date when the rest of the town was so crowded.

Parents felt the loosening of all authority and the lowering of every moral standard. Every girl felt that her boy might die; therefore she aimed to please. The rapidly changing dates became the same dream, only with a different face, and perhaps from another wartime service. There were many Lili Marlenes, under the lamp-posts, and by the barracks-gates.[9]

And so the tempo of life in the capital quickened. In the outports, the traditional, communal way of life, already undermined in the hungry 1920s and 1930s, kept crumbling as more and more men left the fishery. Newfoundland would not quickly forget this taste of the good life.

Throughout the war years Newfoundland's unrepresentative and temporary Commission Government proved to be singularly ill-equipped to protect the country's long-term interests in the tough haggling that went on among the great powers. The near colonial status of Newfoundland was now a decided advantage to Britain, which could make important concessions to the United States and Canada without engaging in prolonged discussions with the puppet government in St John's. Any participation by Newfoundland in significant wartime decisions was more formal than real, and it was recognized that quite apart from its anomalous constitutional position, the Commission Government was understaffed and unaccustomed to conducting negotiations speedily. Its chief interest in any case seems to have been in avoiding unpleasant publicity at home rather than in the substance of agreements and arrangements among the Allies. Among the most diffident of the letters from the Newfoundland government during the period was one written by Sir Wilfred Woods, commissioner for public utilities, asking Canadian authorities for a 'complete statement of the places in Newfoundland ... in which bases had been established by the Canadian Government.'[10] With leadership of this quality, it was not surprising that by the end of the war the United States and Canada had been granted large territorial concessions in Newfoundland. In 1933 Newfoundland was an independent country; in 1945 one could be forgiven for thinking her little more than a military outpost of North America.

If there was any respect shown by other powers during the war years for Newfoundland's tarnished nationhood, it was shown by Canada, which was careful not to appear anxious 'to manoeuvre Newfoundland into federation.'[11] The appointment of a Canadian high commissioner to Newfoundland in 1941, for example, would appear to be an acknowledgment of her autonomy, and there seems to be more than token recognition of Newfoundland's equality as a nation in Canadian official documents. Nevertheless, throughout the war Newfoundland was being slowly drawn into Canada's orbit, and in Ottawa a careful eye was kept on the extent of American interest in the country. Canadian wartime leaders from Mackenzie King down suspected that confederation was a distinct possibility, but many factors including the bad impression created by Canadian soldiers stationed on the island did not make the option of joining Canada immediately attractive to many people. The governor, Humphrey Walwyn, reported on public sentiment about confederation in this note in 1943: 'Little or no interest is taken on the question of confederation, and it is hardly discussed at all. If anything, they are so dazzled by American dollars, hygiene and efficiency that many of the public rather play up to America in preference to Canada. However they universally want to be on their own with a comfortable grant-in-aid, and little responsibility.'[12]

Behind the scenes, however, Newfoundland was being steered towards the 'enlarged vision'[13] of becoming a province of Canada. By the end of the war a majority of the Commissioners favoured confederation, and imperial Britain, as the historian Peter Neary has stated, 'was about to turn to the long and painful task of calling her proconsuls home.' The man who provided the energy to push Newfoundland in the direction which Britain wanted, and which, on reflection, a majority of Newfoundlanders wated too, was J.R. Smallwood. In his unrelenting oratory during the years 1946–8 he kept reminding the people of the vision of prosperity they had seen during the war years. The choice he presented was simple: to choose Canada, or to 'turn our back upon the North American continent beside which God placed us, and resign ourselves to the meaner outlook and shabbier standards of Europe, 2000 miles across the ocean.'[14] In 1948, with the memory of the

1930s and the post-war slump fresh in their minds, the people chose Canada.

The economic and social changes which the war brought to Newfoundland were reflected in the island's literary life, which showed signs of awakening after the torpor of the 1930s. In fact, there was in the period 1942–8 the same kind of quickened intellectual activity that characterized the first decade of the century, and the cause of this renewal was the same as in the earlier period: nationalism. The relinquishing of self-government in 1934 was a source of shame to many patriots, and now that it was obvious that a decision was imminent about the ultimate fate of the country, there was an outburst of writing full of pride and anxiety. Newfoundland had a tradition of minor poetry since before the turn of the century, but there was a new stirring even among established bards during the war years. Among the poets now turning out regionalist work inspired by landscape and history, the ablest were Gregory Power and Michael Harrington, but Bertille Tobin, R.J. Connolly, Ike Newell, and others wrote verses that were not unpleasing. [15] But the real signs of a literary reawakening were the new magazines, which gave the outraged patriots an outlet and provided a forum for discussions of the island's future. The most stridently nationalistic of these journals was the *Courier*, a monthly which began in 1941 and survived for more than five years, continuing briefly after 1946 under a new title, *Newfoundland Profile*. It was founded and edited by Herbert Cranford, a musician and writer who was born in St John's in 1916, and it featured the writing of Cyril Knight and John D. Devine, the latter a fierce and skilful advocate of a return to self-government. For mesmerizing rhetoric, Devine had few equals in Newfoundland. Here is one of his attacks on 'the supine thinking of the defeatists' who opposed the policy of self-government:

I suppose there will always be the modern descendants of the money-changers to whom everything under heaven, including patriotism, is just a question of 'how much is it worth?' who see no difference between a country and a cargo of fish if the price is right. But this mentality must not be allowed to lead us. Newfoundland is no chattel to be mortgaged, swapped or lease-loaned away. It is something entirely different; it is a spiritual force symbolic of the ties of blood and soil which call to the hearts of men even across the world; it is the free winds across our forests, and the thunder of surf on craggy headlands; it is the keen wit and come-all-ye's of the outport chimney corner; it is the tubby sealer challenging the grinding ice-floes; it is Jackman on the Labrador, and

Ricketts, v.c. ... It is the khaki line at Beaumont Hamel and the trail of the Caribou. ... It is the defense of Carbonear Island – and the Forts of Ferryland. ... It is the crash of tall timber, and fishing boats on lonely waters. It is the spires of little churches on village hilltops, and the voices of children singing 'God Guard Thee Newfoundland.'[16]

As this heady material was being loosed upon the people of St John's, the old *Newfoundland Quarterly* marched sedately onward, not altogether impervious, however, to the outburst of local patriotism.[17] In January 1945 another new magazine appeared entitled *Atlantic Guardian, a Magazine of Newfoundland.* Published originally in Montreal, the *Atlantic Guardian* was founded by 'three young Newfoundlanders who have left Newfoundland in body but not in spirit.' These were journalist Brian Cahill, a native of St John's who nevertheless claimed Placentia as 'my home town by heredity as well as by somewhat intermittent residence;' and Ewart Young and Arthur Scammell, the first another journalist, the second a teacher, both natives of Notre Dame Bay. In 1945 all three were residing in Montreal. The background of these three relocated men is important, for it is the source of the dominant mood in their magazine: the mood of indulgent, uncritical nationalism, born of a sense of exile from an embattled homeland. The little monthly advertised itself as 'worth having – worth keeping,' and set out to make Newfoundland 'better known at home and abroad,' deliberately staying out of local political discussions. In opposition to certain Canadian journalists who pointed to the 'gaudy poverty' in Newfoundland and claimed that the island was 'a slum and a hopeless slum,' the *Atlantic Guardian* maintained gallantly that it was 'something more than a slum and that the future for the country is anything but as black as it has been painted.'[18] This moderate, earnest tone was typical of its pages. It comprised feature articles on small Newfoundland communities, biographies of local notables and Newfoundlanders who had succeeded abroad, reflections on the island's future, songs, photographs of Newfoundland scenes, memories, stories, jottings – an inviting potpourri, not very taxing to the intellect, lively, and topical. The mixture proved popular, and the *Guardian* endured for over a decade.

In November 1945 the first issue of *Protocol* was published in St John's. It was founded by two brothers, Charles and Harold Horwood, and it appeared in six more issues during the next four years. This was the avant-garde journal of the day, distinguished from other magazines by the awareness shown in it of the larger literary and intellectual world beyond Newfoundland. As Harold Horwood explained in an essay written in 1949, writers in *Protocol* 'search deep within the human heart, always through the mind of a single character, stir the emotions, and find their answers within the soul of man, sometimes through long, tortuous, stream-of-consciousness techniques.'[19] One notes the grandiose purpose, a cut above the parochial outlook of other local authors. The editors of *Protocol* set out, with juvenile derring-do, to provide a 'soul' for the emerging nationalist spirit in Newfoundland. 'In the forefront of every national movement,' they said, 'there must be an artistic movement.' However, it was not their intention to 'specialize in platitudes for the illiterate,' and they would choose subject matter far removed from 'the fishbawns of Famish Gut' and oppose those 'who venerate the already-created culture and civilization.'[20] *Protocol*'s literary offerings by such writers as 'John Avalon' (Irving Fogwill) and 'William Noble' (Harold Horwood) tended to be experimental and provocative.

Hot on the heels of *Protocol* came four new magazines, all started in 1946, and all devoted to regional interests. These were *Newfoundland Companion*, *The Newfoundland Writer*, *Newfoundland Story*, and *The Islander*. Of these ephemeral journals, the most promising was *The Islander*, edited by Rupert Jackson, which lasted for two issues. 'Newfoundland's hope lies in the future,' Jackson stated in outlining the purpose of his magazine, 'and we should set ourselves a goal, and march towards it with a steadfast step. That is the aim of this magazine – to look forward to the future, and to use the past and present as a springboard to greater achievements.'[21] Among the items included in *The Islander* were an important early story by Ted Russell and a critical column by Grace Butt, a playwright who in 1937 had founded the theatrical group known as the St John's Players.

These fugitive publications reflected the bewilderment and hope of an old nation on the brink of a new life. They also introduced Newfoundland to four of the five most significant native writers of the post-war period.

THE OUTPORT AS IDYLL:
ARTHUR SCAMMELL AND RON POLLETT

The turmoil of the war and the accelerated rate of change which it provoked in Newfoundland society led to a literary examination of the traditional life of the country by natives of the Newfoundland outports. In part, this was a defence against the mockery and abuse directed at Newfoundlanders by foreign military personnel stationed on the island – it was during the war that soldiers began using the derisive term 'Newfies' to describe the people[22] – and a response to derogatory accounts of Newfoundland by visiting jornalists.[23] But perhaps the main reason for the appearance of a literature of nostalgia was the undeniable deterioration in outport life. Even a sympathetic observer like the Englishman Patrick Job could not help but notice the evidence of decay and depression in the outports he visited in 1947. A 'family's social standing,' he noted, 'could be judged by the size of the heap of empty tins beside the house.'[24] Such evident and lamentable change would be especially apparent to natives of the outport who had left their homes permanently in the early decades of the century to get an education and make a living in urban settings, and who had stayed in touch with outharbour developments during the intervening years. It was from two such men that a new kind of sentimental writing would come. Their way of coming to terms with the changes that were taking place in Newfoundland, and with the dislocations they experienced in their own lives by leaving their homes, was to reconstruct the outport way of life they had known, or fancied they had known, in their childhood. They recreated the outport as a pastoral idyll. The principal vehicle for the expression of such sentiment was the *Atlantic Guardian*, and the writer who set the tone for the *Guardian* was Arthur Scammell.

Scammell was born at Change Islands in 1913 and during his boyhood wrote the song for which he is best known, 'The Squid-Jiggin' Ground.' Following his education at home and at Memorial College in St John's, he taught school at a number of small communities: Harbour Deep, Harbour Buffet, Woody Point, Belleoram, and Pinchard's Island. In 1939 he left Newfoundland to attend McGill University, and he decided to stay in Montreal to continue his teaching career. Although he returned to his home for numerous summer visits, he lived outside Newfoundland for the next thirty-one years, coming back for good in 1970. He published short volumes of verse in 1940 and 1945, but his best work was in the *Guardian*. Scammell is an important figure in Newfoundland letters. He was not, of course, the first outharbourman to write books. Men like Pratt, Prowse, and Smallwood – all born in outports – had preceded him, but none of these had been fully immersed in the traditional culture, and they were, in essence, urban men. So too Job Barbour's *Forty-eight Days Adrift* (1932) and Nicholas Smith's *Fifty-two Years at the Labrador Fishery* (1936) were works by outport men that predated Scammell's efforts. But these were totally unself-conscious works, more documentaries than literature, limited to bald, factual narration, and expressing cultural attitudes only by inference, like the Newfoundland ballads. These books are perfect in their way, and impress by their homeliness, simplicity, and lack of literary sophistication; but they are wholly within the culture, not about the culture. There are still other examples of outporters who wrote books before Scammell. But he was the first significant writer with deep roots in the traditional outport way of life to reflect on that way of life and try to recreate it in imaginative literature. The essay which expressed the principal theme of his writing appeared in the *Atlantic Guardian* in 1945. It was called 'Outport Heritage':

... hundreds of little Newfoundland communities, far removed from the rush and bustle of city life, are rich in true social and spiritual values. I have read some stories about Newfoundland outport life, written by visitors from other countries, and most of them played up the pathos of the hard, unrelenting struggle for existence. It made the reader feel as if he should do something for these poor, benighted people. Knowing something of the social picture both in Canada and the United States, I can assure these writers that their well-meaning sympathy could be far better spent on their own countries.

Newfoundlanders in their little communities have built up something worthwhile, something not measured by the size of the churches or the material beauty of the homes. Those of us who are fortunate enough to be able to claim one of these little communities as our birthplace, look back with humble gratitude to what we owe them. Daily lessons in co-operation and kindliness, taught by rude fishermen who wouldn't know a vitamin if they met one, but who did know that 'man does not live by bread alone.' Studies in industry and hard work, taught by example more powerfully than by precept. A delightful sense of humour, real humour of character and situation, that bubbled in the darkest days. Like the old fellow who told me when I asked him how his legs were: 'Not very good b'y. But I s'pose I shouldn't complain. I'm eighty years old and this is the same pair I started life with.' ...

And we had a lot of fun. Maybe we didn't get our quota of orange juice. Perhaps our food was a bit short sometimes on calcium or phosphorus. We were so busy catching tomcods, 'copying' pans in the Spring, doing chores, sailing boats, etc., that we didn't have time to chase all our vitamins. No doubt we'll suffer for it some day. But we learnt many important lessons of life from the humble folk around us, that all the inventions and discoveries of modern civilization cannot lessen or cheapen.

If you have ever lived in a Newfoundland Outport, be proud of it – and grateful. If you were born in one, be prouder still. For myself, when summer holidays come I want to spend them in one of these little villages by the sea – my home, where I can be rejuvenated, physically, mentally, and spiritually.

Above the deep boom of the sea you can hear the melody of human hearts – and the music is sweet.[25]

Here we have the essential ingredients of Scammell's viewpoint: stubborn pride, manly resentment of outsiders' misguided criticisms, and a bypassing of the cruelties of outharbour life. And above all, a sense of loss, a sense of 'something worthwhile,' 'something not measured,' which the outport possessed and the big city did not. This is the old outport seen from a distance of time and space, through the distorting prism of middle age, with the pain filtered out. It is the product of expatriate sentimentality.

There is an artlessness in Scammell's writing that is appealing, and it hardly needs saying that there is in his version of the old outport a great deal of insight. Throughout his stories and songs, which were collected in a volume called *My Newfoundland* (1966), one can see all that was good in the life of the pre-confederation outport. Leaving out the hardship, dependence, poverty, isolation, and peril – leaving the bad out no doubt made the good more conspicuous. But the good was still there, a 'something worthwhile' not easy to define. One notes especially in Scammell the emphasis upon communal life, for there are no heroes in his work, just 'fishermen gathering'[26] and sharing in a whole, integrated, natural existence. There is too an understanding of what the outport, at its best, offered in the way of human satisfaction; for in spite of all its drawbacks, the old outport gave a man the opportunity of mastery over tremendous, non-human forces. Such triumph as the bedlamer boy achieves in Scammell's song 'The Six Horsepower Coaker' is not readily available to those who pass their existence in the dull security of city employment.

Scammell's writing in the *Atlantic Guardian* soon attracted attention and imitation. In July 1946 Ron Pollett published his first sketch in the magazine, a piece significantly entitled 'The Outport Millionaire.' Two months later, Ewart Young reported that he had heard someone say that he would rather read Pollett than Shakespeare.[27] Thereafter, Pollett's writing became one of the leading attractions of the magazine, and it was subsequently reprinted in pamphlets and in a book entitled *The Ocean at my Door* (1956). Pollett was born in New Harbour, Trinity Bay, in 1900. Seeing no future for himself in the fishery, at the age of sixteen he chose one of the few escape routes from the old outport by becoming a school teacher. After three years of teaching, he moved to a better paying job with the pulp and paper company in Grand Falls, and in 1923 proceeded to Montreal, where he learned the trade of linotype operator. Soon afterwards he emigrated to New York, and went to work in the job printing division of the *New York Times* as a typesetter. He settled and raised his family in the Fort Hamilton section of Brooklyn, choosing to be near the harbour so that, as he said afterwards, he could 'smell the salt water.' He began coming back to Newfoundland for summer visits in the early 1930s, and continued them during and after the war, returning for the last time in 1951. From 1946 onwards he was seriously ill. He died in 1955. In Pollett's life we see a pattern that repeated itself in the biographies of thousands of his fellow countrymen, who uprooted themselves from familiar rural settings to puruse, at great cost, economic opportunity in urban North America. Part of Pollett's value as a writer is that he speaks for a mute multitude of emigrant Newfoundlanders.

Many of his autobiographical sketches recreate his boyhood in New Harbour. No 'robust boy,' he wrote, selecting his words carefully, 'could ever have chosen a more interesting spot in which to come into the world.' Fully aware that he was breaking new ground in literature, he set out to record 'the comings and goings, the ins and outs, the ups and downs of family life in the outport village, as seen through the eyes of a boy.'[28] As seen by a boy and, we might add, as reconstructed by Pollett's middle-aged memory. If we can trust that memory, his boyhood was a veritable feast of gambol and delight. However, the sweetened versions of the outport that form the bulk of his writing resemble Scammell's, and we have to turn elsewhere to appreciate the unique contribution of Pollett to local literature. His most important pieces are those in which he reflects upon his life in New York, and what makes these distinctive is his unhesitant display of alienated adult consciousness. In New York Pollett knew how far he had removed himself, not just geographically but mentally, from the anchor of his life, his outport home; and he conveyed, sometimes by rueful directness but more often by inference, his sense of bewilderment. His homely efforts at self-assessment leave the reader with a poignant awareness of a simple man stopped on the road between one life and another, uncertain of what lay ahead, but knowing he could not go back. Not that there was melancholy in Pollett. He had, indeed, grounds for melancholy, but he evaded it by vivid and joyous recollection, good humour, and a kind of barely achieved acceptance. His sense of cultural shock is conveyed with great intensity in essays such as 'On Going Home Again,' 'Up in the Big City,' and the minor classic 'Memories of "Didder Hill." ' The concluding paragraphs of 'Up in the Big City' are his most chilling account of what living in New York had done to him:

> Time goes fast in the city. You settle here a youth and before you know it you're out of breath as an old man. You're scooting around all the time shooting with both barrels – you have to be in order to knock down a living – and you can't afford to lie up for a rest. Close, lifelong friendships such as flourish in the village are rare in New York, where a man's neighbour is too often entirely different either in race or interests, and old age can be lonesome because of that. As a plodding worker you live among strangers, and when you stop living you're buried among strangers – and you are soon forgotten as though you had never been born.
>
> As for me, all I'm waiting for is the pension, when I can clew up in New York and go back to the outport and spend the summers fishing again – this time for fun.[29]

Here he edges away from gloom by a vision of pleasant retirement which he elsewhere dismisses as fantasy. Pollett was such an unaffected writer, so full of contradiction and manly honesty, that his 'compositions' (as he called them, using the old name for school exercises) really do have in them more of the uncertainty of a living voice than the artifice of a designing author.

The limitation of Scammell's and Pollett's versions of the old outport is that they remain focused upon the domestic and the anecdotal. Their tendency is to prettify, to reduce the human story which unfolded in Newfoundland over the centuries to the level of whimsical reminiscence. And so a heroism that went beyond mere eccentric survival is not explored. Still, they are authentic voices that deserve a hearing, for in their modest literary productions we see the language and idiom of ordinary people, and hear the accents of a race long inarticulate, now rubbed by change into self-expression.

TED RUSSELL

Ted Russell is sometimes linked with Scammell and Pollett in critical commentary, and in some ways his life and writing resemble theirs. Russell was born in the small Conception Bay community of Coley's Point in 1904, and received his formal education at home, at Bishop Feild College in St John's, and at Memorial College, where he became qualified to be a teacher. He taught school in a number of communities between 1920 and 1935, starting his career in remote Pass Island in Hermitage Bay. Russell's daughter, Elizabeth Miller, has suggested that Pass Island was possibly the model for the outport Russell later made famous in his stories, 'Pigeon Inlet.'[30] Among his painful memories of Responsible Government, Russell later recalled in his published memoirs, were two cuts in the paltry pittance paid as salaries to him and his fellow teachers: a 10 per cent reduction in 1928, and another of 40 per cent in 1932.[31] So far, then, his life was following the pattern set by Pollett and Scammell. But Russell did not leave Newfoundland. Instead, in 1935 he joined the magistracy and spent what he called 'the five hungriest years of the hungry thirties' in Green Bay. Commenting later on the Commission Government's eventual surplus of over forty million dollars, Russell noted that the surplus 'had been distilled from the life-blood of hungry Newfoundlanders living on six cents a day.' He left the magistracy in 1943 to become Director of Co-operatives under the Commission, a job he loved because it took him, as he said, 'to the remotest parts of the island, among the people I knew and liked best.' As Director of Co-operatives, he was continually involved with the problem of making the outports economically viable. He would, he wrote later, spend 'many nights till long after midnight around a stove in a school classroom or a net-loft, discussing with ten or twenty men whether they should use their thrift-club savings to finance some economic venture. If it was to pack a few cases of rabbit, we worked out to the exact cent what price per rabbit they might hope to get as a result.'[32] This scrupulous attention to practical detail and dedication to communal effort reveal much about Russell's mentality.

Although Russell favoured the retention of the Commission Government, he was invited by Smallwood to join his administration, and was provincial minister of natural resources between 1949 and 1951. Profound disagreement with Smallwood's policies led to his resignation from the cabinet in March 1951, and for the next six years Russell made his living principally as an insurance salesman. Drawing upon his considerable previous experience as a radio commentator while Director of Co-operatives, Russell now began broadcasting on the local CBC, speaking as the outport character 'Uncle Mose.' Selling insurance, he commented drily years afterwards, 'left me with many unused faculties which demanded an outlet of some kind. Uncle Mose provided an ideal outlet.' Between 1954 and 1960 he produced around eight hundred of these stories, and two selections from them have been published, *The Chronicles of Uncle Mose* (1975) and *Tales from Pigeon Inlet* (1977). Russell also wrote a number of radio plays, the best known of which is *The Holdin' Ground*, published in 1972. In later years he returned to teaching and gave up the 'hobby' of writing 'because the faculties I needed for writing were pretty well used up in the classroom'[33] He died in 1977.

Russell's life, then, was marked by prolonged and intense involvement with rural Newfoundland, and by a desire to renovate it. He is thus to be distinguished from Scammell and Pollett, who in most of their sketches were preoccupied with the past. Russell's attention was centred on the living outport. The definitive statement of his attitude to outport life is his little known story 'The Builder,' printed in *The Islander* in 1946. The story pictures three stages in the development of a community called 'Port Carson,' and in each of these stages we see Russell's idea of the outport as it used to be, as it might become in the new age of 'prosperity,' and as it ought to be, given the opportunities now at hand. First, the old Port Carson, inaccessible except by an old slide-path from the main road that led 'through boulders, and bog, and rotted logs':

At the far end of the marsh and close by the east side of the harbour's entrance were the twenty dilapidated buildings that housed the hundred-odd villagers. These, with a weather-beaten school chapel and a few ramshackle fishing stages made up the settlement. You saw no gardens, no sheep, cattle nor live stock of any description; but on a calm evening you heard the mournful howling of the hungry dogs that lay around the doors or scavenged the beach at low tide. ... The very sight of the place ... depressed you ...

Next we see Port Carson after ten years of 'prosperity':

Milligan's new fish plant stood where old Joe Kelland's stage had once been. A hundred new families had moved in from Squid Rocks, Thompson's Beach, Curlew Point and the other tiny settlements along the shore. Shacks had been built for them – temporary, of course, until such time as proper dwellings could be erected. But somehow that time hadn't come and shack life was assuming an air of permanency. Meanwhile fish were abundant and prices good. The people had more money than they had ever seen before. The slide track from the highroad was as rough as ever, but now the coastal boat called there weekly and from her upper deck you could get a close-up of Port Carson and its inhabitants. The newspapers always spoke of it as 'a fast-growing and enterprising centre of the fresh fish industry.' A Thing had come to Port

Carson – a thing that unthinking people called Prosperity. But you were appalled at the pinched faces of the children, the stench of the place and the numerous evidences of every deficiency disease known to mankind. Murden's beer-parlour was doing a thriving business and from it you could sometimes hear the raucous blare of the juke box.

And then we see the Port Carson that Russell hoped would be a model for rural Newfoundland in the future:

You reach it easily from the highroad. The old slide-track has long since grown over but there's a good secondary road into which you can turn your car with confidence. The people of Port Carson keep this road in good shape. They welcome you and wish to make your coming easy. The road takes you near Butler's Pond but you see that the pond is fenced and a giant notice-board bears the words, 'PUBLIC WATER SUPPLY.' You stare in amazement as the harbour's entrance comes into view over the ridge. Gone are the old houses of thirty years ago and the shacks of a decade later. Gone are the stages, the fish-plant and the chapel, and gone all trace of Murden's beer-dive. Only two houses remain – the lighthouse, and the dwelling of old Ben Kelland.

A few yards further and you notice that the intervening marsh has disappeared and in its place are a hundred acres of pasture where cattle and sheep are peacefully grazing. But you see no other sign of human habitation until you have passed the foot of Butler's Pond. Then you look down the slope towards the basin and you see Port Carson as it is today. You feel glad you came. You feel the urge to spend a few days here and get to know the place. You want to go aboard those fishing boats that ride so proudly at their moorings, to be shown through the fish-plant which processes every local variety of edible fish; to walk their main street which parallels the waterfront, and the branch roads that run at right angles to it. You want to admire their well-kept cottages, their gardens, their water and sewerage system, their street lights, their playground, school, church and the hall where their Council meets each Monday evening. Above all, you want to get to know these people and learn the epic story of their twenty years of progress.

With these descriptions as background, Russell went on to explain how the improvement had come about. It had happened through the initiative of a fisherman named Jim Pennell, who inspired his fellow citizens to join together, pool their resources, and build a new town. The resulting community was built only when every inhabitant of Port Carson had 'played a part.'[34]

Judged as literature, Russell's story does not amount to much more than a co-operative tract. Yet it contains the germ of all his later work. The 'Uncle Mose' stories were not written solely to amuse the CBC audience, although Russell did indeed later describe them as 'amusing stories of outport life' and, like Scammell and Pollett, deliberately did not write about the harsher aspects of outport existence. 'I could tell an equal number [of stories] far less amusing,' Russell wrote in 1966, remembering his grim experiences in Green Bay, 'but they are better left untold.'[35] But the ones he did tell nevertheless had the serious purpose of reminding outport people of the value of their way of life, and of warning them not to throw what they had overboard in favour of some vulgar idea of progress. They were written, not in opposition to the new ideas and new technology of the post-confederation period, but rather to show people how to make the best use of these manifestations of change. He tried to answer the 'big' question asked in his second 'Uncle Mose' story: 'What's wrong with a place like Pigeon Inlet if people can't make a decent living here?'[36] Russell's answers were by no means revolutionary, or even startling. He urged individual initiative and self-respect rather than dependence on government; he emphasized education, community spirit, hard work, persistence, and faith. Faith in the outport as a place that could provide the amenities and opportunities of advancing civilization. Russell was not enamoured of the old. He wanted a dynamic and useful outport. In his stories there is no huffing and puffing about the uniqueness of the outport, the unsung heroism of the fishermen, or the sanctity of old traditions. Pigeon Inlet, he said, 'is much about the same as ... any small place anywhere on the Mainland'; and as for the vaunted bravery of Newfoundlanders, 'a lot of this talk about some people bein' brave and others bein' cowardly is a pack of nonsense.'[37] Russell's heroes are common men and women, like Jim Pennell in 'The Builder,' who 'wasn't impressive.' Yet within such durable men, Russell believed, was the stuff needed to ensure that the outport could become a sufficient and comfortable home. They had inside them a spirit 'that could never be beaten.'[38]

The imaginative side of Russell's work was the creation of the character of Uncle Mose and the various other fictitious residents of Pigeon Inlet. All Russell's people have the look of observed reality. They cling to no foolish, romantic notions about the past, nor do they moan and groan about the perils of innovation. They are not coarse, loud, drunken, primitive, bigotted, hostile, or elemental. They simply carry on the even tenor of their ways, driving the system of life onwards from year to year, living quietly, hoping for improvements, yet knowing such improvements will occur slowly. They are of the earth, earthy. And Uncle Mose himself, for the first time in literature, gave outport Newfoundland a living voice, a voice with a true ring, gentle and whimsical, but shrewd, accepting but knowing. This was Russell's humble achievement. He intruded into the strident 'develop or perish' rhetoric of the 1950s with his calm, reassuring reminder that to vulgarize was not to prosper, and that whatever technocrats and politicians were trying to do with the surface of Newfoundland life, they should not violate 'the good holdin' ground below.'[39]

HAROLD HORWOOD

When *Protocol* was begun in 1945 Harold Horwood was twenty-two years of age and already a promising writer. Horwood claims descent from an old Carbonear family of master mariners, but he was born and reared in St John's and educated in a city school, Prince of Wales College. One of his essays expresses his pride in being a 'St. John'sman.'[40] His father, Andrew Horwood, is himself a writer of considerable reputation in Newfoundland. Harold Horwood did not attend university, choosing instead to educate himself further through private study. Despite his desire, expressed in *Protocol*, to steer clear of local politics, and despite his apparent early contempt for J.R. Smallwood,[41] Horwood, like other young intellectuals of the day, was drawn into the fight for confederation, and became in 1949 the first member representing Labrador to sit in the House of Assembly. He did not, however, contest the election in 1951. The reasons for this reluctance to continue in the legislature of the new province are not clear. Although Horwood would hint differently some years later,[42] the reason for his quick exit from politics does not appear to have been hostility to Smallwood or his policies. Possibly he had grown tired of the day-to-day drudgery of political life in Newfoundland and wished to resume his literary career. In 1952 he complained about the flood of mail from constituents which descended daily upon MHAS. 'The politician's nightmare,' he wrote, 'is the letter beginning in some such direct manner as "Dear Sir, I want a horse."' [43] In any event, Horwood's life from 1951 onwards was almost exclusively a literary one. On 1 April 1952 he began a daily column entitled 'Political Notebook' in the St John's *Evening Telegram* under the pseudonym 'vox.' Four months later, the pseudonym was dropped, and the column was continued, with occasional brief interruptions, under Horwood's own name until 23 June 1958. Thus we have a permanent record of Horwood's political and other opinions during the period in which Smallwood was 'dragging Newfoundland kicking and screaming into the twentieth century.'[44] It is a highly revealing series of columns, providing a key to the attitudes displayed in Horwood's later important works of fiction.

Once he joined forces with Canada, Smallwood plunged ahead with his scheme to industrialize Newfoundland, and Horwood, in his early columns in the *Telegram*, was inclined to applaud the Premier's efforts. We find him praising 'the magic touch of Smallwood salesmanship' and supplying information about imminent industrial projects from sources within the cabinet. '$24,000,000 have been spent or committed on new industries, and 11 factories are being built,' he noted approvingly in June 1952. He also told the public that Smallwood's prediction that a chemical industry would be established 'based on fresh air' was not 'as crazy as it sounds.' In July, Horwood offered his support for a proposal to build a 'cat farm' on the island, and told the public to 'look out for the announcement soon of another big industry for Newfoundland.' 'We agree with economic development,' he stated emphatically in September, 'we have no quarrel with Premier Smallwood's economic development policy.' And so it went, Horwood obviously being caught up with the prevailing orthodoxy of the day, and believing that this was the era of 'Newfoundland's great awakening.' His earliest columns on Labrador show little concern over the effects of new developments upon native peoples. 'The shift toward a white culture is something in which the government need take no hand,' he wrote.[45] In addition, we see examples of an astonishing political naïveté in some of the early columns, as when he protested against the 'entirely unworthy innuendo' behind the suggestion that the federal government was distributing Senate seats to gain political advantage. 'Surely,' he wrote, 'no one is base enough to believe that anything of that kind goes on in Canada.' As late as 1955 Horwood was telling his readers 'how fundamentally decent most men in public life really are.'[46] His disenchantment with Smallwood and his policies was gradual, and to some extent it was an understandable response to the Premier's attacks on the *Telegram* for venturing an occasional mild criticism of his government. Smallwood blasted the *Telegram* on 1 May 1952, and his personal antagonism towards the paper continued throughout his premiership. But in 1954 Horwood was still assuring Smallwood of his support. We 'would like once again to assure the Premier,' he wrote, 'that there is no malice toward him or his government from this quarter.' 'Matter of fact,' he added, 'we like Joey a lot. ... He's a great little guy.' In 1955, despite a series of attacks on

Smallwood's new industries in February, the attempt to maintain some degree of harmony and objectivity continued, and Horwood explained somewhat uneasily on 30 May that his column would lose its 'effectiveness' if it were to become 'merely a voice of opposition.' But on 3 April 1956 he wrote a piece on 'the great Tory party of Canada,' and two days later announced that 'if there is any question that I resigned as a member of the Smallwood Party, I hereby do so now.' Thereafter he became a partisan. His criticism of Smallwood tended to be outspoken and scathing, and we hear that the financial affairs of the province are in a 'mess,' that the government is tainted by 'scandal,' and that Horwood himself is fed up with 'tiresome accounts of industries that flopped and dreams that never materialized.' By 1958 Horwood had become, in columnist Ed Finn's view, Smallwood's 'most influential and articulate opponent,' and Finn suggested in public that Horwood 'take over the reins' of the opposition Progressive Conservative party, and go on to be 'the next premier of Newfoundland.'[47]

Contempt for Smallwood implied contempt for those who kept electing him to office. As we have seen, Horwood in *Protocol* appeared to have no love for the 'Famish Guts' of Newfoundland. Quite early in 'Political Notebook,' he wrote this deeply revealing piece upon what was being referred to as 'Newfoundland culture':

Among Newfoundland's favourite myths is the belief that we have in this Province a very distinctive and flavourful culture which should be preserved at all costs. Even the Government subscribes to the belief, offering annual prizes for the encouragement of arts and letters.

We have no quarrel with the prizes, provided it is realized that we are trying to interest people in laying the foundations for a cultural tradition rather than building upon a foundation which already exists. The truth is that Newfoundland has no literature, no music, no art, little philosophy and less science. The only culture which we have is the culture of the fish flake, though even that isn't our own, having come with our peasant ancestors from England and the Channel Islands.

People who rhapsodize about Newfoundland culture are usually orating for a purpose. It is a type of oratory closely associated with pine clad hills. True, we have some thousands of folk songs, but 99 and 44/100 percent of them are slightly garbled versions of traditional English and Irish tunes. Ask the rhapsodists to come down to earth and they're stumped. Usually they can get no further than 'We'll Rant and We'll Roar' and 'The Star of Logy Bay.' The former is a crude parody, both as to words and music, of a traditional English sea chaunty. The latter is an unaltered Irish air which has reappeared, slightly changed in 'Molly Bawn.'

Perhaps four hundred years of drudgery and barter have not been conducive to the flight of the imagination. There is something incurably prosaic about trading in fish, and the stages and stores, while they may look quaint and picturesque to the tourist gazing across a fishing harbour, take on quite a different aspect to those who remember nights spent in them by the light of a kerosene oil lamp, ankle deep in blood and guts. ...

The only Newfoundlanders who ever had a culture of their own were the Indians and Eskimos. That we set out deliberately to destroy. Having exterminated the Beothucks, we proceeded to kill spiritually the Montagnais and the Eskimos. Having turned them into beggars, we forbade them their tribal laws and customs, passed local regulations against their traditional dances, and converted them, wherever possible, into imitation white men. The process is still going on.[48]

In the later years of the column, Horwood's distaste for outharbour life became on occasion even more explicit. After the federal general election in 1958, which saw a massive PC majority across the country, he noted that the continued strength of the Liberal party in Newfoundland was due to Smallwood's efforts and showed that 'he can still appeal to the ignorant, the stupid, the illiterate, and the purely selfish.' A day later, he explained that what had saved the Liberals locally 'was the solid block of captive votes in places such as White Bay, St. Barbe, Trinity North, and the little villages of Notre Dame Bay, where they still think they are voting for Baby Bonus, and are under the impression that Joey is Prime Minister of Canada.'[49] This lingering hatred for what he thought was outport meanness and narrowness was probably a product of his upbringing. In one of his essays he recalled visiting Carbonear as a boy and viewing those who lived along the North Shore – the very people praised by Laurence Coughlan for their 'very bright Genuis' – as 'the Snopeses of Conception Bay.'[50] (The Snopeses are an upstart group of hillbilly ignoramuses in William Faulkner's novels. One critic has described them as 'a species of pure sons of bitches.'[51]) This new frankness about Smallwood's outport supporters was typical of Horwood's fearlessness in the later columns of 'Political Notebook.' We note the reappearance of the young iconoclast and egotist of *Protocol*, expressing itself in, among other things, the posture of being above politics. Politics, he wrote, 'tends to make honest men into miscreants.' In 1958 he stated that to enter the political fray against Smallwood 'would be like stepping into a pig sty to collar a pig.' In answer to Ed Finn's suggestion that he should become premier, Horwood said that 'My ambitions are very much higher than that, and they do not fall in the field of politics. I have never regarded politics as anything more than a sideline interest.'[52] But behind the posturing and excess of these later columns, we can also see serious intellectual development. Especially noteworthy are worries about the effects of industrial pollution upon the environment and a genuine concern over the fate of the province's native peoples.

After relinquishing his column and other editorial duties with the *Telegram* in 1958, Horwood became a free-lance writer, and turned his attention to the study of the natural world and the writing of miscellaneous articles and fiction. Despite initial difficulties ('my income fell to almost zero for a couple of years,' he noted in an interview in 1971),[53] his talent was soon recognized, and he began selling items to national magazines and the CBC. Some of his articles on the province were later collected in a book called *Newfoundland* (1969). But the two major achievements from his first decade as an independent man of letters were a novel, *Tomorrow Will Be Sunday* (1966), and a study of the environment of Newfoundland, *The Foxes of Beachy Cove* (1967). The novel, Horwood's most ambitious and laboured work, was by far the most impressive imaginative recreation of Newfoundland outport life to be attempted since confederation. Why he would undertake to write at all about people for whom he felt such obvious and open lack of sympathy is a question which cannot easily be answered. It was a sign, perhaps, of Horwood's idea of himself as an author of international stature who should be impervious to the effects of his writing upon local sensibilities, rather like Joyce writing about Ireland. Yet Joyce did at least know the part of Ireland he wrote about. Horwood has written in an unpublished comment that 'I did not grow up in a Newfoundland outport, or go to an outport school, or make my living as a fisherman, or, in fact, ever live through any of the experiences outlined in the book except, in a very general sense, the sexual experiences, which were, in fact, developed in a very different context from that given here.' He added that his portrait of the outport, to the extent that it 'is drawn from life at all,' was based on his father's and sister-in-law's memories.[54] Thus his novel violates one of his own stated rules of writing, namely, that 'to really write effectively about anything, you have to be there.'[55] Nevertheless, the book was not only written, but also, one gathers, toiled over with infinite patience and scrupulousness. It went through five revisions in manuscript, and three titles (the earlier ones being 'The Day of the Lord' and 'Habitation of Dragons'), before Horwood was satisfied with his product.

In the earliest draft of the book, written in 1962, Horwood's version of the outport of Caplin Bight was, on the whole, sympathetic, and indeed at times poignant and beautiful.[56] Subsequent revisions, however, rooted the sympathy out, and we presumably are to interpret that earlier feeling of warmth as some kind of literary affectation which the author eventually came to see as sham, and discarded. The novel as published must be taken as representing his true sentiments, arrived at after much cogitation and revision. To judge *Tomorrow Will Be Sunday* as an interpretation of outport life in the 1930s – and we are justified in taking this approach, which might seem to some an unfair one in treating a fictional work, because Horwood himself boasted that his book 'managed to capture the essential nature of Newfoundland outports.'[57] – if we take the book at this level, then it surely is a libel upon outport people. 'Caplin Bight,' the locale of the story, is pictured as one of 'the backwaters of civilization,' where ignorance, intolerance, and fanaticism reign supreme. The ordinary people are a smelly and benighted race, 'almost a lower species' when compared to somebody like Christopher Simms, the son of a local retired magistrate who has been away to 'the magic world of the cities' and received a university education. They are held captive by sexual taboos and fear of novelty, and lead emotionally constricted lives, all the consequence, in Horwood's view, of being 'cooped up in a little harbour with nothing but rocks and Bibles and hymnbooks' to feed their minds. As we might expect, Horwood places little value on the traditional skills and knowledge which outport people developed over the centuries to enable them to cope with a harsh environment, and even less on what he scornfully called Newfoundland 'culture' in his newspaper column. To be educated properly, his young hero, Eli Pallisher, is emphatically told, means throwing off the sexual taboos 'along with all the other lumber that your ignorant parents piled on your young back.' The most powerful of the 'invisible walls' which stand in the way of enlightenment in Caplin Bight is evangelical Christianity, which Horwood excoriates with the ferocity and disdain that one could see bubbling in *Protocol*. The particular sect which held sway in Caplin Bight taught Eli that 'sex was sin' and left him with 'a deep and abiding sense of guilt.' This was another burden he had to throw off in order to be educated. And Eli does indeed manage to skin off what Horwood regards as the ancient slough of outport narrowness and bigotry, and he learns the new code which Horwood is preaching. At the end of the book we see him on the eve of his departure from his outport home, emerging from his symbolic swim in the cold ocean, 'washed clean,' 'primordial and renewed.'[58] He has overcome.

When we ask what exactly it is that Eli has learned, we can see the author of *Tomorrow Will Be Sunday* for what he really is – a romantic idealist, whose novel is probably more a reflection of the *Zeitgeist* of the 1960s than a realistic depiction of an actual outport. Horwood, always attentive to intellectual developments outside Newfoundland, was deeply stirred by the 'youth movement' in North America, and in his young hero we see his hope that a new generation was appearing that would change the world for the better; a generation which sexual liberation, intellecutal curiosity, and education would set free. The author of this book was clearly on his way to joining the 'counter-culture.' The spokesman for his views in *Tomorrow Will Be Sunday* is Christopher Simms, the 'Christ' figure in the book's symbolism, who preaches the new message of redemption in his role as teacher in Caplin Bight. Under his tutelage, Eli's mind expands beyond the limits enforced by outport drudgery and religion to explore the wonders of science and the delights of the natural world. He learns to overcome his emotional restraint, to become responsive, candid, and loving; and he learns that sex is 'something to be enjoyed with a carefree heart, like a picnic, or a swim in the ocean.' With Christopher as guide, Eli is led through the novel from one 'adventure of the mind' to another, through books that seem to Eli's father to be 'full o' heathen lies,'[59] books such as *The Golden Bough* and the Greek dramatists, until he becomes at the end as uplifted as the eagle – a stock romantic image, reminding us again in whose company we are travelling. *Tomorrow Will Be Sunday* is a paean to youth that reminds us of Blake and Twain, or of any thinker who indulged in the naïve belief that one generation would be more enlightened than any other, or who believed that evil in men springs from external tyrannies. *Tomorrow Will Be Sunday*, far from being, as some readers thought, a corrupting book, is a restatement of romantic hopes, so disarmingly innocent and uncritical that one feels tempted to describe Horwood's intellectual history as a journey, not from idealism to cynicism, but from naïveté to more naïveté.

At the novel's end Eli, having taken his baptismal dip in salt water, is fully prepared for his immersion in the larger world beyond Caplin Bight. Precisely what role he is to play in that world is not indicated, since romantics typically shy away from examining the dull compromises and absurdities of adult life. But Horwood does throw out hints about Eli's imminent elevated position. He will become an engineer, perhaps, since he is a mathematical prodigy; or maybe 'a professor or a research worker' in science, a lawyer, or even a politician. Certainly, he does not belong 'in a trap boat' but is destined to 'make a pretty big noise in the world.'⁶⁰ But although Horwood later claimed that he once wanted to make Eli 'just a drifter,'⁶¹ in the novel as published we are left, finally, guessing as to what this young marvel will accomplish, and in fact we get only fleeting glimpses of what precisely 'the magic world of the cities' to which he is heading consists of. We even see in the book indications that what he is moving to may be no better than what he is moving from. 'Sooner or later, I believe,' Christopher tells him, 'you'll find that life is better and fuller here than in any city.' It is a startling comment, showing uncertainty, not in Christopher, but in Horwood himself. Nor is this the only such remark, for Horwood, amidst his portrayal of the outport as overwhelmingly stifling, even permits Christopher to say, albeit somewhat grudgingly, that 'There's nothing wrong with being a fisherman.'⁶² These are not just cracks in the edifice of romantic propaganda that Horwood inflicted upon the outport in *Tomorrow Will Be Sunday*. They are signs of his own distaste for the North American industrial society which was beginning to cast a shadow over Newfoundland and which he, as a journalist, had been among the first to embrace. This distaste is expressed with some force in the original draft of *Tomorrow Will Be Sunday*, where Horwood has Eli return to Caplin Bight twenty-five years after his departure and complain at great length that rural Newfoundland was becoming contaminated by 'the false gospel of the huxters from over the sea to the south and west,' 'the cheap, tawdry world handed down from America, with all the blowsiest elements of American civilization.'⁶³ Reading the earlier and later versions of the book consecutively, one gets the sense of a writer not certain which way to turn.

In *The Foxes of Beachy Cove*, Horwood turned inward. This is a book of meditation and observation, written by an intellectual in deliberate retreat from the workaday world of men and machines that he has come to loathe. Inviting comparison with Thoreau in *Walden*, Horwood pictures himself as having withdrawn from the 'passing scourge' of men to Beachy Cove in Conception Bay, 'at the back door of civilization' where he can commune with nature in solitude and in the company of young people. This may seem like posturing, but the book is in fact a beautifully written and evocative work, insightful and unpretentious, and as free as one could reasonably hope from the intrusion of Horwood's strident editorializing. Horwood takes us on walks through woods and on canoe trips up Newfoundland's rivers, making us see what, perhaps, we have never before learned to look for, and impressing us with the thoroughness of his knowledge of external nature. Though there are a number of acid comments on the havoc wreaked on nature by 'civilized man,' there is luckily no theorizing about the retarded condition of outports, and we can only wonder at the kind of book he would have written if he had given to ordinary people the same degree of sympathy and attention that he here gives to owls and weasels. But this is a minor masterpiece of love and vision, and even the forlorn remains of human settlement that he comes upon in his meanderings are viewed with warmth and pity. At one point he finds an abandoned clearing in the woods and the remains of an old root cellar, and he is reminded of the laborious days of the early pioneers. 'It seemed,' he wrote, 'wrong – even tragic – that the structure they had built with loving care should lie abandoned now, the roots of trees seeking between its stones the crumbs of soil that winds and worms and years had planted there.' He continued: 'And what of the abandoned fields? How did the labour of men change the land? Was anything left by their passing, or will it all vanish, like the smoke of their wood-fires?' Though he later refers to this field as a 'scar' which nature would change to 'a thing of beauty,' yet the signs of sympathy for forgotten human endeavour are apparent. No such sympathy, however, is wasted on the modern renovators, surveyors, and drivers of bulldozers who brazenly intrude on nature to build shopping centres and subdivisions. Be assured, he warns all such men, 'the earth waits, and will, almost with a wave of its green fingers, wipe from sight and memory all the marks of the works of man.' This doomsday prophesying is not typical of the book. The romanticism is. He leads us gently towards the delusion that somehow the external world can offer sufficient comfort to the troubled heart of man, and that among animals living by blind instinct and unwitting savagery, we will discover 'the innocence and simplicty that have never been more than a few steps off the beaten trail.'[64]

By the late 1960s, possibly because he was influenced by the views of his friend Farley Mowat, Horwood's distaste for industrialism had developed into fierce hatred. In an essay published in 1969 he welcomed the hippies to eastern Canada, declared them 'bronzed and bearded and barefooted and beautiful,' and expressed the belief that 'they will succeed in tearing down at least a good part of the filthy, fart-ridden mess that we were brought up to regard as man's highest achievement.'[65] Horwood had by now joined the 'counter-culture' and was describing himself as 'a head' or 'a freak.'[66] He had become 'something of a mentor'[67] for young people, and went around in long hair and jeans, bare-footed when possible. He had been led to this epiphany, he explained, by a nephew, who suspected that 'I might be the only person of my generation in Newfoundland who might be *capable* of being converted.' His talk was now full of the cant of the hippies, and he believed that 'It's a very sad fact that the only possible hope of rescuing North American society from a total state of decadence and stagnation is the success of the revolution.' That revolution, he said, had come to Newfoundland, and he maintained stoutly that 'there's a larger number of heads per capita around St. John's than any other city in the Maritimes unless you include Truro.' Horwood's new beliefs affected his writing, and he apparently wrote a book called 'The Toslow Fire Sutra' in which he 'tried to translate into a novel the true experience of the current generation, the real experience of the revolution that goes on in your soul rather than outside, the real experience of the counter-culture.'[68] The book, perhaps fortunately for Horwood's reputation, was not published.

The radicalized Horwood next turned his attention to the most primitive part of the province, the coast of Labrador, and produced his second novel, *White Eskimo* (1972). The book tells the story of a white man, Esau Gillingham, who tries to inspire the Innuit people to return to their wholesome, pre-Christian way of life. In essence, it is another expression of Horwood's incorrigible romanticism, this time taking the form of a celebration of the life of the 'noble savage' and a denunciation of 'the sickness of Western society.' He castigates the Moravian missionaries as 'white racists,' Grenfell (disguised as 'Dr. Tocsin') as a liar and exploiter, and the Newfoundland government as 'nincompoops.' He is especially hard on Protestantism, which is described as 'the religion of the illiterate' and 'a terrible creed – ruthless, sick and sentimental.' The Innuit are urged to return to the primitive gods of their forefathers and to their elemental connection with the land and ocean. Among the debasing creeds which Christians have inflicted upon the Innuit is their notion of sin: 'Eskimos are not much impressed with the idea of sin. It is a concept foreign to their culture. About the nearest the pagan Eskimo can get to this concept is the fear that he may make the spirit of the seal angry by hunting seals in the wrong way, or the fear that he might drive off the caribou from the coastal plain by showing disrespect for the animal he had killed. No feelings of guilt are ever instilled in Eskimo babies or children. Sex play at all ages is indulged and encouraged. Girls are expected to be pregnant, or even to give birth, before marriage. And friends who never swapped husbands and wives would be looked on as a little odd.' Unwilling as Horwood was to concede that outport Newfoundlanders had a 'culture,' he was perfectly content to confer one on the Innuit. Horwood in *White Eskimo* has not only turned against such white man's corruptions as Christianity and capitalism; he also seems inclined to reject what, in *Tomorrow Will Be Sunday*, he admired, namely, formal education and science. One character is said to have come to Labrador 'with his two useless degrees,' and at the end of the book a spokesman for the Innuit states that his people are now ready 'to shake off the past that had been inflicted upon us, the two hundred years of the scientific myth and the Christian superstition and the other trappings of colonialism.'[69] It is a conclusion from which not even Christopher Simms could take much consolation.

Since 1972 Horwood has continued his dedicated career as a writer in Newfoundland, and he has done much to encourage other talented authors to publish their work. His own books since *White Eskimo* have been exercises in conventional modes: an unimportant coffee-table book on the Great Northern Peninsula, a collection of stories, and a biography of Bob Bartlett.[70] But one cannot review the career of this, perhaps Newfoundland's most gifted, living writer, without a sense of regret. Horwood's radicalism and incurable romantic pursuit of lost causes and literary fashions have separated him from the mainstream of Newfoundland's development since confederation. However sincere his feelings, he has since the early 1960s stood on the sidelines shouting jeremiads about the evidences of progress that the people themselves have welcomed, and the slow march of the province towards North American material prosperity has gone remorselessly onward. There can be no turning back now, Horwood or no Horwood, and by backing himself into romantic corners, he has denied himself a full hearing among people who could have used mature counsel. What he has succeeded in doing, as the reviews of his first novel show, is provide a distorted picture of Newfoundland to foreign readers.[71]

PERCY JANES

To turn from Horwood's work to that of his contemporary, Percy Janes, is to find yet another expression of alienation and dismay. Janes was born in St John's in 1922, and though his life, like

Horwood's, was an urban one, he nevertheless had close ties to the outport through his father and mother. His father was Eli Janes, a blacksmith, who was born in Clarke's Beach in Conception Bay and grew up in nearby Bryant's Cove. His mother was a native of Spencer's Cove, on Long Island, Placentia Bay. Eli Janes had moved from Bryant's Cove to St John's to escape the economic insecurity of life in his outport home. When Percy Janes was only seven years of age, his father decided to move again, this time to Corner Brook, where work was available at the new pulp and paper mill. Janes passed the formative years of his boyhood in this frontier boom town, to which outporters were flocking in their search for steady employment at good wages. A scholarship enabled him to attend Memorial College, and he spent two years (1938–40) following the 'very cautious, very reserved, very British'[72] curriculum which the fledgling institution offered by way of literary study. In 1940 he published a poem entitled 'To Robert Burns' in the college yearbook.[73] At the age of eighteen, Janes left Corner Brook and went to Montreal, where he enlisted in the Canadian navy, serving the next four years in the medical corps of that service. He then enrolled at Victoria College of the University of Toronto and became acquainted with modern literature. After completing his studies in 1949, he taught at a private school in Ontario for two years, but decided that he would prefer the life of a writer, and moved to England. His life thereafter was one of writing and travelling. 'I have lived,' he said in 1971, 'in more sordid single housekeeping rooms in more great cities of the world than any other Canadian writer.'[74] His first published novel was *So Young and Beautiful* (1958), an interesting book of no relevance to Newfoundland. In the mid-1960s, following the death of his father, he decided to write an autobiographical novel about his years in Corner Brook, and the result was 'House of Hate, the Story of a Newfoundland Family, by A Newfoundlander.'[75] This was the original title of Jane's manuscript, and it seems obvious that he intended to publish the work anonymously. However, when the book was eventually published in 1970, the title was shortened to *House of Hate* and, at the request of the publisher,[76] the author's name was given. Janes now resides and writes in St John's.

Janes admits that *House of Hate* 'is based on my own family life,' but adds that although 'rooted in autobiography,' the book 'is not a literal transcript of my own or my family's life.'[77] 'I have added, subtracted, altered, arranged and invented,' he has insisted.[78] He thus claims the usual privileges granted to a writer of novels. How far he is entitled to this literary protection with respect to his own family may be left for others to judge.[79] But while the book is occupied chiefly with the inner life of the 'Stone' family, that life is seen in the context of Newfoundland society as a whole, so much so that at the end we see Janes advance a sociological interpretation of the entire development of the Newfoundland people in order to shed light on the book's main character, the father, Saul Stone. As his notebooks show, he pointedly extended the theme of his novel beyond the family to include 'Newfoundland past and present,'[80] and if Janes is himself willing to act as commentator and make generalized observations about Newfoundlanders, then the common reader is surely justified in asking whether or not that commentary is convincing. It is too much to ask that we view the 'Newfoundland' of this novel as simply one component in a self-contained, imaginative world of fiction, when the author deliberately steps outside those boundaries to editorialize about the real world.

House of Hate is an exploration of the life of the Stone family in 'Milltown,' Newfoundland. Saul Stone had come to Milltown from a menial occupation in St John's, to which he had been initially driven from his birthplace, a 'God-forsaken' outport, 'Raggedy Cove,' Conception Bay:

Raggedy Cove was aptly named, being in fact a ragged V cut into the coastline of solid rock. It composed no more than a few shelterless houses that stood deep in the mouth of the cove and backed onto a stretch of grey rocky barrens sparsely dotted with fir trees and blueberry bushes. Here the child Saul grew up and here, from the time when he could turn a fish or trench a potato, he knew one thing only: work.

Bodily labour was the condition and the law of his existence, and the boy accepted this as long as there was some kind of living to be drawn from the sea or scratched from the gritty soil. When that was no longer the case he bundled up the one change of clothes he owned and set out ...

The mother, Gertrude Stone, had been similarly compelled to leave her home in 'Haystack,' Placentia Bay (the name of a now abandoned outport on Long Island), where she too had known only hunger and dependence: 'When she was an old woman she could still hear herself and her eleven brothers and sisters clamouring at their mother for 'bread-and-lassie, bread-and-lassie,' and could still see her harassed mother pitifully yet half-reluctantly drawing a loaf of bread from the oven, cutting twelve small slices, spreading a dab of the viscous blackstrap molasses over each and having them snatched from under her hands before she could even finish warning the children to eat it slowly because they would be nothing else before dinner time.'[81] Gertrude and Saul meet in Milltown, and their subsequent life together is the subject of Janes's book. What happens to the Stone family is appalling in its simplicity and in its ugliness. Saul brings up his children in an atmosphere of hatred, recrimination, and violence, turns all of them against him, and poisons their lives. The book is filled with domestic scenes of frightening rawness: beatings, vulgar shouting between father and mother, hateful backbiting, drunken grovelling, punishing labour around the home imposed by the father on his sons, ominous periods of bitter silence, angry homecomings, and joyless card games. Such scenes are conveyed with an intensity and daring that suggest real genius. But more chilling than all of this is the mood of hatred and fear that pervades the life of the family. With considerable artfulness, Janes traces the life of each of the children from childhood to maturity, and illustrates how all of them have been coarsened and twisted by their upbringing. The 'arctic void which the Old Man created around himself'[82] descends upon them all. Having been starved of love in their childhood, they have none in adulthood to give to others, or even to themselves. They turn into drunks, emotional cripples, and bullies. All but one, Flinksy, the daughter, who by sheer force of character manages to build a decent life for herself.

If life within the family is bleak and forbidding, that outside the walls of the house of hate is not much better. Milltown itself, a 'Hell-Hole' contaminated by 'insularity and the village virus,' is altogether repellent: 'I could not remember a time when my foremost and altogether obsessive desire was anything but escape from the place, from the sleet and mud in spring, from the greyish clogged heaps of slop and garbage that stood and stank in the ditches outside our homes all summer, and above all from the paralyzing cold of the long winter.' Saul's work in the blacksmith's shop at the mill is not described in detail, but apparently it amounted to endless days of 'drag and dehydration.' Social life in the community consists mostly of boozing, fornicating, fighting, and gossiping. In general, Milltown is a scene of 'human darkness and chaos' and 'grinding materialistic horror.' Neither does Janes waste any sentiment on the smaller villages of Newfoundland. 'Flowery Cove,' a northern outport to which one of the children goes to work as a teacher, is described as 'narrow and barbarous.' Isle aux Morts, a community on the south coast, is said to consist of 'a few frame houses huddled together on kelpy boulders.' 'Baywops' are generally seen throughout the novel as semi-retarded and contemptible. As for the regional dialect or 'local *patois*,' it is regarded as 'the gobbled syntax of unlettered Newfoundlanders.'[83] The language of the Stone family, brilliantly conveyed in Janes's book, is itself marked by vehemence and obscenity, and there is hardly an image or scene which expresses real joy or even ordinary satisfaction. Such humour as there is partakes of satire and low comedy. It is hard to think of any work that keeps the reader so persistently close as this to sour human anger, misery, and discontent.

The key figure in the book is Saul, a tyrant feared and loathed by his children, who unwittingly passes on to them the dark legacy of his hate. Janes has made it clear since the publication of his novel that the source of Saul's incorrigible cantankerousness is not the difficulty he experiences in adjusting to the industrial life in Milltown. The damage to his character, he has stated, had been done prior to his journey to the west coast.[84] Towards the end of the book, Janes reaches for some explanation of Saul's character, and he finds his 'clue' in Saul's own upbringing and in the history of Newfoundland:

From there my mind travelled back to all I had heard of the horror of his ancestry in Ireland and his own childhood and youth in Raggedy Cove, Conception Bay. I thought of the frightful circumstances under which he had been born a semi-orphan, and of how harsh and bitter must have been his fight for the right just to go on living. Many grim tales I had heard and read of life in our island home over these years. Our father's daily companions and his great unresting enemies had been hunger and insecurity, which perhaps had left neither to him nor those close to him any inclination or indeed any strength for the indulgence of the softer emotions; it was grimness and battle all the way through his early life on the east coast of this island and Labrador, where each day's food must be won from a capricious ocean or a niggardly cold and rocky soil. It was mostly a famine and rarely a feast for anyone then living in the Raggedy Coves of our crazy coastline. Not until our father had been some years in the economic haven of Milltown was he ever liberated from this fret and fear of a screaming stomach. And then it was too late.

Was there any truth in my idea that by some strange process of diffusion this physical misery and the implacable hardness it gave him somehow passed into his moral and emotional and spiritual nature as well? Did it leave in his mind and heart a substratum of fear that made him invincibly shy of revealing himself or exposing himself so that he might receive still more hurt in the human relationships of daily life?

Poverty, and its Siamese twin ignorance, must have caused him endless humiliations of spirit long before he was a man, and bred in him that profound modesty which is such a distinguishing mark of our people as a whole that it amounts to an island-wide inferiority complex. Emotional constriction – and from such causes – has always been a well-known feature of Newfoundland life. It was as though all the hardship and hunger our fathers collectively endured had materialized in the form of a spectre which dogged them through all their days and was forever warning them to put no trust in this life nor in anyone connected with it or with them for as long as life endured.[85]

The thesis is proposed tentatively, and with pity, and it contains some truth – more, perhaps, than most Newfoundlanders would be willing to concede. There is such grim honesty in Janes that one prefers his sombre generalizations to those of the sentimentalists and the glib formulae of Horwood's *Tomorrow Will Be Sunday*. Here, clearly, is a writer of a different cast, insistent to the point of obsessiveness, determinedly his own man, indifferent to applause. Yet doubts remain. To place the blame for Saul's senescent spleen upon the burdensome history of Newfoundlanders may be to reach for a ready-made, facile solution to a problem whose roots lie closer to home, in some pent-up frustration with industrial stresses, or in a solitary, savage misanthropy. It is to saddle the distant past with our present incapacities. One recoils instinctively from Janes's incautious reading of the Newfoundland character and the complex pattern of Newfoundland history. And the thought lingers that in this historical and racial theorizing we are seeing a further expression of the gloomy, bitter, private vision of life that darkens the whole of this compelling novel.

OUTSIDE LOOKING IN:
FARLEY MOWAT AND FRANKLIN RUSSELL

Throughout the twentieth century, as in the nineteenth, Newfoundland and Labrador have continued to be 'discovered' by writers from the outside world, and the result has been a steady stream of books and articles, some condescending and insulting, some inspired, all but a few limited. Of those written in the pre-confederation period, two merit brief attention, both by Americans. George Allan England's *Vikings of the Ice: being the Log of a Tenderfoot on the Great Newfoundland Seal Hunt* (1924) describes the author's experiences on a sealing voyage on the *Terra Nova* in the spring of 1922. England was a superbly gifted reporter, with curiosity, persistence, and detachment, and his achievement was that he put the reality of the Newfoundland seal fishery on record, in prose crackling with excitement and packed with images. Another impressive book by an outsider was Elliott Merrick's *True North* (1933), which described his escape from the 'great stone desert'[86] of an American city to what he considered to be the simpler and better life on the Labrador coast. Merrick was among the first of the fugitives from North America and elsewhere who have tried to discard their sorry past and seek in Newfoundland their version of the New Jerusalem. One of the ironies of post-confederation Newfoundland, and especially of the 1960s, was the spectacle of many similar orphans turning up among the people, fleeing from the very industrial life which Newfoundlanders themselves were seeking, pursuing simplicities long outgrown. One such traveller, the Canadian, Farley Mowat, has become the chief literary interpreter of modern Newfoundland to the world at large.

Mowat was born in Belleville, Ontario, in 1921, and has made a career out of writing largely on one theme: primitive societies, and the impact of modern civilization and technology upon such societies. Himself a product of central Canada, he has been drawn to the potency and assurance of traditional peoples, and has expressed open, withering contempt for complicated, urban, industrial living. And so many of his books are set on the fringes of industrial nations, for example, in the North, Siberia, and in Newfoundland. Mowat visited Newfoundland first in 1957, and the following summer readers of the *Evening Telegram* were informed that he had 'fallen in love' with the island:

Farley is delighted with its atmosphere of rugged individualism, the colorful and distinctive characteristics of its people, and the leisurely, unhurried tenor of life as it is lived in most of our communities. His greatest dread now is that Newfoundland, too, will eventually succumb to what he calls 'the disease of creeping Americanism.' He is afraid that if Newfoundlanders are exposed for long to the influences of u.s. movies, books and television, together with the baby bonus and old-age pension cheques from Ottawa, they will lose their initiative and vigor and become passive absorbers of the American entertainment media, as so many other Canadians have become.

'I visited Newfoundland for a few weeks last summer,' he said, 'and in a few East Coast outports I detected the first incipient signs of the disease already. It will be a catastrophe if it is allowed to spread unchecked.'[87]

Thus it did not take Mowat long to detect what was going wrong with modern Newfoundland, and his writing on the province consists of endless repetitions of one theme. The province, in his view, was becoming a victim to North American lunacy, 'its disruptive infatuation with change for its own sake; its idiot dedication to the bitch goddess, Progress.' An admirable people, 'a people out of time' who 'partook of the primal strength of rock and ocean,' were dangerously tottering towards the rootlessness of the industrial age and becoming infected with the disease of 'compulsive consumerism.'[88] Soon after settling in Newfoundland in 1962, Mowat set about becoming their saviour. He would ultimately find that his was a perilous undertaking.

After no doubt careful analysis, Mowat laid the blame for Newfoundland's troubles at the feet of J.R. Smallwood. In *This Rock Within the Sea* (1968) and *A Whale for the Killing* (1972) he lambasted the Premier for harrying the people towards progress and inflicting upon them 'psychic and spiritual havoc.'[89] Newfoundland, he wrote,

... was stampeded into joining Canada. Smallwood won the decisive vote by the slimmest of margins as islanders of all classes fought desperately for the retention of their independence, impoverished as it was. For these dissenters, independence was of greater worth than flash prosperity. Smallwood, on the other hand, regarded independence as an insufferable barrier to progress. Most Newfoundlanders, he once contemptuously said, did not know what was good for them and would have to be hauled, kicking and screaming, into the twentieth century. He was just the man to do the hauling.

He became the island's first provincial Premier and during the next twenty-two years ran Newfoundland almost single-handedly, according to his personal concept of what was good for it. It was a simple concept: industrialize at all costs. This meant that all the island's mineral, forest and human resources were to be made available, virtually as gifts, to any foreign industrial entrepreneurs who would agree to exploit them. Smallwood demanded that Newfoundland turn its back on the ocean which had nurtured the islanders through so many centuries.

'Haul up your boats ... burn your fishing gear!' he shouted during one impassioned speech directed at the outport men. 'There'll be three jobs ashore for every one of you. You'll never have to go fishing again!'

Many believed him, for he was a persuasive demagogue, and he had the silver tongue.[90]

While his analysis contains a germ of truth, the general picture given of developments in post-confederation Newfoundland has to be rejected as simple-minded. The forces that were driving Newfoundland towards some kind of industrial life were at work long before Smallwood came to power, and the simple fact is that Smallwood, the greatest populist in the province's history, could do what he did only with the consent of the people. The progress that he facilitated and initiated, the people themselves wanted. This is the bitter pill that primitives and romantics like Mowat must swallow. It is only fair to add that Smallwood denies ever having made three of the four statements ascribed to him in the above passage, and now regards Mowat as 'one of the greatest liars alive.' Mowat started attacking him, he has said, when he discouraged the Canadian writer's plan to write his biography.[91]

Mowat's sporadic residence in Newfoundland lasted form 1962 to 1967, when an event occurred which ended his love affair with the island. In January 1967 a large female finback whale stranded itself by pursuing bait fish into a deep salt water pond near Burgeo, close to Messer's Cove, where Mowat was residing. Shortly afterwards, a number of young fishplant workers (according to Mowat) proceeded to the pond with high-powered rifles and began shooting at it. These men, wrote Mowat bitterly, 'were representative of the new Newfoundlanders envisaged by Premier Smallwood – progressive, modern men only too anxious to deny their outport heritage in favour of adopting the manners and mores of 20th-century industrial society.' Significantly, to him, while the men had been born in the outports, 'they had all spent some years away, either in Canada or the United States.' The whale, probably doomed anyway, was wounded by the rifle fire, and despite Mowat's frantic efforts to save it, the animal perished early in February. Through his connections with the mainland media, Mowat made the event into an international news story and created a storm of unfavourable publicity. In *A Whale for the Killing* he indicated that the act of butchery would not have been committed by the older generation of Newfoundlanders, but only by the tainted young. He makes the incident into a parable telling of the growing chasm between modern man and the animal kingdom. 'I wept,' he writes, that an opportunity to bridge that chasm 'had perished in a welter of human stupidity and ignorance – some part of which was mine'[92] The admission of his own partial responsibility seems like an attempt to disarm criticism. Whoever or whatever was responsible for killing the animal, surely he had done his best to rescue it.

The event certainly does seem to have symbolic value, but one may question whether Mowat has placed the right interpretation upon it. Judging the incident in retrospect, it is obvious that something from the outside, something corrupt, something that did not belong, had indeed intruded into the living outport that welcomed Mowat as a resident. That intrusion was sentimental excess, together with the obscenity of mass publicity; and the intruder was none other than Mowat himself. For he was wrong to suppose that the ancientry of Newfoundland regarded animal life with the same sympathy that coddled city dwellers expend on dumb animals such as seals and whales. The old outporter lived by killing, which came as instinctively to him as eating, and the pressures of his harsh environment left little room for the luxury of sentiment. He was a killer, not from cruelty, but through exigency. Mowat in Burgeo was just another muddled outsider, imposing upon the people the baggage of his own preconceptions. *A Whale for the Killing*, which concluded with a mawkish appeal to the general public 'to make amends to the whale nations,'[93] became a popular book among the army of North American environmentalists. But the events of 1967 alientated him from Newfoundlanders, and he left the province. In a recent humorous public comment he referred to Burgeo as 'Bugaro.'[94]

The environmental movement of the 1960s led to a questioning of the value of economic growth and keen anxiety about the effects of such growth upon the natural world. In this context it was to be expected that a new interest would be taken in the still primitive corners of the continent, and in the forms of life there surviving. Mowat's visitation was one sign of this new interest. Another was the arrival in Newfoundland of a much more important writer, Franklin Russell. Russell was born in 1926 in Christchurch, New Zealand, where his Scottish father had settled to avoid what he thought would be the disastrous consequences of the First World War.[95] He grew up on a New Zealand farm, but received much of his education abroad, in Australia and England. After working at a variety of occupations, he became a newspaperman in 1948, eventually coming to Canada, where he became a citizen. From there he emigrated to the United States, and he lives now in New York. His interest in Newfoundland was aroused in the mid-1950s, when he came to the island on assignment for a Canadian magazine and realized that this was a province which 'the rest of Canada not only knew nothing about but didn't give a damn.'[96] He returned in the early 1960s for three summer visits, and the result was a book, *The Secret Islands*, published in 1965. Though the work describes his experiences in a number of islands on the Atlantic coast of Canada, it is mainly focused on Newfoundland.

Since the turn of the twentieth century, and increasingly since confederation, Newfoundland has been slowly but surely changing from a primitive, rural cluster of communities to something resembling North American industrial society. What Franklin Russell tried to do in his own life was to seek a deliberate, if temporary, reversal of this process. Rootless, cosmopolitan, and discontent, fed up with 'the city and its perversions,' he wanted 'affirmation of an older order of life, before the megalopolis.'[97] He wanted contact with the elemental and savage. And so in Newfoundland he sought out the bleakest and most barren parts of the shoreline, relishing solitude, fleeing the company of men like himself. He tried to reconnect his life with that of the animals. He communed with birds, touched them, took them into his hands, spent dark nights with them on lonely islands. He went alone into the desert places of the province, all the while looking inward as well in search of knowledge of himself and refreshment for his jaded spirit. *The Secret Islands* is an intimate journal of a life as well as a description of Newfoundland. There is nothing quite like it in our literature, for Russell was an inspired naturalist as well as a self-knowing man, and was able to evoke with brilliant accuracy and great power the feel of life in Newfoundland's primeval corners.

The 'loneliest, the least accessible, the most fascinating and repellent' of all the islands he visited was Funk Island, the tiny spot of granite about thirty miles off the northeast coast of the province. He went there in midsummer, when the island was covered with screaming murres and gannets, and stank incredibly of rotten eggs, rotting, regurgitated fish, bird excrement, dead bodies, and the suffocating smell of overabundant life. The constant, riotous motion and noise overwhelmed his senses. Russell wrote that about a hundred thousand birds were in the air at any given time. About a million perched and moved on land. The murres, when disturbed, would fly clumsily for a short space, collide with one another, and come crashing down on other birds, trampling on the little nestlings – or, as he calls them, 'murrelings' – and sending eggs toppling from precarious nesting places. The fluffy murrelings too came crashing to their deaths into the putrid water of a small gulch, or got fatally jammed in crevices. Russell was struck by the primitive energy of life on the Funks, but he and his companion, a fisherman named Willie, also saw death:

In the middle of the murre mass, standing on slightly higher ground, was a group of gannets. These birds, though inferior in number, occupied the best territory. Though dominant, they seemed to have an amicable relationship with the murres. In places, murres and gannets were mixed together; murrel-ings gathered around gannets as though they were murres.

A gannet on a nest had reached down casually for one of these nearby murrelings, and as I watched, upended it and swallowed the struggling youngster. It was not the sight of such casual destruction that was shocking; it was the sound of the murreling dying.

It screamed when it was seized by the gannet's beak, which was bigger than the murreling's entire body. It screamed as it was hoisted into the air. Horrifyingly, it screamed loudest as it was being swallowed. The gannet, though a big, powerful bird, had to swallow hard to get the murreling down. Its neck writhed and its beak gaped and all the time the awful screams of the murreling came up out of the gannet's throat. The cries became fainter and fainter.

'Horrible,' Willie said. 'Oi never gets used to it.'

On the Funks, Russell wrote, 'Death is nothing. Life is nothing.' No niceties of culture or touches of compassion were evident there, only nature red in tooth and claw. There was no comfort, only appetite. Russell saw no sign of God either. The roar of the bird colony, he wrote, 'cries out to a heedless sky.'[98] Russell on the Funks seemed to be transported back to the green slime out of which the ancestors of man had crawled to begin their ascendancy over the creatures of the earth. It was an appalling experience. He perceived, as he later explained, that 'in the wilderness there's more terror and horror than in Manhattan.'[99]

Russell went to Newfoundland looking for birds, and instead 'found Newfoundlanders.'[100] The fishermen he met, especially the older ones, filled him with admiration. Their hands, 'ripped by hooks, burning ropes, and dogfish teeth,' were the product of elemental struggles. 'Their bodies,' he wrote, 'concealed a kind of dynamic strength that came from a will to do and an acceptance.' When he went to their homes, he mourned for the lost lives back in American cities. One 'can only feel disquiet,' he wrote, 'at the subversion of the spirit in city slums, where human beings, far better off, far more sophisti-cated, cannot cope with life.' When he measured himself by the fishermen's standards, 'when I put my life against theirs, I suffered by comparison.' He sensed and unashamedly stated that some of the fishermen he met were mysteriously gifted, from having passed their lives close to the elements of wind, tide, and crag. One man looked at him and said: 'I do believe, sir, that you are going to have hard times.' Not long afterwards, when hard times did indeed strike him, he remembered the remark, and marvelled. But Russell also saw that the old, instinctive Newfoundland life was passing. He found disquiet in the children especially, and met men who felt it their duty to lead the Newfoundland people forward. All this he saw with regret, but he accepted it as inevitable. 'The singing commericals have arrived,' he noted, 'The fishermen will winter in Paris. The barrens will be plowed or forested.' Newfoundlanders, he told his readers, want 'to be like the rest of us.'[101]

Seeing such a gifted man retreating from Manhattan, the so-called centre of North American civilization, to seek meaning and comfort on Newfoundland's hard edges, may tempt critics to view *The Secret Islands* as yet another exercise in mainland sentiment. This would be to misread the book, for there is no maudlin note struck in it, nor, at bottom, any indulgence in fantasy about the possibility of retreating now to a happy life close to nature. Russell was too wise to offer to Newfoundlanders, or to any race, the hope of a return to some fake Arcadian condition of simplicity and security. He knew that nature held no answers for men. He saw that the life of the oldtime New-foundlanders, though admirable in many ways, was attended by such economic hardship that they would naturally want to leave it, and that the path which the new generation was following would bring gains as well as losses. In any case, he was not a moralist passing judgment. He saw Newfoundlanders on a journey which, for good or ill, it was their destiny to travel.

The case of George Tuff

A CONCLUDING NOTE

In the grim spring of 1914, a Bonavista Bay man, George Tuff, thirty-two years of age, was second hand on the sealing vessel the S.S. *Newfoundland*. He was, though young, a veteran seal hunter, having first gone to the ice at the age of sixteen and having already lived through the *Greenland* disaster of 1898. Through hard work and caution, Tuff had done well. He was known as a careful man. Even Captain Abram Kean, the aristocrat of the sealing industry, knew and trusted him. As second hand, he did not have to go on the ice to kill a single seal. Success indeed! His job was to ensure the smooth operation of the ship itself. Nevertheless, on 31 March, at the prompting of his young captain, Wes Kean, Abram's son, Tuff volunteered to lead the *Newfoundland*'s crew a distance of about four or five miles over rough ice to Abram Kean's ship the *Stephano*, where the main patch of seals appeared to be. There he would be given orders by the great man himself. Tuff did his job. After four and a half weary hours, with the weather becoming dirtier and more ominous, he and his men – except for thirty-four, who wisely chose to leave the group and head back to their ship – reached the *Stephano*, where in view of the weather most of the men thought they would spend the coming night. But Old Man Kean, impatient to get on with his own hunt, and thinking no storm was in sight, had different plans. After bringing the *Newfoundland*'s men near a small patch of seals two miles closer (as he thought) to their own ship, he told Tuff to get his crew underway and to head for the seals. Tuff would have to get his men back to the *Newfoundland* before nightfall, in weather that was looking worse and worse. By this time Tuff could not, in fact, see his own ship, but though worried by the increasing snowfall he said quietly: 'I don't want to delay you, sir.' In a few minutes he and his crew of one hundred and thirty-one men were on the ice, the *Stephano* disappeared into the surrounding snow, and, as his men started to question his leadership, the full horror of his situation struck home in Tuff's mind:

'There's a starm on, George.'
'What we doin' here?'
Then an accusation, 'George, ye're our leader, ye brought us here.'
'What's goin' to happen to we, George?'
The situation, the magnitude of the responsibility, hit George Tuff perhaps for the first time. He was in charge now. He was no longer taking orders from Captain Kean, or from anyone else. There was nobody to take orders from. Slowly he was coming to realize the peril in which they had been placed. The anxious faces, the questioning eyes of the men clustering around him were too much. He was a man of limited capabilities, and to be responsible for them – many of them personal friends – was overwhelming. Tears rolled down his cheeks. 'Cap'n Kean give me orders to kill seals an' go back to our own ship,' he pleaded.
A murmur went through the crowd and reached Cecil Mouland and his buddies on the outskirts. 'Tuff is cryin',' they said in wonderment.[1]

The incident is related in Cassie Brown's fine book, *Death on the Ice* (1972). Like so many other episodes described in Newfoundland literature, episodes such as George Cartwright's slaughter of bears on the Eagle River, Norman Duncan's encounter with Uncle Zeb on the Great Northern Peninsula, Franklin Russell's visit to the Funks, and many more, Tuff's disastrous decision to take the crew of the *Newfoundland* onto the ice in perilous conditions seems a symbolic moment, rich with meaning. What are we to make of it? Is Tuff's obedience to Abram Kean a sign of social deference and the yoke of a dependent spirit inherited from the old outport way of life? An expression of the fatalistic mood we note in one of the melancholy Newfoundland ballads?

The best thing to do is to work with a will;
For when 'tis all finished you're hauled on the hill,
You're hauled on the hill and put down in the cold,
And when 'tis all finished you're still in the hole,
And it's hard, hard times.[2]

Or are we rather seeing in the incident another spirit entirely, a manly but unspoken confidence of success and determination against great odds? Tuff, after all, was no callow youth, but an experienced seal hunter. He had confronted rough weather, knobby ice, cold, and risky situations time after time, and had not only survived but done wonderfully well. Was he thinking that he had survived the *Greenland* tragedy, and that surely he would never again have to experience such a horror? Was he acting in the spirit of another ballad, full of a sense of mastery and power?

> I'se the b'y that builds the boat,
> And I'se the b'y that sails her!
> I'se the b'y that catches the fish
> And takes 'em home to Lizer.[3]

Judgment balks. We are left with an episode of great dramatic power, make of it what we will. One thing we know. The long history of the Newfoundland people includes more than story-telling in the twine loft and cavorting on the landwash. It includes seventy-seven frozen bodies of the *Newfoundland*'s dead sealers. And George Tuff's tears.

To explore the whole of Newfoundland's printed literature is to become aware of the richness of a body of writing long neglected, and to learn caution in interpreting it. It is also to be left with a sense of the utter inadequacy of familiar catch phrases often used by authors, phrases such as 'the nature of Newfoundland life' or 'the shape of Newfoundland history.' So little is known about the true history of Newfoundland, and indeed about the character and motivation of many of those who tried to influence or describe it, that any writer who summarily reduces the complexity of Newfoundland's past or present to a ready formula must be regarded with great suspicion. The literature we have examined mirrors, rather than resolves, that complexity. If it lacks the symmetry and universality of great art, it is none the less important in what it reveals. Through it we see, at times only faintly, the epic story of a people's struggles against overwhelming natural forces and economic adversity. The fleeting illuminations we receive of men such as George Tuff fill us with admiration, awe, pride, and, on occasion, bitter regret and anger.

Now, thirty years into the Canadian confederation, the people of Newfoundland have at long last found a way out of economic uncertainty and hardship. What the future holds, who can tell? And who can say with confidence how much Newfoundland society has changed, in its essence, in the past three decades? One commentator has spoken with authority of the 'overall influence' of the new mass

media, pointing out that the effect 'has been not only to put Newfoundlanders more closely in touch with North America but to make
them part of it.'[4] This note has been sounded as well by other observers, who worry about the loss of the Newfoundlander's distinctiveness, and hold out a future of assimilation. Yet these may be percep-
tions based on imperfect observations. To look closely at Newfoundland life as it is lived, rather than fancied, is to be struck with the force
of continuity rather than change. Writers come and go; but whatever
has changed, the elements of wind, tide, and crag remain; and the
people may be already too irresistibly altered, the stamp of an old land
too firmly implanted in them, to respond as readily as some think to
new influences. Their character, perhaps, has been formed, and

> ... will go onward the same
> Though Dynasties pass.[5]

It is at least possible that, in opting as they did, in 1948, for a chance at
a decent and secure mode of life, the people may have chosen, not
assimilation, but a kind of freedom. If this is so, their old history may
find a new beginning, and writers will discover in men like George
Tuff the materials for a living literature.

Notes

CHAPTER 1: 'IT PASSETH ENGLAND'

1 This account of Cabot's voyage is based on John Day's Spanish letter
   to (possibly) Christopher Columbus, late in 1497. See L.A. Vigneras, 'The
   Cape Breton Landfall: 1494 or 1497,' *Canadian Historical Review*, XXXVIII
   (1957), 219–28.
2 H.P. Biggar, *The Precursors of Jacques Cartier* (Ottawa: Government
   Printing Bureau 1911), 9–28
3 *Ibid.*, 63–7
4 See S.E. Morison, *The European Discovery of America: the Northern Voyages* (New York: Oxford University Press 1971), 56. Other references: *The
   Voyages and Colonising Enterprises of Sir Humphrey Gilbert*, ed. D.B.
   Quinn, 2 vols. (London: The Hakluyt Society 1940), II, 281; Shakespeare,
   Othello, I, iii, 144–5; Whitbourne, *A Discoerus and Discovery of New-
   found-land* (London 1623), sigs. P3–P4; Richard Hakluyt, *Voyages*, 8 vols.
   (London: Everyman ed. 1926), V, 346.
5 The phrase 'new fund Yle' is from William Dunbar's poem 'Of the Warldis
   Instabilitie,' dated c. 1503. See Dunbar, *Poems*, ed. W. Mackay Mackenzie
   (London: Faber 1967), 30. For other early references, see E.H. Sugden, *A
   Topographical Dictionary to the Works of Shakespeare and his Fellow
   Dramatists* (Manchester: University Press 1925), 363. See C.F. Klinck, ed.,
   Literary History of Canada (Toronto: University of Toronto Press 1970), 6.
6 J.A. Williamson, *The Voyages of the Cabots and the English Discovery of
   North America under Henry VII and Henry VIII* (London: The Argonaut
   Press 1929), 73
7 *Ibid.*, 104–5; Biggar, *Precursors of Jacques Cartier*, 167
8 H.P. Biggar, ed., *The Voyages of Jacques Cartier* (Ottawa: King's Printer
   1924), 273–7

9 *Ibid.*, 22
10 Barlow, *A Brief Summe of Geographie*, ed. E.G.R. Taylor (London: The Hakluyt Society 1932), 180
11 Anthony Parkhurst's phrase, in Hakluyt, *Voyages*, v, 346
12 *Ibid.*, 343–9
13 Quinn, *Sir Humphrey Gilbert*, I, 17
14 W.G. Gosling, *The Life of Sir Humphrey Gilbert* (London: Constable 1911), 211
15 Quinn, *Sir Humphrey Gilbert*, I, 61–2
16 Hayes's narrative, like Parkhurst's, was first printed in Hakluyt's *Principall Navigations* of 1589. I quote from Quinn, *ibid.*, II, 385–423.
17 *The New Found Land of Stephen Parmenius*, ed. D.B. Quinn and N.M. Cheshire (Toronto: University of Toronto Press 1972), 89, 93
18 *Ibid.*, 149
19 I quote the Hakluyt translation of Parmenius's letter, *ibid.*, 174–6.
20 Quinn, *Sir Humphrey Gilbert*, II, 383. Peckham himself wrote *A true reporte of the late discoveries ... By that valiaunt and worthye Gentleman, Sir Humfrey Gilbert Knight* (London 1583), an account based on Hayes. For Richard Clarke's account of the wreck of the *Delight* and the sufferings of the survivors, see Hakluyt, *Voyages*, vi, 38–42.
21 Quinn, *ibid.*, II, 420
22 Keith Matthews, *Lectures on the History of Newfoundland: 1500–1830* (St John's: Memorial University of Newfoundland 1973), 89
23 Rogers, *Newfoundland* (Oxford: Clarendon Press 1911), 67. Donne's line 'O my America! my new-found-land!' is in his 'Elegy XIX. Going to Bed,' but imagery dealing with discovery, maps, globes, &c., is found in other poems. Shakespeare's *The Tempest* (c.1610) may well be, at one level of interpretation, a comment upon the possibilities offered to European man by the 'brave new world' unfolding to the west. Drayton alludes to the 'plenteous Seas, and fishfull Havens' of Newfoundland in his *Poly-Olbion* (1622), Song XIX, l. 305. Bacon's essay 'Of Plantations' was included in *The Essayes or Counsels* (1625).
24 Mason, *A Brief Discourse of the New-found-land* (Edinburgh 1620), in J.W. Dean, ed., *Capt. John Mason, the Founder of New Hampshire* (Boston: Prince Society 1887), 151
25 T.C., *A Short Discourse of the New-found-land* (Dublin 1623), sig. c
26 Vaughan, *The Golden Fleece* (London 1626), 5–9
27 Hayman, *Quodlibets, lately come over from New Britaniola, Old Newfoundland* (London 1628), 31
28 Whitbourne, *Discoerus and Discovery of New-found-land*, 27, 49, 51–2, [64–5]

29 *Ibid.*, sigs. R_2–R_3
30 The phrase is Orwell's, in *The Collected Essays: Journalism and Letters of George Orwell*, ed. S. Orwell and I. Angus, 4 vols. (Harmondsworth: Penguin Books 1970), I, 547. Guy's letter is in Samuel Purchas, *Hakluytus Posthumus or Purchas His Pilgrimes*, 20 vols. (Glasgow: James MacLehose 1905–7), XIX, 410–16; Powell's is in D.W. Prowse, *A History of Newfoundland* (London: Macmillan 1895), 129–30; Wynne's is in Whitbourne, *Discoerus and Discovery of New-found-land*, sigs. Q–Q_2.
31 See Purchas, *Hakluytus Posthumus*, XIX, 418–24.
32 Gillian T. Cell, *English Enterprise in Newfoundland, 1577–1660* (Toronto: University of Toronto Press 1969), 66, 70
33 L.C. Wroth, 'Tobacco or Codfish: Lord Baltimore Makes His Choice,' *Bulletin of the New York Public Library*, LVIII (1954), 527
34 Yonge, *The Journal of James Yonge (1647–1721)*, ed. F.N.L. Poynter (London: Longman's 1963), 136, 55–60
35 Prowse, *A History of Newfoundland*, 20
36 Farley Mowat, *The Grey Seas Under* (Boston: Little, Brown & Co. 1958), 20

CHAPTER 2: FISHERS OF MEN

1 Matthews, *Lectures on the History of Newfoundland*, 103–10
2 Keith Matthews, *Collection and Commentary on the Constitutional Laws of Seventeenth Century Newfoundland* (St John's: Memorial University 1975), 4
3 Matthews, *Lectures*, 139
4 Thomas Hardy, *The Dynasts* (New York: St Martin's Press 1965), 6
5 B. Lacy, *Miscellaneous Poems Composed at Newfoundland* (London 1729), 17–18
6 See C. Grant Head, *Eighteenth Century Newfoundland: A Geographer's Perspective* (Toronto: McClelland and Stewart 1976), 82–94; Matthews, *Lectures*, 121–9, 189–97.
7 Matthews, *ibid.*, 196
8 Head, *Eighteenth Century Newfoundland*, 245; Hardy, *Collected Poems* (London: Macmillan 1930), 100
9 Griffith Williams, *An Account of the Island of Newfoundland* (London 1765), 9
10 Head, *Eighteenth Century Newfoundland*, xiii
11 Peter Kropotkin, *Memoirs of a Revolutionist*, 2 vols. (London: Smith, Elden 1899), I, 250
12 Ruth M. Christensen, 'The Establishment of S.P.G. Missions in New-

foundland, 1703–1783,' *Historical Magazine of the Protestant Episcopal Church*, xx (June 1951), 211–12

13 Society for the Propagation of the Gospel in Foreign Parts, MSS. Series 'B,' vol. 6, letter #157 – hereafter abbreviated to SPG B6

14 SPG B6, #158

15 SPG B6, #162, 163, 168

16 SPG B6, #172

17 SPG B6, #174, 178

18 SPG B6, #161

19 Cited in Governor John Byron's letter to the inhabitants of Harbour Grace, Mosquito, and Carbonear on 18 July 1770. Colonial Secretary, Letter Books, IV, 237–8, Provincial Archives of Newfoundland and Labrador – hereafter abbreviated to PANL

20 Lambeth Palace Library, Fulham Papers 21, f. 11, 14, 13. I am grateful to Mr E.G.W. Bill, Librarian, Lambeth Palace Library, for this information. Coughlan's missionary bond is contained in the Fulham Papers 33, f. 221.

21 *A Sermon Preached before the Incorporated Society for the Propagation of the Gospel in Foreign Parts* (London 1768), 43

22 C.H. Crookshank, *History of Methodism in Ireland*, 3 vols. (Belfast: Allen & Allen 1885–8), I, 100, 107; John Wesley, *Letters*, ed. John Telford, 8 vols. (London: Epworth Press 1960), IV, 56

23 Crookshank, *ibid.*, 149; Arthur Young, *A Tour in Ireland*, ed. Constantia Maxwell (Cambridge: University Press 1925), 136–7

24 John Wesley, *Journal*, 4 vols. (Everyman ed. 1906), II, 435; Wesley, *Letters*, IV, 204, 289–90

25 Wesley, *Letters*, IV, 290; V, 109; 101–3

26 In William Myles, *A Chronological History of the People called Methodists* (London 1813), 447, the period of Coughlan's formal connection with Wesley's movement is given as 1755–65.

27 *A Sermon Preached before the Incorporated Society* (1768), 44

28 *Arminian Magazine*, VIII (Sept. 1785), 491

29 Coughlan, *Account of the Work of God in Newfoundland* (London 1776), 7–12, 15

30 *Ibid.*, 16

31 Warwick Smith, 'Rev. Laurence Coughlan,' MS. A.C. Hunter Library, St John's [Appendix], 4

32 *Account of the Work of God*, 14

33 Smith, 'Rev. Laurence Coughlan,' Appendix, 2

34 SPG MSS. Series 'C', Box 1, #5; Jacob Parsons, 'The Origin and Growth of Newfoundland Methodism,' unpublished MA thesis, Memorial University of Newfoundland, 1964, p. 20

35 *A Sermon Preached before the Incorporated Society for the Propagation of the Gospel in Foreign Parts* (London 1774), 18
36 Letters to Coughlan from his Methodist followers are in *An Account of the Work of God*, 50 ff.
37 *Arminian Magazine*, VIII (Sept. 1785), 491
38 *Account of the Work of God*, 16–17
39 *Ibid.*, 17–19, 13
40 A.H. McLintock, *The Establishment of Constitutional Government in Newfoundland, 1783–1832* (London: Longmans 1941), 14
41 SPG MSS. 'Journals,' vol. 20, p. 213; vol. 21, pp. 5, 292–3, 409; SPG C1, #40
42 SPG B6, #207
43 SPG 'Journals,' vol. 21, p. 263; SPG B6, #215. Governor Edward's order relating to Balfour's right to enter 'two Chapels within his mission' (dated 1 Sept. 1779) is in Colonial Secretary, Letter Books, vol. 7, pp. 118–19, PANL.
44 SPG B6, #231
45 McLintock, *Constitutional Government in Newfoundland*, 14
46 Parsons, 'Origin and Growth of Newfoundland Methodism,' 36–40
47 For an account of Thoresby's early career, see his *A Narrative of God's Love to William Thoresby*, 2nd ed. (Redruth 1801), 3–31. A memoir of George Smith by his son William Bramwell Smith is in the *Wesleyan Methodist Magazine*, 3rd Series, XII (1833), 1–13, 73–82.
48 *A Narrative of God's Love*, 50, 52–3, 59
49 *Ibid.*, 89, 94
50 *Ibid.*, 88, 77
51 *Ibid.*, 55, 95
52 *Ibid.*, 101
53 Matthews, *Lectures*, 265
54 Hardy, *Collected Poems*, 302

CHAPTER 3: WALKING NEW GROUND

1 McLintock, *Constitutional Government in Newfoundland*, 198; W.H. Whiteley, 'James Cook and British Policy in the Newfoundland Fisheries, 1763–7,' *Canadian Historical Review*, LIV (1973), 254
2 Burke, *Works*, 12 vols. (London: John C. Nimmo 1887), I, 320; see W.H. Whiteley, 'Governor Hugh Palliser and the Newfoundland and Labrador Fishery, 1764–1768,' *Canadian Historical Review*, L (1969), 141–63; also, *An Account of the European Settlements in America*, 2 vols., 2 ed. (London 1758), 280–2 (this work is attributed to Burke).
3 Whiteley, 'James Cook,' 251

4 Whiteley, 'Palliser,' 149
5 *Ibid.*, 148; G.O. Rothney, 'The Case of Bayne and Brymer: An Incident in the Early History of Labrador,' *Canadian Historical Review*, xv (1934), 264–75
6 D.W. Zimmerly, *Cain's Land Revisited: Culture Change in Central Labrador, 1775–1972* (St John's: Memorial University 1975), 44–5; British Privy Council, *In the Matter of the Boundary between the Dominion of Canada and the Colony of Newfoundland in the Labrador Peninsula*, 12 vols. (London 1927), III, 959 – hereafter called *Labrador Boundary Papers*
7 *Labrador Boundary Papers*, III, 1013
8 *Memoir of the Life of Br. Jens Haven* (London [n.d.]), 2–4
9 W.H. Whiteley, 'The Establishment of the Moravian Mission in Labrador and British Policy, 1763–83,' *Canadian Historical Review*, xlv (1964), 34–5
10 *Labrador Boundary Papers*, III, 1059
11 George Cartwright, *A Journal of Transactions and Events, during a Residence of nearly Sixteen Years on the Coast of Labrador*, 3 vols. (Newark 1792), I, vi – hereafter called *Journal*. For accounts of Cartwright, see C.W. Townsend, *Along the Labrador Coast* (Boston: Dana Estes & Co. 1907), 217–28; *Captain Cartwright and his Labrador Journal*, ed. C.W. Townsend (Boston: Dana Estes & Co. 1911), xix–xxxiii; W.T. Grenfell and others, *Labrador: the Country and the People* (New York: Macmillan 1922), 24–7; F.D. Cartwright, *The Life and Correspondence of Major [John] Cartwright*, 2 vols. (London: Henry Colburn 1826), II, 158–60; Prowse, *History of Newfoundland*, 598–601; and W.G. Gosling, *Labrador* (London: Alston Rivers, Ltd. 1910), 222–50.
12 *Journal*, I, [1]
13 *Ibid.*, 21
14 *Ibid.*, II, 134, 213; 82–3, 85
15 Townsend, *Along the Labrador Coast*, 227
16 *Ibid.*, 228
17 *Journal*, II, 342–8
18 *1 Henry IV*, I, iii, 295–6
19 *Journal*, I, 184; II, 470; I, 244–5; III, 103; I, 145
20 J. P. Howley, *The Beothucks or Red Indians* (Cambridge: University Press 1915), 59
21 Falconer, *Poetical Works* (London: George Bell 1887), 7
22 *Journal*, II, 88–9; III, 222–3; II, 84
23 F.D. Cartwright, *Life and Correspondence of Major Cartwright*, II, 159.
24 *Journal*, II, 139, 235, 137
25 *Labrador Boundary Papers*, III, 1058–73
26 *Journal*, II, 361–4

27 *Ibid.*, III, 189–90
28 Howley, *The Beothucks*, 53
29 George Cartwright, *Labrador, A Political Epistle* (Doncaster: C. Plummer 1785), [1]. The poem was also appended to the third volume of the *Journal*.
30 J.D. Rogers, *Newfoundland*, 140
31 Williams, *Account of the Island of Newfoundland*, [1]–2; A.M. Lysaght, ed., *Joseph Banks in Newfoundland and Labrador* (London: Faber 1971), 132; Whiteley, 'James Cook,' 266
32 Howley, *The Beothucks*, 29
33 George Cartwright, *Journal*, I, 7
34 Howley, *The Beothucks*, 41–4
35 *Ibid.*, sketch III, facing p. 241
36 For accounts of Cormack, see J.R. Smallwood, *The Book of Newfoundland*, 6 vols. (St John's: Newfoundland Book Publishers, Ltd. 1937–67), III, 411–13; Michael Harrington, 'The Trailblazer,' *Atlantic Advocate*, LVI (Sept. 1965), 105–8; and Howley, *The Beothucks*, 234–8. The *Dictionary of Canadian Biography* contains an account of Cormack by G.M. Story.
37 Howley, *ibid.*, 274
38 *Edinburgh Philosophical Journal*, X (1824), 156–62. I refer throughout to this edition: W.E. Cormack, *Narrative of a Journey across the Island of Newfoundland in 1822*, ed. F.A. Bruton (London: 1928) – hereafter called *Journey*.
39 See Cormack's map accompanying his article in the *Edinburgh Philosophical Journal*.
40 *Journey*, 23
41 *Ibid.*, 28–9
42 *Ibid.*, 62
43 Rogers, *Newfoundland*, 159
44 *Journey*, 63. The agreement with Sylvester is printed in Howley, *The Beothucks*, 237.
45 *Journey*, 65, 80, 81, 85, 86, 113
46 Norman Duncan, *The Way of the Sea* (New York: McClure, Phillips & Co. 1903), 99
47 Lowell, *The New Priest in Conception Bay*, 2 vols. (Boston: Phillips, Sampson and Company 1858), I, [9]

CHAPTER 4: THE TRIUMPH OF SENTIMENT

1 S.J.R. Noel, *Politics in Newfoundland* (Toronto: University of Toronto Press 1971), 4

2 Keith Matthews, *Lectures on the History of Newfoundland*, 204
3 William Wilson, *Newfoundland and its Missionaries* (Cambridge, Mass. 1866), 76
4 Ruth M. Christensen, 'The Establishement of s.p.g. Missions in Newfoundland,' 215–16; F.W. Rowe, *The Development of Education in Newfoundland* (Toronto: Ryerson Press 1964), 28–9
5 C. Grant Head, *Eighteenth Century Newfoundland*, 199
6 Cartwright, *Journal*, iii, 215
7 Prowse, *A History of Newfoundland*, 366
8 *Ibid.*, 377
9 See Matthews's lecture 'The Origins of Newfoundland Nationalism,' in *Lectures*, 265–70.
10 Matthews, 'Historical Fence Building: A Critique of Newfoundland Historiography' (1971), 3. This highly original paper, a revised version of which has been published in the *Newfoundland Quarterly*, lxxiv, 1 (1978), 21–30, is in the Centre for Newfoundland Studies, mun Library. Matthews's paper provided the starting point for my own investigations in this area. I am also indebted to Peter Neary's paper, 'The Writing of Newfoundland History: An Introductory Survey,' also available in the Centre for Newfoundland Studies. See also F.W. Rowe, 'Myths of Newfoundland,' *Newfoundland Quarterly*, lxxiv, 4 (1979), 3–16.
11 Reeves, *History of the Government of the Island of Newfoundland* (London 1793), [1]
12 See G.O. Rothney, *Newfoundland: A History* (Ottawa: Canadian Historical Association 1973), 7
13 Reeves, *History*, 15–16, 20–1
14 *Ibid.*, 149, 152, 164–5, [i]–cxvi
15 *Collection and Commentary on the Constitutional Laws of Seventeenth Century Newfoundland*, 10, 183
16 Prowse, *A History of Newfoundland*, 190–6, 205–8
17 Reeves, *History*, 93, 110, 31
18 Matthews, *Collection and Commentary*, 209–10; Head, *Eighteenth Century Newfoundland*, 244 (my italics)
19 Carson, *A Letter to the Members of Parliament of the United Kingdom* (Greenock 1812), 14
20 *Ibid.*, 4, 5–6, 19
21 Carson, *Reasons for Colonizing the Island of Newfoundland* (Greenock 1813), 14, 16
22 See Charles Pedley, *History of Newfoundland* (London: Longman 1863), 119
23 *Reasons for Colonizing*, 9, 20, 8

24 Morris, *Observations on the Government, Trade, Fisheries, and Agriculture of Newfoundland* (London 1824), 4–5

25 Morris, *Remarks on the State of Society, Religion, Morals, and Education at Newfoundland* (London 1827), 8, 10, 6–7, 17

26 Morris, *Arguments to Prove the Policy and Necessity of granting to New-foundland a Constitutional Government* (London 1828), 11–12, 16

27 Morris, *Observations*, 12, 28

28 Morris, *Remarks*, 6

29 *Ibid.*, 55–6; *Observations*, 17–18

30 *Ibid.*, 7; *Remarks*, [3]–5

31 Morris, *Arguments*, 16–17

32 M'Gregor, *British America*, 2 vols. (Edinburgh: Blackwood 1832), I, 181

33 Murray, *History of British America*, 2nd ed., 3 vols. (Edinburgh: Oliver and Boyd [n.d.]), II, 283–4

34 Chappell, *Voyage of his Majesty's Ship Rosamond* (London: J. Mawman 1818), 142, 139, 140, 144, 54

35 *Ibid.*, 51–2, 72, 173, 27

36 Anspach, *A History of the Island of Newfoundland* (London 1819), 228–43

37 *Ibid.*, 107

38 *Ibid.*, 356, 358, 360, 367, 357, 379, 388, 206

39 M'Gregor, *British America*, I, 260–2

40 Anspach, *History*, 438, 422, 462ff.

41 Wix, *Six Months of a Newfoundland Missionary's Journal* (London 1836), 169, 85

42 Jukes, *Excursions in and about Newfoundland during the Years 1839 and 1840*, 2 vols. (London: John Murray 1842), II, 346; I, 82; II, 351–2

43 *Ibid.*, I, 165, 155

44 *Ibid.*, 184, 195. See his comments on Conception Bay communities, *ibid.*, 41.

45 *Ibid.*, II, 85

46 *The Taming of the Shrew*, III, ii, 32

47 See Jukes, *Excursions*, I, 262; see pp. 250–322 for his account of his sealing adventure.

48 *Ibid.*, II, 169–70, 173

49 *Ibid.*, I, 241, 244

50 See Prowse, *A History of Newfoundland*, 431; Rogers, *Newfoundland*, 190

51 Jukes, *Excursions*, II, 125, 173

52 Bonnycastle, *Newfoundland in 1842*, 2 vols. (London: Henry Colburn 1842), I, 3, 5; II, 66

53 *Ibid.*, I, 5, 162, 186, 258; II, 43, 154; I, viii

54 Morris called Newfoundland 'the oldest ... Transatlantic possession belonging to his Majesty' in 1827. *Remarks*, 5–6

55 Bonnycastle, *Newfoundland*, I, 160, 4–5
56 *King Lear*, V, iii, 15
57 Rogers, *Newfoundland*, 217–25. See Peter Neary, 'The French and American Shore Questions as Factors in Newfoundland History,' MS, Centre for Newfoundland Studies, MUN Library.
58 See Matthews's comments in *Lectures*, 254.
59 Morris, *A Short Review of the History, Government, Constitution, Fishery and Agriculture of Newfoundland* (St John's 1847), 69. Jukes in 1839 reported that 'a tolerably good understanding' was maintained between French and English settlers on the west coast, 'more especially among the lower orders of each nation.' *Excursions*, I, 202–3
60 Prowse, *A History of Newfoundland*, 404–7
61 Wilson, *Newfoundland and its Missionaries*, 390–4; letters from James Crowdy, Colonial Secretary, to the magistrates in Harbour Grace, dated 4 Feb. and 25 Feb. 1833 (from my private collection).
62 R.T.S. Lowell, *The New Priest in Conception Bay* (Toronto: McClelland and Stewart 1974), 5
63 Private collection
64 Letters from Thomas Hutchings to Robert Pinsent (magistrate), 9 and 22 Feb. 1854, 22 Jan. 1855 (private collection)
65 Philip Tocque, *Newfoundland: As It Was, and As It Is in 1877* (Toronto: John B. Magurn 1878), 190
66 Bonnycastle, *Newfoundland*, I, 337
67 March, *The Present Condition of Newfoundland* (St John's 1854), 4, 19, 23, 17, 22–3, 26
68 Gertrude E. Gunn, *The Political History of Newfoundland, 1832–1864* (Toronto: University of Toronto Press 1966), 182
69 See Murray and Howley, *Geological Survey of Newfoundland* (London: Edward Stanford 1881); for the history of the period, see J.K. Hiller, 'A History of Newfoundland, 1874–1901,' unpublished PH D thesis, Cambridge University, 1971
70 D.W. Prowse, quoted in G.M. Story, 'Judge Prowse: Historian and Publicist,' *Newfoundland Quarterly*, LXVIII, 4 (1972), 23
71 See a biography of Pedley in *The Dissenting Church of Christ at St. John's, 1775–1975* (St John's, n.d.), 81–5.
72 Pedley, *History*, 82, 56, 197–8, 200
73 Morris, *Short Review*, 69; Pedley, *History*, 196
74 Wilson, *Newfoundland and its Missionaries*, 79–80; Moses Harvey, *Textbook of Newfoundland History* (Boston: Doyle and Whittle 1885), 79
75 See accounts of Harvey in H.Y. Mott, *Newfoundland Men, A Collection of Biographical Sketches* (Concord, NH: T.W. & J.F. Cragg 1894), 129; *Evening*

Telegram, 3 and 4 Sept. 1901 (by D.W. Prowse); a somewhat unflattering treatment, Alison J. Earle, 'From Natural Philosophy to Natural Science: A Case-study of the Giant Squid,' unpublished MA thesis, Memorial University of Newfoundland, 1977, pp. 55 ff.; and Bob Osmond, 'Nineteenth Century Newfoundland's Most Important Man of Letters,' MS, Maritime History Group, MUN. Osmond's paper contains an incomplete bibliography of Harvey. Dr F.A. Aldrich of Memorial University is now writing Harvey's biography.

76 Some of Harvey's early ruminations were printed in St John's and elsewhere: for example, *Thoughts on the Poetry and Literature of the Bible* (1853); *The Testimony of Nineveh to the Veracity of the Bible* (1854); *Lectures on the Harmony of Science and Revelation* (1856); and *Lectures on Egypt and its Monuments* (1857).

77 *Evening Telegram*, 4 Sept. 1901

78 Harvey, *Where are We and Whither Tending?* (Boston: Doyle and Whittle 1886), 102. 'Human Progress – Is it real?' appeared in *Stewart's Quarterly*, V (1871), 225–41. Harvey was a regular and voluminous contributor to foreign newspapers and magazines, and wrote articles on Newfoundland and Labrador for the *Encyclopedia Britannica*. He founded a local newspaper, *The Evening Mercury*, in 1882, but stepped down as editor in 1883. Among his local publications, three pamphlets, *Across Newfoundland with the Governor*, *A Visit to our Mining Region*, and *This Newfoundland of Ours*, were printed together in 1879.

79 *Stewart's Quarterly*, V (1871), 235, 237

80 Earle, 'From Natural Philosophy to Natural Science,' 59

81 A bibliography of McGrath has been prepared by Melvin Baker, and is available at the Centre for Newfoundland Studies, MUN. For a biography, see Mott, *Newfoundland Men*, 255; an obituary is in the *Newfoundland Quarterly*, XXIX, 1 (1929), 16.

82 Harvey, 'A Geological Discovery in Newfoundland,' *Stewart's Quarterly*, III (1869), 60; for similar arguments, see 'Newfoundland as it is,' *ibid.*, 287–304.

83 Harvey, *Across Newfoundland with the Governor* (St John's 1879), 93

84 See Hiller, 'A History of Newfoundland,' 70, 82, 104

85 Harvey, *Across Newfoundland with the Governor*, 49

86 *Ibid.*, 8, 73; 'More about Newfoundland,' *Stewart's Quarterly*, IV (1870), 28; 'The Shortest Route to and from Europe – via Newfoundland,' *Maritime Monthly*, I (1873), 504; Joseph Hatton and Moses Harvey, *Newfoundland* (Boston: Doyle and Whittle 1883), 92

87 *Stewart's Quarterly*, IV (1870), 28

88 See Harvey, 'The Devil-fish in Newfoundland Waters,' *Maritime Monthly*, III (1874), 193–212. Harvey described the squid in many other places. For

an evaluation of his role in the science of the giant squid, see Earle, 'From Natural Philosophy to Natural Science,' 94–5.

89 Tocque, *Wandering Thoughts or Solitary Hours* (London: James Richardson 1846), 196, 14

90 See Eliot Warburton, *Hochelaga*, 2 vols. (London: Henry Colburn 1846), I, 31–2; E.J. Devereux, 'The Beothuck Indians in Newfoundland in Fact and Fiction,' *Dalhousie Review*, L (1970), 350–62. The best account of the Beothucks is F.W. Rowe's *Extinction* (Toronto: McGraw-Hill Ryerson 1977).

91 Harvey, 'Memoirs of an Extinct Race; or, the Red Indians of Newfoundland,' *Maritime Monthly*, V (1875), 498–514

92 Tocque, *Newfoundland: As It Was, and As It Is*, 210, 235, 195, 456

93 Tocque, *Kaleidoscope Echoes* (Toronto: Hunter, Rose, Co. 1895), 109, 123, 278, 36, 129–30

94 Prowse, *A History of Newfoundland*, xiv–xv, 20, 35, 61, 70–1, 174. For an account of Prowse, see G.M. Story, 'Judge Prowse,' *Newfoundland Quarterly*, LXVIII, 1 (1971), 15–25.

95 *A History of Newfoundland*, 195, 145, 530, 495, 512

96 *Ibid.*, xvii; F.E. Smith (Lord Birkenhead), *The Story of Newfoundland* (London: Horace Marshall [1898]), 12.

CHAPTER 5: THE LURE OF THE NORTH

1 R.T.S. Lowell, *The New Priest in Conception Bay*, I, [9]

2 For example, Edmund Spearman, 'Sacrificing the First-born: England and Newfoundland,' *Westminster Review*, CXXXVII (1892), 403–21; Isabella F. Mayo, 'The Tribulations of Newfoundland,' *The Victorian Magazine* (Aug. 1892), 694–704; Charles W. Dilke, 'Newfoundland,' *Nash's Pall Mall Magazine*, XVIII (1899), 211–16; H.C. Goldsmith, 'Newfoundland and the French Fishery Question,' *The National Review*, XV (1890), 404–11; Donald Morison, 'The Discontent in Newfoundland,' *Forum and Century*, IX (1890), 694–704; see also F. Heinr Geffcken, 'North American Fisheries Disputes,' *Fortnightly Review*, LIII (1890), 741–60; 'St. John's, Newfoundland,' *Harper's Weekly*, XXXV (1891), 250–1; William Greswell, 'The Crisis in Newfoundland,' *Fortnightly*, LXIII (1895), 467–74. I want to thank Melvin Baker for letting me use his collection of articles on Newfoundland.

3 Edmund Gosse, in Prowse, *A History of Newfoundland*, x–xi

4 Jukes, *Excursions*, I, 6; Eliot Warburton, *Hochelaga*, I, 19; Bayard Taylor, *At Home and Abroad: A Sketch-book of Life, Scenery and Men* (New York: Putnam 1860), 247, 267

5 *Macmillan's Magazine*, LXXIV (1896), 33

6 Spearman, 'Sacrificing the First-born,' 412

7 Ballantyne, *The Crew of the Water Wagtail* (London: James Nisbet & Co.

[1889]), 155–7; Hatton, *Under the Great Seal* (London: Hutchinson & Co. [1893]), 5–8. Harvey had himself tried to fictionalize the giant squid incident in the *Maritime Monthly*, III (1874), 541–56.

8 Connolly, *The Crested Seas* (New York: Charles Scribner's Sons 1907), 153

9 For an account of English, see *Evening Telegram*, 3 June 1959; for Spencer, see Ewart Young, 'Sickly Fortune Youth Climbed Ladder of Success in London's "Street of Ink,"' St John's *Daily News*, 8 April 1939; also Ronald Rompkey, 'Newfoundland's Forgotten Storyteller,' Memorial University *Gazette* (June 1977), 10.

10 Noble, *After Icebergs with a Painter* (New York: D. Appleton and Co. 1861), 84. Many nineteenth-century sketches of Newfoundland scenes are reproduced in Charles P. deVolpi's book, *Newfoundland: A Pictorial Record* (Toronto: Longman 1972).

11 For example: R.L. Dashwood, *Chiploquorgan; or, Life by the Camp Fire* (Dublin: Robert T. White 1871); S.T. Davis, *Caribou Shooting in Newfoundland* (Lancaster, Pa.: New Era Printing House 1895); Sir William R. Kennedy, *Sport, Travel, and Adventure in Newfoundland and the West Indies* (Edinburgh and London: Blackwood 1885); Wakeman Holberton, 'A Trip to Newfoundland,' *Outing* (Jan. 1892), 332–6

12 For example: John Mullaly, 'A Trip to Newfoundland,' *Harper's New Monthly Magazine*, XII (1855), 45–57, an account also published as a book, *A Trip to Newfoundland* (New York: T.W. Strong 1855); Bayard Taylor's *At Home and Abroad* (1860) was also an account of 'a telegraphic trip to Newfoundland.'

13 Lady Blake, 'On Seals and Savages,' *The Nineteenth Century*, XXV, pt. i (1889), 513–26. Lady Blake wrote an account of 'The Beothucks of Newfoundland' in *ibid.*, XXIV, pt. ii (1888), 899–918. See Grenfell's able defence of the sealers in 'The Seal Hunters of Newfoundland,' *Leisure Hour Monthly Library*, XXVII (1897–8), 290.

14 Roberts, *The Canadian Guide Book* (New York: D. Appleton and Co. 1891), 233

15 See a list of Grenfell's books in J. Lennox Kerr, *Wilfred Grenfell: his Life and Work* (New York: Dodd, Mead & Co. 1959), 258–9.

16 Grenfell, *What Christ Means to me* (London: Hodder and Stoughton 1927), 19

17 *Ibid.*, 31, 61. The date of Grenfell's initial conversion is given as 1883 in *What Christ Means to me* and 1885 in his autobiography, *A Labrador Doctor* (London: Hodder and Stoughton [1920]), 31.

18 Grenfell, 'Work among Labrador Fishermen,' *The Canadian Club* (17 April 1905), 161; Norman Duncan, *Dr. Grenfell's Parish* (New York: Fleming H. Revell Co. 1905), 50

19 Taylor, *At Home and Abroad*, 273

20 Grenfell, *A Labrador Doctor*, 103

21 Dashwood, *Chiploquorgan*, 247; Mullaly, *A Trip to Newfoundland*, 30, 48

22 Julian Moreton, *Life and Work in Newfoundland* (London: Rivingtons 1863), 27; Taylor, *At Home and Abroad*, 294; F.E.J. Lloyd, *Two Years in the Region of Icebergs* (London: Society for Promoting Christian Knowledge [1886]), 30

23 W. Wingfield-Bonnyn, *The Newfoundland Colonisation Hand Book* (London: Newfoundland Colonisation and Mining Co. [1888]), 16

24 Lady Blake, 'On Seals and Savages,' 515

25 Lady Blake, 'A Chat about Newfoundland,' *North American Review*, CLII (1891), 716; J.G. Mountain, *Some Account of a Sowing Time on the Rugged Shores of Newfoundland* (London: Society for Promoting Christian Knowledge 1857), 32–3. Mountain found, however, 'fine specimens of fishermen' in other places. *Ibid.*, 32

26 David Kennedy, *Kennedy's Colonial Travel* (London: Edinburgh Publishing Co. [1876], 437

27 The Earl of Dunraven, 'A Glimpse at Newfoundland,' *Living Age*, XXXIII (1881), 423. Dunraven noted, however, that in general the 'hardy Newfoundland fisherman' leads 'a poor, and too often a miserable life.' *Ibid.*, 422

28 McCrea, *Lost Amid the Fogs* (London: Sampson Low 1869), 127, 110, 132, 297

29 Harvey, 'More about Newfoundland,' *Stewart's Quarterly*, IV (1870), 28. Harvey added that the people 'sorely need education.'

30 Moreton, *Life and Work in Newfoundland*, 23, 26–7, 40

31 Lloyd, *Two Years in the Region of Icebergs*, 29–30. See Mountain, *Some Account of a Sowing Time*, 10–38.

32 *The Newfoundland Journal of Aaron Thomas*, ed. Jean M. Murray (Don Mills: Longmans 1968), 137

33 Lady Blake, 'A Chat about Newfoundland,' 714–22; George Patterson, 'Notes on the Dialect of the People of Newfoundland,' *Journal of American Folk-Lore*, VIII (1895), 27–40; IX (1896), 19–37. See also Patterson's 'Notes on the Folk-Lore of Newfoundland,' *Journal of American Folk-Lore*, VIII (1895), 285–90.

34 The Earl of Dunraven, 'A Glimpse at Newfoundland,' 410–11; for a similar statement on the 'breed of fisher-folk,' see Spearman, 'Sacrificing the First-born,' 413.

35 Prowse, *A History of Newfoundland*, 514–20

36 J.K. Hiller, 'A History of Newfoundland,' 151

37 Richard Howley, 'The Fisheries and Fishermen of Newfoundland,'

Month, LXI (1887), 489, 490, 494–6, 497–8. For another striking article by Howley, see 'Newfoundland,' *Month*, LXIV (1888), 210–30. Howley was a Doctor of Theology, a professor at All Hallow's College in Dublin, and vice-president of St Bonaventure's College in St John's. For a biography, see H.M. Mosdell, *When Was That? A Chronological Dictionary of Important Events in Newfoundland* (St John's: Trade Printers and Publishers 1923), 60; also an obituary by M.F. Howley, *Newfoundland Quarterly*, XII, 3 (1912), 16. His bibliography has not been investigated.

38 McGrath, 'The Fisherfolk of Newfoundland,' *Outing*, XLIV (1904), 306. See also Norman Duncan, 'Newfoundlanders of the Outports,' *Outing*, XXXIX (1901), 271–8; Grenfell, 'The Fisher Folk of Labrador,' *The Canadian Club* (4 March 1907), 98–104. The St John's native Frederick Woods, however, in a sermon entitled *A Strange Country in the Waters*, delivered in 1893, claimed that Newfoundlanders 'are decidedly English in their ways' (p. 20).

39 Prowse, 'From an Island. With Some Gleams of its Humour,' *Newfoundland Magazine*, I, 1 (1900), 16

40 Colonial Secretary, Letter Books, Series S 2, vol. LIV, p. 1104, PANL. I have written a biography of Lowell in my introduction to the New Canadian Library reprint of *The New Priest in Conception Bay* (1974).

41 In the 'Forewords' to a revised edition of *The New Priest in Conception Bay* (Boston: Roberts Brothers 1889)

42 A large number of favourable reviews are appended to a later edition of Lowell's book, *The Story of the New Priest in Conception Bay*, 2 vols. (Boston: E.P. Dutton and Co. 1864).

43 Philip Hiscock, 'Dialect Representation in R.T.S. Lowell's novel *The New Priest in Conception Bay*,' in H.J. Paddock, ed., *Languages in Newfoundland and Labrador* (St John's MUN 1977), 81–9. Another story by Lowell that skilfully reproduces local dialect was called 'A Raft That No Man Made.' See *Atlantic Monthly*, IX (1862), 365–72.

44 Lowell, *The New Priest in Conception Bay*, I, 196–8

45 Lowell, *Poems* (Boston: E.P. Dutton and Co. 1864), 72

46 Lowell, *Fresh Hearts that Failed Three Thousand Years Ago* (Boston: Ticknor and Fields 1860), 100

47 *The New Priest in Conception Bay*, II, 97, 139, 169–71

48 Duncan, *Dr. Grenfell's Parish*, 128; Thomas Moore, 'A Biography of Norman Duncan,' unpublished MA thesis, Memorial University, 1977, 34–5

49 See Grenfell's brief 'Appreciation' of Duncan in Duncan's *Battles Royal Down North* (New York: Fleming H. Revell 1918), 5–8

50 Duncan, *Dr. Grenfell's Parish*, 103.

51 *Ibid.*, 83–102, [7]
52 Duncan, however, denied that Dr Luke was modelled on Grenfell. *Ibid.*, [8]
53 Duncan, *The Way of the Sea*, 35, 129
54 Duncan, *Battles Royal Down North*, 7. Grenfell's observation that Duncan 'loved the sea passionately' (*ibid.*, 8) is sentimental overstatement. See Moore, 'A Biography of Norman Duncan,' 34.
55 *The Way of the Sea*, 69
56 *Dr. Grenfell's Parish*, 104
57 *The Way of the Sea*, 110, 309
58 *Ibid.*, 107–8, 129
59 *Ibid.*, 65–6
60 *Ibid.*, 185, 309–32
61 See his comment in *Dr. Grenfell's Parish*, 79.
62 Hardy, *The Return of the Native* (London: Macmillan 1970), 14
63 Duncan, *Dr. Luke of the Labrador* (New York: Fleming H. Revell 1904), 124
64 *Dr. Grenfell's Parish*, 106
65 *Ibid.*, 123–4
66 John McLean, *Notes of a Twenty-five Years' Service in the Hudson's Bay Territory* (1849), ed. W.S. Wallace (Toronto: The Champlain Society 1932), 229–30
67 F.H. Herrick, *Audubon the Naturalist*, 2 vols. (New York: D. Appleton and Co. 1917), II, 50, 46–7
68 J.J. Audubon, *Letters*, ed. Howard Corning, 2 vols. (Boston: Club of Odd Volumes 1930), I, 240
69 Randle F. Holme, *A Journey to the Interior of Labrador, July to October, 1887* (London: Royal Geographical Society 1888), 13; Henry G. Bryant, *A Journey to the Grand Falls of Labrador* (Philadelphia: Geographical Club 1892), 42
70 Packard, *The Labrador Coast* (New York: N.D.C. Hodges 1891), 78, 176
71 Hind, *Explorations in the Interior of the Labrador Peninsula*, 2 vols. (London: Longman 1863), I, 234–5
72 A.P. Low, *Report on Explorations in the Labrador Peninsula* (Ottawa: Geological Survey of Canada 1896), 17. Stearns's book was *Labrador: a Sketch of its Peoples, its Industries and its Natural History* (Boston: Lee and Shepard 1884).
73 [anon.], 'Three Months in Labrador,' *Harper's New Monthly Magazine*, XXII (1861), 761
74 Holme, *A Journey in the Interior of Labrador*, 10
75 Quoted in Bryant, *A Journey to the Grand Falls*, 9
76 *Ibid.*, 8–9

77 J.P. Cilley, *Bowdoin Boys in Labrador* (Rockland, Maine: Rockland Publishing Co., n.d.), 47–8
78 Quoted in Bryant, *A Journey to the Grand Falls*, 43
79 McLean, *Notes*, 212–14
80 See Holme, *A Journey in the Interior of Labrador*, 3, and Low, *Report on Explorations in the Labrador Peninsula*, 17. Dillon Wallace, however, after making 'inquiries' in Labrador, was convinced that the priest did not go overland. See Wallace, *The Lure of the Labrador Wild* (New York: Fleming H. Revell 1905), 24.
81 Wallace, *ibid.*, 17, 24, 15
82 *Ibid.*, 17
83 For an account of Mina Hubbard's expedition, see Pierre Berton, *The Wild Frontier* (Toronto: McClelland and Stewart 1978), 177–208. See Mina Hubbard, *A Woman's Way through Unknown Labrador* (New York: The McClure Co. 1908), and Dillon Wallace, *The Long Labrador Trail* (Toronto: Fleming H. Revell Co. 1907).
84 McLean, *Notes*, 227–8
85 Wallace, *The Lure of the Labrador Wild*, 111, 141
86 *Ibid.*, 212–13
87 Mina Hubbard, *A Woman's Way*, 241
88 Wallace, *The Lure of the Labrador Wild*, 172. See also his remarks in his diary, in Mina Hubbard, *ibid.*, 241
89 *Ibid.*, 234–5

CHAPTER 6: EMIGRANT MUSE

1 J.K. Hiller, 'A History of Newfoundland, 1874–1901,' 368
2 *Ibid.*, 28, 91
3 Shannon Ryan, 'The Newfoundland Cod Fishery in the Nineteenth Century,' unpublished MA thesis, Memorial University, 1971, pp. 24, 197
4 For discussions of the causes of the bank crash, see Hiller, 'A History of Newfoundland,' 182–4; Ryan, 'The Newfoundland Cod Fishery,' 194–204.
5 S.J.R. Noel, *Politics in Newfoundland*, 26–7
6 Ryan, 'The Newfoundland Cod Fishery,' 8
7 Peter Neary and S.J.R. Noel, 'Newfoundland's Quest for Reciprocity, 1890–1910,' in Mason Wade, ed., *Regionalism in the Canadian Community, 1867–1967* (Toronto: University of Toronto Press 1969), 210–26
8 Comment by Governor T.N. O'Brien (appointed 1889); quoted in Hiller, 'A History of Newfoundland,' 234
9 *Ibid.*, 368–9

10 Beckles Wilson, *The Tenth Island* (London: Grant Richards 1897), 31
11 Hiller, 'A History of Newfoundland,' 183
12 E.J. Pratt Library, Victoria University, Pratt MSS, Box 9-69.2, p. 1. I wish to thank Dr Robert C. Brandeis, Librarian, Victoria University Library, for permission to quote from the Pratt MSS.
13 Ryan, 'The Newfoundland Cod Fishery,' 195
14 Peter Neary, ed., *The Political Economy of Newfoundland, 1929–1972* (Toronto: Copp Clark 1973), 16
15 *Report of the Commission appointed by the Government to Deal with and Report upon the Subject of Public Health in the Colony of Newfoundland* (St John's: Association for Prevention of Consumption 1911), 4. For statistics on tuberculosis, see this pamphlet and other material in the Centre for Newfoundland Studies, MUN, file no RA 644 T7A8.
16 *Newfoundland Quarterly*, IX, 2 (1909), 18
17 *Newfoundland Magazine*, I, 3 (1900), 238
18 Rogers, *Newfoundland*, iii–iv
19 'The Passing of the Founder,' *Newfoundland Quarterly*, XLIV, 3 (1944), 33
20 'Just Among Ourselves,' *ibid.*, VII, 4 (1908), 17
21 *Ibid.*, I, 4 (1902), 6–8; III, 3 (1903), 14
22 *Ibid.*, II, 3 (1902), 17; VIII, 4 (1909), 11–12
23 Isabella Rogerson, *The Victorian Triumph and Other Poems* (Toronto: William Briggs 1898); M.F. Howley, *Poems and Other Verses* (New York: Fischer & Bro. 1903); F.B. Wood, *Songs of Manhood* (London: Routledge 1908); R.G. McDonald, *From the Isle of Avalon* (London: Frank H. Morland 1908)
24 *Newfoundland Quarterly*, II, 2 (1902), 18
25 Mildred Claire Pratt, *The Silent Ancestors* (Toronto: McClelland and Stewart 1971), 23, 143
26 Pratt MSS, Box 69.2, p. 1
27 E.J. Pratt, *Newfoundland Verse* (Toronto: Ryerson Press 1923), 17; Pratt MSS, Box 12.D, p. 3
28 E.J. Pratt, 'Memories of Newfoundland,' in J.R. Smallwood, ed., *The Book of Newfoundland*, II, 56
29 M.C. Pratt, *The Silent Ancestors*, 20
30 Pratt, 'Memories of Newfoundland,' 56
31 M.C. Pratt, *The Silent Ancestors*, 182
32 H.W. Wells and C.F. Klinck, *Edwin J. Pratt: the Man and his Poetry* (Toronto: Ryerson Press 1947), 8
33 Pratt MSS, Box 9-69.5, p. 1
34 Pratt MSS, Box 9-70.2, p. 6
35 *Newfoundland Verse*, 51
36 Pratt, *Here the Tides Flow*, ed. D.G. Pitt (Toronto: Macmillan 1962), 41–58.

The original publication was *Rachel; a sea story of Newfoundland in verse* (New York: [privately printed] 1917), to which a 'Conclusion' was added in *Newfoundland Verse*, 115–21.Extracts from the poem *Rachel* in *Here the Tides Flow*, from *Newfoundland Seaman* and *Newfoundland* in *Collected Poems of E.J. Pratt*, are reprinted by permission of the Macmillan Company of Canada Limited.

37 Pratt was fond of drawing attention to the 'Elizabethan qualities of character' in Newfoundlanders. See Pratt MSS, Box 9-68.1, pp. 1–3.

38 Pratt MSS, Box 9-69.2, p. 1

39 *Newfoundland Verse*, 87

40 Pratt MSS, Box 12-D, pp. 2–3

41 Pratt MSS, Box 8-62, p. 5. See also *Newfoundland Verse*, 9–14. The passage from 'Clay' is quoted by permission of Mrs Viola L. Pratt.

42 Pratt MSS, Box 8-62, p. 2

43 Pratt MSS, Box 9-69.4, p. 4

44 Pratt, *Many Moods* (Toronto: Macmillan 1932), 10.*Erosion*, in *Collected Works of E.J. Pratt*, is reprinted by permission of the Macmillan Company of Canada Limited.

45 Pratt, *Here the Tides Flow*, 25

46 Sandra Djwa, *E.J. Pratt: The Evolutionary Vision* (Toronto: Copp Clark 1974), 46–9

47 *Here the Tides Flow*, 25

48 Wells and Klinck, *Edwin J. Pratt*, 19

49 Tom Marshall, 'E.J. Pratt,' *Canadian Forum*, LVII, 675 (1977), 19

50 Pratt MSS, Box 9-68.1, p. 11

51 Pratt MSS, Box 9-68.1, p. 4

52 In 'Overheard in a Cove,' *Newfoundland Verse*, 47–63, there are a couple of usages showing a Newfoundland flavour. However, the only authentic Newfoundland word is 'swilin',' and Pratt prepares the reader for this at the beginning with the headnote: 'Swiles = seals.' There are a number of valuable comments on Pratt's language and themes in George Whalley's lecture, *Birthright to the Sea* (St John's: Memorial University 1978).

53 M.C. Pratt, *The Silent Ancestors*, 183

54 Pratt MSS, Box 9-69.2, p. 1

55 Pratt MSS, Box 9-68.3, p. 15

56 *English Studies in Canada*, II (1976), 486

CHAPTER 7: BRIDGING TWO WORLDS

1 A.B. Keith, *The Sovereignty of the British Dominions* (London: Macmillan 1929), 17–18

2 David Alexander, 'Newfoundland's Traditional Economy and Development to 1934,' *Acadiensis*, v (1976), 65

3 Horace G. Hutchinson, *A Saga of the 'Sunbeam'* (London: Longmans 1911), 119

4 R.A. Mackay, ed., *Newfoundland, Economic, Diplomatic, and Strategic Studies* (Toronto: Oxford University Press 1946), 509 ff.

5 See J.R. Smallwood, *The New Newfoundland* (New York: Macmillan 1931), 22–4, 54–8; on Labrador, see 'The Possibilities of Labrador,' *Newfoundland Quarterly*, xxvii, 1 (1927), 9–11, also P.T. McGrath, 'Labrador and what it means to us,' *ibid.*, 11–16, and xxvii, 2 (1927), 17–23; see also 'Progress at Buchans Mine, Newfoundland,' *ibid.*, xxix, 3 (1929), 17

6 P.T. McGrath, *Newfoundland in 1911* (London: Whitehead, Morris, & Co. 1911), 251–4; Smallwood, *The New Newfoundland*, 20–1; Alexander, 'Newfoundland's Traditional Economy and Development to 1934,' 69–71

7 MacKay, *Newfoundland*, 133; Smallwood, *The New Newfoundland*, 222–3; S.J.R. Noel, *Politics in Newfoundland*, 131

8 *The New Newfoundland*, 211–24

9 J.L. Paton, 'Newfoundland: Present and Future,' *International Affairs*, xiii (1934), 396

10 *The New Newfoundland*, 232

11 Thomas Lodge, *Dictatorship in Newfoundland* (London: Cassell 1939), 21

12 Noel, *Politics in Newfoundland*, 147

13 *The New Newfoundland*, 8

14 MacKay, *Newfoundland*, 132

15 *The New Newfoundland*, 233

16 *The Log of Bob Bartlett* (New York: Putnam's 1928), 102–3

17 See Ian McDonald, 'W.F. Coaker, and the Balance of Power Strategy: The Fishermen's Protective Union in Newfoundland Politics,' ms, Centre for Newfoundland Studies, mun Library, pp. 3–7

18 Smallwood, *The New Newfoundland*, 1

19 Smallwood, *I Chose Canada* (Toronto: Macmillan 1973), 195

20 Noel, *Politics in Newfoundland*, 184n, quoting *The Times* of London in 1927

21 Margot Duley Morrow, 'Margaret Duley 1894–1968,' in Margaret Duley, *Highway to Valour* (Toronto: Griffin House 1977). Other recent comments on Margaret Duley and her work are: Linda Whalen, 'Margaret Duley: A Critical Analysis,' *Newfoundland Quarterly*, lxxi, 3 (1975), 27–9; G.M. Story, 'Margaret Duley: 1894–1968,' *ibid.*, 15–16; Margaret-Ann Maher, 'Margaret Duley,' ms, Centre for Newfoundland Studies, mun Library. Duley's bibliography has not been investigated. See her story, 'Mother Boggan,' *Fortnightly*, cliii (1940), 401–10. Professor Alison Feder of Memorial University is now completing a biography of Duley.

22 Maher, 'Margaret Duley,' [1]
23 See R.B. Job, *John Job's Family* (St John's: Telegram Printing Co. 1949), 11
24 Maher, 'Margaret Duley,' 3, 2
25 Margaret Duley, 'Glimpses into Local Literature,' *Atlantic Guardian*, XIII, 7 (1956), 26
26 Rockwell Kent, *It's Me, O Lord* (New York: Dodd, Mead & Co. 1955), 279–302.
27 *The Eyes of the Gull* (London: Arthur Barker Ltd. 1936), 122, 10, 50, 144, 87
28 *Ibid.*, 49, 81, 103, 122, 81–3
29 *Cold Pastoral* (London: Hutchinson [1939]), 7–8, 15, 34, 163–4
30 *Ibid.*, 59, 125, 262–3, 232, 235, 292, 333
31 Duley, 'Glimpses into Local Literature,' 26
32 *Highway to Valour* (Toronto: Macmillan 1941), 28–9
33 *Ibid.*, 2, 63, 162, 306, 64
34 *Ibid.*, 173–4
35 *Ibid.*, 1, 26–7
36 *Saturday Review of Literature*, XXIV, 25 (11 Oct. 1941), 13
37 *The Tempest*, III, ii, 129
38 *Highway to Valour*, 221–2
39 *Atlantic Guardian*, XIII, 7 (1956), 20–6
40 See M.D. Morrow, 'Margaret Duley 1894–1968,' for an account of local reception of her novels. A scrapbook containing many flattering foreign reviews of her work is in the Centre for Newfoundland Studies, MUN Library.
41 Paton, 'Newfoundland: Present and Future,' 397, 405
42 *Newfoundland Royal Commission 1933 Report* (London: H.M. Stationery Office 1933), 77–8
43 Gertrude Gunn, *The Political History of Newfoundland, 1832–1864*, 180
44 Kent, *It's Me, O Lord*, 287

CHAPTER 8: VISIONS AND REVISIONS

1 *Evening Telegram*, 16 Feb. 1941. For assessment of the Commission, see S.J.R. Noel, *Politics in Newfoundland*, 221–43; Peter Neary, *The Political Economy of Newfoundland*, 66–8; R.A. MacKay, *Newfoundland, Economic, Diplomatic, and Strategic Studies*, 212–18.
2 Noel, *ibid.*, 242
3 *Evening Telegram*, 29 Jan. 1941
4 Paul Bridle, ed., *Documents on Relations between Canada and Newfoundland* (Ottawa: Department of External Affairs 1974), 7, xlv. Other military

statistics quoted are taken from the introduction to this book, pp. xix–lxiii.

5 *Ibid.*, 3, lv
6 *Evening Telegram*, 12 Feb. 1941
7 Bridle, *Documents*, 1345, 1351, 1337
8 *Evening Telegram*, 20 Feb. 1941
9 Duley, *The Caribou Hut* (Toronto: Ryerson Press, n.d.), 16–17
10 Bridle, *Documents*, 391
11 *Ibid.*, 212
12 I am grateful to Peter Neary for letting me use this letter from his scholarly files.
13 Bridle, *Documents*, 204
14 Neary, *The Political Economy of Newfoundland*, 103, 114
15 For an account of Newfoundland literature in the pre-war period, see Harold Horwood, 'Newfoundland Literature has Vigor, Character,' *Saturday Night*, LXIV (March 1949), 10. The poets of the day favoured 'simplicity,' 'contemplation of nature,' and 'solitude.' See Clyburn Duder, 'Some Thoughts on Literature,' *Newfoundland Quarterly*, XLIV, 1 (1944), 25–6. Michael Harrington's work is displayed in his book *Newfoundland Tapestry* (Dallas: The Kaleidograph Press 1943). A book containing poems by the other writers listed is Michael Harrington, ed., *Poems of Newfoundland* (St John's: F.M. O'Leary, Lt. 1953). For earlier poetry, see J.R. Smallwood, *Book of Newfoundland*, II, 456–86. For a comment on Gregory Power, with a selection from his poetry, see Daphne L. Benson, 'Power, Politics, and Poetry: An Unlikely Alliance,' *Newfoundland Quarterly*, LXXIV, 4 (1979), 26–31.
16 *Courier*, I, 5 (Aug. 1942), 14–15. For an account of the *Courier*, see *The Newfoundland Herald TV Week* (14 Feb. 1979), 4–5.
17 See, for example, A.F. Binnington, 'I Like Newfoundland (A Meditation),' *Newfoundland Quarterly*, XLIV, 1 (1944), 22–4. The founder of the *Quarterly*, John J. Evans, died in November 1944.
18 *Atlantic Guardian*, I, 1 (1945), 12, 20, 12; I, 11 (1945), 48
19 *Saturday Night*, LXIV (March 1949), 10
20 *Protocol*, 1 (Nov. 1945), [2]; 2 (Jan. 1946), 1–2
21 *The Islander*, I, 1 (Oct. 1946), 3
22 See Margaret Duley, *The Caribou Hut*, 11.
23 Typical opinions have already been cited. For an interesting later comment, see George Woodcock, 'The Lost Dominion,' *The New Statesman* (23 July 1949), 92.
24 Patrick Job, *The Settlers* (London: Constable 1957), 15
25 *Atlantic Guardian*, I, 5 (1945), 12–13

26 'O this is the place where the fishermen gather' is the first line of 'The Squid-Jiggin' Ground.' See Scammell, *My Newfoundland* (Montreal: Harvest House 1966), 118.
27 *Atlantic Guardian*, II, 9 (1946), 1. This comment is contained in a brief biographical sketch of Pollett. I have received additional information about Pollett from his son, Ron Pollett, Jr., of New York.
28 Pollett, *The Ocean at my Door* (St John's: Guardian Ltd. [1956]), [7]
29 *Ibid.*, 240–1
30 Elizabeth Miller is currently preparing a biography of her father. This suggestion was made in a private conversation. See her Introduction to Russell's *Tales from Pigeon Inlet* (St John's: Breakwater Books 1977), ix–x; see Harold Horwood's remarks on Russell in the *Evening Telegram*, 15 Feb. 1956.
31 *Evening Telegram*, 28 Oct. 1966
32 *Ibid.*, 4 Nov., 28 Oct. 1966
33 *Ibid.*, 18 Nov., 28 Oct. 1966
34 *The Islander*, I, 2 (Nov. 1946), 7–25. For another early story by Russell, see *Newfoundland Story*, I, 4 (1947), 12–19.
35 *Evening Telegram*, 4 Nov. 1966
36 Peter Neary and Patrick O'Flaherty, eds., *By Great Waters* (Toronto: University of Toronto Press 1974), 247
37 *Tales from Pigeon Inlet*, 91, 45
38 *The Islander*, I, 2 (Nov. 1946), 10
39 Russell, *The Holdin' Ground* (Toronto: McClelland and Stewart 1972), 46
40 Horwood, *Newfoundland* (Toronto: Macmillan 1969), 93–102
41 See *Protocol*, 4 (May–June 1946), 1
42 See the *Evening Telegram*, 5 April 1956; *Quill & Quire* (Aug. 1972), 3.
43 *Evening Telegram*, 4 April 1952
44 Smallwood acknowledges having applied this common tag to Newfoundland, and many writers attribute it to him. See Farley Mowat, *A Whale for the Killing* (Boston: Little, Brown and Co. 1972), 27.
45 *Evening Telegram*, 18 April, 28 June, 10 April, 16 July, 28 July, 10 Sept., 11 Oct., 23 Oct. 1952 (see also his column on 9 March 1956)
46 *Ibid.*, 12 Dec. 1952; 2 April 1955 (see also the column on 20 Dec. 1955)
47 *Ibid.*, 1 April 1954 (see also the column for 2 April); 3, 6, 13 April 1957; 3 April 1958
48 *Ibid.*, 11 Sept. 1952
49 *Ibid.*, 1 and 2 April 1958
50 Horwood, *Newfoundland*, 159
51 Dorothy Tulk, *Crowell's Handbook of Faulkner* (New York: Thomas Y. Crowell Co. 1964), 91

52 *Evening Telegram*, 14 April 1956 (see also his column on 14 May 1958); 21 and 5 April 1958
53 *Quill & Quire* (Aug. 1972), 3
54 'Tomorrow Will Be Sunday, Original manuscripts with author's notes and editor's suggestions,' MS, A.C. Hunter Library, St John's, introductory note. I wish to thank Mr Harold Horwood for permitting me to quote from this MS.
55 *Quill & Quire* (Aug. 1972), 3
56 The original 105 page MS is in the A.C. Hunter Library.
57 *Quill & Quire* (Aug. 1972), 3
58 Horwood, *Tomorrow Will Be Sunday* (New York: Doubleday 1966), 166, 112, 153, 311, 166, 4, 374
59 *Ibid.*, 311, 116, 148
60 *Ibid.*, 347, 114–5
61 *Quill & Quire* (Aug. 1972), 10
62 *Tomorrow Will Be Sunday*, 206, 147
63 'Tomorrow Will Be Sunday,' MS, 105
64 Horwood, *The Foxes of Beachy Cove* (Toronto: Doubleday 1967), 21–2, 171–3, 174, 154
65 Andy Wainwright, *Notes for a Native Land* (Toronto: Oberon Press 1969), 108–9
66 *Quill & Quire* (Aug. 1972), 3. This interview with Horwood was conducted in June 1971.
67 *Atlantic Advocate*, LXI, 11 (1971), 43
68 *Quill & Quire* (Aug. 1972), 3, 10, 3. See also *Atlantic Advocate*, LXI, 11 (1971), 43, where it is announced that Horwood is also writing a book called 'Slouching Toward Bethlehem' on a similar theme. A portion of this work appeared in his collection of stories, *Only the Gods Speak* (St John's: Breakwater Books 1979), 102–13.
69 Horwood, *White Eskimo* (Don Mills: General Publishing Co. 1973), 88, 90, 108–9, 234, 88–9, 63, 85, 276. (This is the Paperjack reprint of the novel.)
70 Horwood, *Bartlett, the Great Canadian Explorer* (New York: Doubleday 1977); Stephen Taylor and Horwood, *Beyond the Road* (Toronto: Van Nostrand Reinhold Ltd. 1976); see note 68, above.
71 See the reviews of *Tomorrow Will Be Sunday* in *Saturday Review* (29 Jan. 1966) and *The New York Times Book Review* (6 Feb. 1966).
72 See a 'Profile' of Janes in *The Newfoundland Herald TV Week* (28 Dec. 1977).
73 *The Cap and Gown* (St John's: Memorial University 1940), 26
74 *Evening Telegram*, 27 Nov. 1971
75 MS, Centre for Newfoundland Studies, MUN Library. The manuscript of

the novel is accompanied by a Notebook indicating its structure and meaning. There is a large collection of Janes's manuscripts in the MUN Library.

76 Interview with Janes, Learning Resources Centre, MUN
77 *Ibid.*
78 Janes, *House of Hate* (Toronto: McClelland and Stewart 1976), x. (This is the New Canadian Library reprint of the novel, with an introduction by Margaret Laurence.)
79 Canon J.E. Loder, who knew 'the author and the Janes family during my twenty-five years as Rector of the Anglican Parish of Corner Brook,' denounced the book as 'the most blasphemous and obscene in content that I have ever examined.' See his letter to the *Atlantic Advocate*, LX, 9 (May 1970), 15.
80 MS, Centre for Newfoundland Studies, MUN Library
81 Janes, *House of Hate* (Toronto: McClelland and Stewart 1970), 159, 11, 15–16
82 *Ibid.*, 317
83 *Ibid.*, 151, 38, 265, 228, 125, 238, 36
84 Interview with Janes, MUN. Claire Mowat misinterpreted the book as a commentary upon industrial life in the *Atlantic Advocate*, LX, 7 (March 1970), 60. See Helen Porter's rejoinder, *ibid.*, LX, 9 (May 1970), 15.
85 *House of Hate*, 318–19
86 Merrick, *True North* (New York: Scribner's 1943), 5
87 *Evening Telegram*, 9 July 1958
88 *A Whale for the Killing*, 18–19, 30
89 Mowat and John de Visser, *This Rock Within the Sea* (Boston: Little Brown and Co. 1968), unpaged
90 *A Whale for the Killing*, 27
91 Remarks made in a private conversation
92 *A Whale for the Killing*, 105–6, 223
93 *Ibid.*, 239
94 In a letter to *Maclean's* (24 July 1978)
95 Biographical information about Russell is supplied from a note appended to his book, and from a personal interview in 1977.
96 Interview with Franklin Russell, Learning Resources Centre, MUN
97 Russell, *The Secret Islands* (Toronto: McClelland and Stewart Ltd. 1965), 14–15
98 *Ibid.*, 23, 103–17
99 Interview with Russell, MUN
100 *Ibid.*
101 *The Secret Islands*, 54, 162, 164, 173, 49

CHAPTER 9: THE CASE OF GEORGE TUFF

1 Cassie Brown, *Death on the Ice* (Toronto: Doubleday 1972), 97
2 *Old-time Songs and Poetry of Newfoundland*, comp. Gerald S. Doyle, 4 ed. (St John's: Gerald S. Doyle, Ltd. 1966), 46
3 *Ibid.*, 28
4 S.J.R. Noel, *Politics in Newfoundland*, 273
5 Hardy, *Collected Poems*, 511

Credits for illustrations

1 Charles P. deVolpi, *Newfoundland: A Pictorial Record* (Toronto: Longman Canada Ltd. 1972), 8 – used with permission of Mr deVolpi
2 *Ibid.*, 11 – used with permission of Mr deVolpi
3 Centre for Newfoundland Studies, MUN
4 Public Archives of Newfoundland and Labrador
5 *Ibid.*
6 *Ibid.*
7 *Ibid.*
8 Dr F.A. Aldrich
9 Ferris Greenslet, *The Lowells and their Seven Worlds* (Cambridge, Mass. 1946), 228
10 Tom Moore Collection, Avondale, Newfoundland
11 Norman Duncan, *Dr. Grenfell's Parish* (New York: Fleming H. Revell Co. 1905), 111
12 *Ibid.*, 101
13 *Ibid.*, 73
14 Private collection (an A.C. Shelton photograph)
15 National Film Board of Canada
16 Public Archives of Newfoundland and Labrador
17 Private collection (an A.C. Shelton photograph)
18 Dr D.G. Pitt
19 Dr Alison Feder
20 Arthur Scammell
21 Ron Pollett, *The Ocean at my Door* (St John's: Guardian Ltd. 1956), frontispiece
22 ETV Photography, MUN
23 Professor Elizabeth Miller
24 Percy Janes
25 G.M. Story

Index

This book

was designed by

ANTJE LINGNER

and was printed by

University of

Toronto

Press